751469

KU-071-879

Ten 'Lost' Plays

———

EUGENE O'NEILL

TEN
'LOST'
PLAYS

With a Foreword by
BENNETT CERF

JONATHAN CAPE
THIRTY BEDFORD SQUARE LONDON

A *Foreword* by

BENNETT CERF

Here are nine one-act plays and one three-act play that are among the very earliest exercises Eugene O'Neill undertook in his self-disciplined apprenticeship to become a playwright. As his mastery of dramatic techniques became surer, as his capacity to express the themes that were most serious to him became more effective, he looked back on these early works without sentimentality. Later in life, he had no desire for them to be preserved at all. But by that time they were out of his hands and they have been published in various editions which are now collectors' items.

Through the courtesy of Mrs. Eugene O'Neill, these ten plays are now made available to the general reader in this standard official edition. For the interested reader, and for the historians of the American theater, they are presented as the "curiosities" that they are: not intrinsic contributions to American drama, but revelations of developing power, thought, and craftsmanship on the part of a man who became the first universally recognized world dramatist America produced.

Contents

THIRST

A Play in One Act

CHARACTERS

A Gentleman

A Dancer

A West Indian Mulatto Sailor

SCENE—A steamer's life raft rising and falling slowly on the long ground swell of a glassy tropic sea. The sky above is pitilessly clear, of a steel-blue color merging into black shadow on the horizon's rim. The sun glares down from straight overhead like a great angry eye of God. The heat is terrific. Writhing, fantastic heat waves rise from the white deck of the raft. Here and there on the still surface of the sea the fins of sharks may be seen slowly cutting the surface of the water in lazy circles.

Two men and a woman are on the raft. Seated at one end is a West Indian mulatto dressed in the blue uniform of a sailor. Across his jersey may be seen the words "Union Mail Line" in red letters. He has on rough sailor shoes. His head is bare. When he speaks it is in drawling sing-song tones as if he were troubled by some strange impediment of speech. He croons a monotonous Negro song to himself as his round eyes follow the shark fins in their everlasting circles.

At the other end of the raft sits a middle-aged white man in what was once evening dress; but sun and salt water have reduced it to the mere caricature of such a garment. His white shirt is stained and rumpled; his collar a formless pulp about his neck; his black tie a withered ribbon. Evidently he had been a first-class passenger. Just now he cuts a sorry and pitiful figure as he sits staring stupidly at the water with unseeing eyes. His *scanty black hair is disheveled, revealing a bald spot burnt crimson by the sun. A mustache droops over his lips, and some of the dye has run off it making a black line down the side of his lean face, blistered with sunburn, haggard with hunger and thirst. From time to time he licks his swollen lips with his blackened tongue.*

Between the two men a young woman lies with arms outstretched, face downward on the raft. She is an even more bizarre figure than the man in evening clothes, for she is dressed in a complete short-skirted dancer's costume of black velvet covered with spangles. Her long blond hair streams down over her bare, unprotected shoulders. Her silk stockings are baggy and wrinkled and her dancing shoes swollen and misshapen. When she lifts her head a diamond necklace can be seen glittering coldly on the protruding collarbones of her emaciated shoulders. Continuous weeping has made a blurred smudge of her rouge and the black make-up of her eyes but one can still see that she must have been very beautiful before hunger and thirst had transformed her into a mocking specter of a dancer. She is sobbing endlessly, hopelessly.

In the eyes of all three the light of a dawning madness is shining.

DANCER (*Raising herself to a sitting posture and turning piteously to the* GENTLEMAN) My God! My God! This silence is driving me mad! Why do you not speak to me? Is there no ship in sight yet?

GENTLEMAN (*Dully*) No. I do not think so. At least I cannot see any. (*He tries to rise to his feet but finds himself too weak and sits down again with a groan*) If I could only stand up I could tell better.

I cannot see far from this position. I am so near the water. And then my eyes are like two balls of fire. They burn and burn until they feel as if they were boring into my brain.

DANCER I know! I know! Everywhere I look I see great crimson spots. It is as if the sky were raining drops of blood. Do you see them too?

GENTLEMAN Yesterday I did—or some day—I no longer remember days. But today everything is red. The very sea itself seems changed to blood. (*He licks his swollen, cracked lips—then laughs—the shrill cackle of madness*) Perhaps it is the blood of all those who were drowned that night rising to the surface.

DANCER Do not say such things. You are horrible. I do not care to listen to you. (*She turns away from him with a shudder*)

GENTLEMAN (*Sulkily*) Very well. I will not speak. (*He covers his face with his hands*) God! God! How my eyes ache! How my throat burns! (*He sobs heavily —there is a pause—suddenly he turns to the DANCER angrily*) Why did you ask me to speak if you do not care to listen to me?

DANCER I did not ask you to speak of blood. I did not ask you to mention that night.

GENTLEMAN Well, I will say no more then. You may talk to him if you wish.

(*He points to the SAILOR with a sneer. The Negro does not hear. He is crooning to himself and watching the sharks. There is a long pause. The raft slowly rises and falls on the long swells. The sun blazes down*)

DANCER (*Almost shrieking*) Oh, this silence! I cannot bear this silence. Talk to me about anything you please but, for God's sake, talk to me! I must not think! I must not think!

GENTLEMAN (*Remorsefully*) Your pardon, dear lady! I am afraid I spoke harshly. I am not myself. I think I am a little out of my head. There is so much sun and so much sea. Everything gets vague at times. I am very weak. We have not eaten in so long—we have not even had a drink of water in so long. (*Then in tones of great anguish*) Oh, if we only had some water!

DANCER (*Flinging herself on the raft and beating it with clenched fists*) Please do not speak of water!

SAILOR (*Stopping his song abruptly and turning quickly around*) Water? Who's got water?

(*His swollen tongue shows between his dry lips*)

GENTLEMAN (*Turning to the* SAILOR) You know no one here has any water. You stole the last drop we had yourself. (*Irritably*) Why do you ask such questions?

(*The* SAILOR *turns his back again and watches the shark fins. He does not answer nor does he sing any longer. There is a silence, profound and breathless*)

DANCER (*Creeping over to the* GENTLEMAN *and seizing his arm*) Do you not notice how deep the silence is? The world seems emptier than ever. I am afraid. Tell me why it is.

GENTLEMAN I, too, notice it. But I do not know why it is.

DANCER Ah! I know now. He is silent. Do you not remember he was singing? A queer monotonous song it was—more of a dirge than a song. I have heard many songs in many languages in the places I have played, but never a song like that before. Why did he stop, do you think? Maybe something frightened him.

GENTLEMAN I do not know. But I will ask him. (*To the* SAILOR) Why have you stopped singing?

(*The* SAILOR *looks at him with a strange expression in his eyes. He does not answer but turns to the circling fins again and takes up his song, dully, droningly, as if from some place he had left off. The* DANCER *and the* GENTLEMAN *listen in attitudes of strained attention for a long time*)

DANCER (*Laughing hysterically*) What a song! There is no tune to it and I can understand no words. I wonder what it means.

GENTLEMAN Who knows? It is doubtless some folk song of his people which he is singing.

DANCER But I wish to find out. Sailor! Will you tell me what it means—that song you are singing?

(*The Negro stares at her uneasily for a moment*)

SAILOR (*Drawlingly*) It is a song of my people.

DANCER Yes. But what do the words mean?

SAILOR (*Pointing to the shark fins*) I am singing to them. It is a charm. I have been told it is very strong. If I sing long enough they will not eat us.

DANCER (*Terrified*) Eat us? What will eat us?

GENTLEMAN (*Pointing to the moving fins in the still water*) He means the sharks. Those pointed black things you see moving through the water are their fins. Have you not noticed them before?

DANCER Yes, yes. I have seen them. But I did not know they were sharks. (*Sobbing*) Oh, it is horrible, all this!

GENTLEMAN (*To the Negro harshly*) Why do you tell
her such things? Do you not know you will
frighten her?

SAILOR (*Dully*) She asked me what I was singing.

GENTLEMAN (*Trying to comfort the* DANCER, *who is still
sobbing*) At least tell her the truth about the
sharks. That is all a children's tale about them eat-
ing people. (*Raising his voice*) You know they
never eat anyone. And I know it.

(*The Negro looks at him and his lips contract grotesquely. Perhaps he is trying to smile*)

DANCER (*Raising her head and drying her eyes*) You
are sure of what you say?

GENTLEMAN (*Confused by the Negro's stare*) Of
course I am sure. Everyone knows that sharks are
afraid to touch a person. They are all cowards. (*To
the Negro*) You were just trying to frighten the
lady, were you not?

(*The Negro turns away from them and stares at the
sea. He commences to sing again*)

DANCER I no longer like his song. It makes me dream
of horrible things. Tell him to stop.

GENTLEMAN Bah! You are nervous. Anything is better
than dead silence.

DANCER Yes. Anything is better than silence—even a
song like that.

GENTLEMAN He is strange—that sailor. I do not know
what to think of him.

DANCER It is a strange song he sings.

GENTLEMAN He does not seem to want to speak to us.

DANCER I have noticed that, too. When I asked him
about the song he did not want to answer at all.

GENTLEMAN   Yet he speaks good English. It cannot be
that he does not understand us.

DANCER   When he does speak, it is as if he had some
impediment in his throat.

GENTLEMAN   Perhaps he has. If so, he is much to be
pitied and we are wrong to speak of him so.

DANCER   I do not pity him. I am afraid of him.

GENTLEMAN   That is foolish. It is the sun which beats
down so fiercely which makes you have such
thoughts. I, also, have been afraid of him at times,
but I know now that I had been gazing at the sea
too long and listening to the great silence. Such
things distort your brain.

DANCER   Then you no longer fear him?

GENTLEMAN   I no longer fear him now that I am quite
sane. It clears my brain to talk to you. We must
talk to each other all the time.

DANCER   Yes, we must talk to each other. I do not
dream when I talk to you.

GENTLEMAN   I think at one time I was going mad. I
dreamed he had a knife in his hand and looked at
me. But it was all madness; I can see that now. He
is only a poor Negro sailor—our companion in misfortune. God knows we are all in the same pitiful
plight. We should not grow suspicious of one another.

DANCER   All the same, I am afraid of him. There is
something in his eyes when he looks at me which
makes me tremble.

GENTLEMAN   There is nothing, I tell you. It is all your
imagination.

(*There is a long pause*)

DANCER   Good God! Is there no ship in sight yet?

GENTLEMAN   (*Attempting to rise but falling back weakly*)   I can see none. And I cannot stand to get a wider view.

DANCER   (*Pointing to the Negro*)   Ask him. He is stronger than we are. He may be able to see one.

GENTLEMAN   Sailor! (*The Negro ceases his chant and turns to him with expressionless eyes*)   You are stronger than we are and can see farther. Stand up and tell me if there is any ship in sight.

SAILOR   (*Rising slowly to his feet and looking at all points of the horizon*)   No. There is none.

(*He sits down again and croons his dreary melody*)

DANCER   (*Weeping hopelessly*)   My God, this is horrible. To wait and wait for something that never comes.

GENTLEMAN   It is indeed horrible. But it is to be expected.

DANCER   Why do you say it is to be expected? Have you no hopes, then, of being rescued?

GENTLEMAN   (*Wearily*)   I have hoped for many things in my life. Always I have hoped in vain. We are far out of the beaten track of steamers. I know little of navigation, yet I heard those on board say that we were following a course but little used. Why we did so, I do not know. I suppose the Captain wished to make a quicker passage. He alone knows what was in his mind and he will probably never tell.

DANCER   No, he will never tell.

GENTLEMAN   Why do you speak so decidedly? He might have been among those who escaped in the boats.

DANCER   He did not escape. He is dead!

GENTLEMAN   Dead?

DANCER   Yes. He was on the bridge. I can remember seeing his face as he stood in under a lamp. It was pale and drawn like the face of a dead man. His eyes, too, seemed dead. He shouted some orders in a thin, trembling voice. No one paid any attention to him. And then he shot himself. I saw the flash, and heard the report above all the screams of the drowning. Someone grasped me by the arm and I heard a hoarse voice shouting in my ear. Then I fainted.

GENTLEMAN   Poor Captain! It is evident, then, that he felt himself guilty—since he killed himself. It must be terrible to hear the screams of the dying and know oneself to blame. I do not wonder that he killed himself.

DANCER   He was so kind and good-natured—the Captain. It was only that afternoon on the promenade deck that he stopped beside my chair. "I hear you are to entertain us this evening," he said. "That will be delightful, and it is very kind of you. I had promised myself the pleasure of seeing you in New York, but you have forestalled me." (*After a pause*) How handsome and broad-shouldered he was—the Captain.

GENTLEMAN   I would have liked to have seen his soul.

DANCER   You would have found it no better and no worse than the souls of other men. If he was guilty he has paid with his life.

GENTLEMAN   No. He has avoided payment by taking his life. The dead do not pay.

DANCER   And the dead cannot answer when we speak

evil of them. All we can know is that he is dead. Let us talk of other things.

(*There is a pause*)

GENTLEMAN (*Fumbles in the inside pocket of his dress coat and pulls out a black object that looks like a large card case. He opens it and stares at it with perplexed eyes. Then, giving a hollow laugh, he holds it over for the* DANCER *to see*) Oh, the damned irony of it!

DANCER What is it? I cannot read very well. My eyes ache so.

GENTLEMAN (*Still laughing mockingly*) Bend closer! Bend closer! It is worth while understanding—the joke that has been played on me.

DANCER (*Reading slowly, her face almost touching the case*) United States Club of Buenos Aires! I do not understand what the joke is.

GENTLEMAN (*Impatiently snatching the case from her hand*) I will explain the joke to you then. Listen! M-e-n-u—menu. That is the joke. This is a souvenir menu of a banquet given in my honor by this club. (*Reading*) "Martini cocktails, soup, sherry, fish, Burgundy, chicken, champagne"—and here we are dying for a crust of bread, for a drink of water! (*His mad laughter suddenly ceases and in a frenzy of rage he shakes his fist at the sky and screams*) God! God! What a joke to play on us!

(*After this outburst he sinks back dejectedly, his trembling hand still clutching the menu*)

DANCER (*Sobbing*) This is too horrible. What have we done that we should suffer so? It is as if one misfortune after another happened to make our agony

more terrible. Throw that thing away! The very
sight of it is a mockery. (*The* GENTLEMAN *throws
the menu into the sea, where it floats, a black spot
on the glassy water*) How do you happen to have
that thing with you? It is ghastly for you to tor-
ment me by reading it.

GENTLEMAN   I am sorry to have hurt you. The jest was
so grotesque I could not keep it to myself. You ask
how I happen to have it with me? I will tell you.
It gives the joke an even bitterer flavor. You remember when the crash came? We were all in the
salon. You were singing—a Cockney song I think?

DANCER   Yes. It is one I first sang at the Palace in London.

GENTLEMAN   It was in the salon. You were singing.
You were very beautiful. I remember a woman on
my right saying: "How pretty she is! I wonder if
she is married?" Strange how some idiotic remark
like that will stick in one's brain when all else is
vague and confused. A tragedy happens—we are in
the midst of it—and one of our clearest remem-
brances afterwards is a remark that might have
been overheard in any subway train.

DANCER   It is so with me. There was a fat, bald-headed,
little man. It was on deck after the crash. Everywhere they were fighting to get into the boats. This
poor little man stood by himself. His moon face
was convulsed with rage. He kept repeating in loud
angry tones: "I shall be late. I must cable! I can
never make it!" He was still bewailing his broken
appointment when a rush of the crowd swept him
off his feet and into the sea. I can see him now. He

is the only person besides the Captain I remember clearly.

GENTLEMAN (*Continuing his story in a dead voice*) You were very beautiful. I was looking at you and wondering what kind of a woman you were. You know I had never met you personally—only seen you in my walks around the deck. Then came the crash—that horrible dull crash. We were all thrown forward on the floor of the salon; then screams, oaths, fainting women, the hollow boom of a bulkhead giving way. I vaguely remember rushing to my stateroom and picking up my wallet. It must have been that menu that I took instead. Then I was on deck fighting in the midst of the crowd. Somehow I got into a boat—but it was overloaded and was swamped immediately. I swam to another boat. They beat me off with the oars. That boat too was swamped a moment later. And then the gurgling, choking cries of the drowning! Something huge rushed by me in the water, leaving a gleaming trail of phosphorescence. A woman near me with a life belt around her gave a cry of agony and disappeared—then I realized—sharks! I became frenzied with terror. I swam. I beat the water with my hands. The ship had gone down. I swam and swam with but one idea—to put all that horror behind me. I saw something white on the water before me. I clutched it—climbed on it. It was this raft. You and he were on it. I fainted. The whole thing is a horrible nightmare in my brain—but I remember clearly that idiotic remark of the woman in the salon. What pitiful creatures we are!

DANCER When the crash came I also rushed to my
stateroom. I took this (*Pointing to the diamond
necklace*), clasped it round my neck and ran on
deck; the rest I have told you.

GENTLEMAN Do you not remember how you came on
this raft? It is strange that you and he should be on
a raft alone when so many died for lack of a place.
Were there ever any others on the raft with you?

DANCER No, I am sure there were not. Everything in
my memory is blurred. But I feel sure we were always the only ones—until you came. I was afraid
of you—your face was livid with fear. You were
moaning to yourself.

GENTLEMAN It was the sharks. Until they came I kept
a half-control over myself. But when I saw them
even my soul quivered with terror.

DANCER (*Horror-stricken, looking at the circling fins*)
Sharks! Why they are all around us now. (*Frenziedly*) You lied to me. You said they would not
touch us. Oh, I am afraid, I am afraid!

(*She covers her face with her hands*)

GENTLEMAN If I lied to you it was because I wished to
spare you. Be brave! We are safe from them as
long as we stay on the raft. These things must be
faced. (*Then in tones of utter despondency*) Besides, what does it matter—sharks or no sharks—
the end is the same.

DANCER (*Taking her hands away from her eyes and
looking dully at the water*) You are right. What
does it matter?

GENTLEMAN God! How still the sea is! How still the
sky is! One would say the world was dead. I think

the accursed humming of that nigger only makes one feel the silence more keenly. There is nothing —that seems to live.

DANCER   How the sun burns into me! (*Piteously*) My poor skin that I was once so proud of!

GENTLEMAN (*Rousing himself with an effort*)   Come! Let us not think about it. It is madness to think about it so. How do you account for your being on the raft alone with this nigger? You have not yet told me.

DANCER—How can I tell? The last thing I remember was that harsh voice in my ear shouting something —what, I cannot recollect.

GENTLEMAN   There was nothing else?

DANCER   Nothing. (*Pause*) Stop! Yes, there was something I had forgotten. I think that someone kissed me. Yes, I am sure that someone kissed me. But no, I am not sure. It may have all been a dream I dreamed. I have had so many dreams during these awful days and nights—so many mad, mad dreams. (*Her eyes begin to glaze, her lips to twitch. She murmurs to herself*) Mad, mad dreams.

GENTLEMAN (*Reaching over and shaking her by the shoulder*)   Come! You said someone kissed you. You must be mistaken. I surely did not, and it could hardly have been that sailor.

DANCER   Yet I am sure someone did. It was not since I have been on this raft. It was on the deck of the ship just as I was fainting.

GENTLEMAN   Who could it have been, do you think?

DANCER   I hardly dare to say what I think. I might be wrong. You remember the Second Officer—the young Englishman with the great dark eyes who

was so tall and handsome? All the women loved
him. I, too, I loved him—a little bit. He loved me
—very much—so he said. Yes, I know he loved me
very much. I think it was he who kissed me. I am
almost sure it was he.

GENTLEMAN Yes, he must have been the one. That
would explain it all. He must have sent away the
raft when only you and this sailor were on it. He
probably did not let the others know of the existence of this raft. Indeed he must have loved you to
disregard his duty so. I will ask the sailor about it.
Maybe he can clear away our doubts. (*To the
Negro*) Sailor! (*The Negro stops singing and looks
at them with wide, bloodshot eyes*) Did the Second Officer order you to take this lady from the
ship?

SAILOR (*Sullenly*) I do not know.

GENTLEMAN Did he tell you to take no one else with
you but this lady—and perhaps himself afterwards?

SAILOR (*Angrily*) I do not know.

(*He turns away again and commences to sing*)

DANCER Do not speak to him any more. He is angry
at something. He will not answer.

GENTLEMAN He is going mad, I think. However, it
seems certain that it was the Second Officer who
kissed you and saved your life.

DANCER He was kind and brave to me. He meant well.
Yet I wish now he had let me die. I would have
way down in the cold green water. I would have
been sleeping, coldly sleeping. While now my
brain is scorched with sun-fire and dream-fire. And
I am going mad. We are all going mad. Your eyes
shine with a wild flame at times—and that sailor's

are horrible with strangeness—and mine see great drops of blood that dance upon the sea. Yes, we are all mad. (*Pause*) God! Oh God! Must this be the end of all? I was coming home, home after years of struggling, home to success and fame and money. And I must die out here on a raft like a mad dog. (*She weeps despairingly*)

GENTLEMAN   Be still! You must not despair so. I, too, might whine a prayer of protest: Oh God, God! After twenty years of incessant grind, day after weary day, I started on my first vacation. I was going home. And here I sit dying by slow degrees, desolate and forsaken. Is this the meaning of all my years of labor? Is this the end, oh God? So I might wail with equal justice. But the blind sky will not answer your appeals or mine. Nor will the cruel sea grow merciful for any prayer of ours.

DANCER   Have you no hope that one of the ship's boats may have reached land and reported the disaster? They would surely send steamers out to search for the other survivors.

GENTLEMAN   We have drifted far, very far, in these long, weary days. I am afraid no steamer would find us.

DANCER   We are lost then!

(*She falls face downward on the raft. A great sob shakes her thin bare shoulders*)

GENTLEMAN   I have not given up hope. These seas, I have heard, are full of coral islands and we surely ought to drift near one of them soon. It was probably an uncharted coral reef that our steamer hit. I heard someone say "derelict" but I saw no sign of one in the water. With us it is only a question of whether we can hold out until we sight land. (*His voice quivers; he licks his blackened lips. His eyes have grown very mad and he is shaking spasmodically from head to foot.*)Water would save us— just a little water—even a few drops would be enough. (*Intensely*) God, if we only had a little water!

DANCER Perhaps there will be water on the island. Look; look hard! An island or a ship may have come in sight while we were talking. (*There is a pause. Suddenly she rises to her knees and pointing straight in front of her, shouts*) See! An island!

GENTLEMAN (*Shading his eyes with a trembling hand and peering wildly around him*) I see nothing— nothing but a red sea and a red sky.

DANCER (*Still looking at some point far out over the water, speaks in disappointed tones*) It is gone. Yet I am quite sure I saw one. It was right out there quite near to us. It was all green and clean-looking with a clear stream that ran into the sea. I could hear the water running over the stones. You do not believe me. You, Sailor, you must have seen it too, did you not? (*The Negro does not answer*) I cannot see it any more. Yet I must see it. I *will* see it!

GENTLEMAN (*Shaking her by the shoulder*) What you say is nonsense. There is no island there, I tell you. There is nothing but sun and sky and sea around us. There are no green trees. There is no water. (*The* SAILOR *has stopped singing and turns and looks at them*)

DANCER (*Angrily*) Do you mean to tell me I lie? Can I not believe my own eyes, then? I tell you I saw it—cool clear water. I heard it bubbling over the stones. But now I hear nothing, nothing at all. (*Turning suddenly to the* SAILOR) Why have you stopped singing? Is not everything awful enough already that you should make it worse?

SAILOR (*Sticking out his swollen tongue and pointing to it with a long brown finger*) Water! I want water! Give me some water and I will sing.

GENTLEMAN (*Furiously*) We have no water, fool! It is your fault we have none. Why did you drink all that was left in the cask when you thought we were asleep? I would not give you any even if we had some. You deserve to suffer, you pig! If any one of the three of us has any water it is you who have hidden some out of what you stole. (*With a laugh of mad cunning*) But you will get no chance to drink it, I promise you that. I am watching you.

(*The Negro sullenly turns away from them*)

DANCER (*Taking hold of the* GENTLEMAN's *arm and almost hissing into his ear. She is terribly excited and he is still chuckling crazily to himself*) Do you really think he has some?

GENTLEMAN (*Chuckling*) He may have. He may have.

DANCER Why do you say that?

GENTLEMAN He has been acting strangely. He has looked as if he wished to hide something. I was wondering what it could be. Then suddenly I thought to myself: "What if it should be some water?" Then I knew I had found him out. I will not let him get the best of me. I will watch him. He will not drink while I am watching him. I will watch him as long as I can see.

DANCER   What could he have put the water in? He has
    nothing that I can discover.

(*She is rapidly falling in with this mad fixed idea of
his*)

GENTLEMAN   Who knows? He may have a flask hidden
    in under his jersey. But he has something, that I
    am sure of. Why is it he is so much stronger than
    we are? He can stand up without effort and we can
    scarcely move. Why is that, I ask you?

DANCER   It is true. He stood up and looked for a ship
    as easily as if he had never known hunger and
    thirst. You are right. He must have something hid-
    den—food or water.

GENTLEMAN (*With mad eagerness to prove his fixed
    idea*)   No, he has no food. There has never been
    any food. But there has been water. There was a
    whole small cask full of it on the raft when I came.
    On the second or third night, I do not remember
    which, I awoke and saw him draining the cask.
    When I reached it, it was empty. (*Furiously shak-
    ing his fist at the Negro's back*) Oh, you pig! You
    rotten pig!

(*The Negro does not seem to hear*)

DANCER   That water would have saved our lives. He is
    no better than a murderer.

GENTLEMAN (*With insane shrewdness*)   Listen. I think
    he must have poured some of the water into his
    flask. There was quite a little there. He could not
    have drunk it all. Oh, he is a cunning one! That
    song of his—it was only a blind. He drinks when
    we are not looking. But he will drink no more, for
    I will watch him. I will watch him!

B

DANCER   You will watch him? And what good will that do either of us? Will we die any the less soon for your watching? No! Let us get the water away from him in some way. That is the only thing to do.

GENTLEMAN   He will not give it to us.

DANCER   We will steal it while he sleeps.

GENTLEMAN   I do not think he sleeps. I have never seen him sleep. Besides, we should wake him.

DANCER   (*Violently*)   We will kill him then. He deserves to be killed.

GENTLEMAN   He is stronger than we are—and he has a knife. No, we cannot do that. I would willingly kill him. As you say, he deserves it. But I cannot even stand. I have no strength left. I have no weapons. He would laugh at me.

DANCER   There must be some way. You would think even the most heartless savage would share at a time like this. We must get that water. It is horrible to be dying of thirst with water so near. Think! Think! Is there no way?

GENTLEMAN   You might buy it from him with that necklace of yours. I have heard his people are very fond of such things.

DANCER   This necklace? It is worth a thousand pounds. An English duke gave it to me. I will not part with it. Do you think I am a fool?

GENTLEMAN   Think of a drink of water! (*They both lick their dry lips feverishly*) If we do not drink soon we will die. (*Laughing harshly*) You will take your necklace to the sharks with you? Very well then, I will say no more. For my part, I would sell my soul for a *drop* of water.

DANCER (*Shuddering with horror she glances instinctively at the moving shark fins*) You are horrible. I had almost forgotten those monsters. It is not kind of you to be always bringing them back to my memory.

GENTLEMAN It is well that you should not forget them. You will value your duke's present less when you look at them. (*Impatiently pounding the deck with one bony hand*) Come, come, we shall both die of thirst while you are dreaming. Offer it to him! Offer it to him!

DANCER (*She takes off the necklace and, musing vacantly, turns it over in her hands watching it sparkle in the sun*) It is beautiful, is it not? I hate to part with it. He was very much in love with me— the old duke. I think he would even have married me in the end. I did not like him. He was old, very old. Something came up—I forget what. I never saw him again. This is the only gift of his that I have left.

GENTLEMAN (*In a frenzy of impatience—the vision of the water clear before his glaring eyes*) Damn it, why are you chattering so? Think of the water he has got. Offer it to him!

DANCER Yes, yes, my throat is burning up; my eyes are on fire. I must have the water. (*She drags herself on hands and knees across the raft to where the Negro is sitting. He does not notice her approach. She reaches out a trembling hand and touches him on the back. He turns slowly and looks at her, his round, animal eyes dull and lusterless. She holds the necklace out in her right hand before his face and speaks hurriedly in a husky voice*) Look, you have stolen our water. You deserve to be killed. We will forget all that. Look at this necklace. It was given to me by an English duke—a nobleman. It is worth a thousand pounds —five thousand dollars. It will provide for you for the rest of your life. You need not be a sailor any more. You need never work at all any more. Do you understand what that means? (*The Negro does not answer. The* DANCER *hurries on however, her words pouring out in a sing-song jumble*)That water that you stole—well, I will give you this necklace—they are all real diamonds, you know—five thousand dollars—for that water. You need not give me all of it. I am not unreasonable. You may keep some for yourself. I would not have you die. I want just enough for myself and my friend—to keep us alive until we reach some island. My lips are cracked with heat! My head is bursting! Here, take the necklace. It is yours.

(*She tries to force it into his hand. He pushes her hand away and the necklace falls to the deck of the raft, where it lies glittering among the heat waves*)

DANCER   (*Her voice raised stridently*)   Give me the water! I have given you the necklace. Give me the water! (*The* GENTLEMAN, *who has been watching her with anxious eyes, also cries: "Yes. Give her the water!"*)

SAILOR (*His voice drawling and without expression*)   I have no water.

DANCER   Oh, you are cruel! Why do you lie? You see me suffering so and you lie to me. I have given you the necklace. It is worth five thousand dollars, do you understand? Surely for five thousand dollars you will give me a drink of water!

SAILOR   I have no water, I tell you.

(*He turns his back to her. She crawls over to the* GENTLEMAN *and lies beside him, sobbing brokenly*)

GENTLEMAN   (*His face convulsed with rage, shaking both fists in the air*)   The pig! The pig! The black dog!

DANCER   (*Sitting up and wiping her eyes*)   Well, you have heard him. He will not give it to us. Maybe he only has a little and is afraid to share it. What shall we do now? What can we do?

GENTLEMAN   (*Despondently*)   Nothing. He is stronger than we are. There is no wind. We will never reach an island. We can die, that is all.

(*He sinks back and buries his head in his hands. A great dry sob shakes his shoulders*)

DANCER   (*Her eyes flaming with a sudden resolution*)   Ah, who is the coward now? You have given up hope, it seems. Well, I have not. I have still one chance. It has never failed me yet.

GENTLEMAN   (*Raising his head and looking at her in amazement*)   You are going to offer him more money?

DANCER   (*With a strange smile*)   No. Not that. I will offer more than money. We shall get our water.

(*She tears a piece of crumpled lace off the front of her costume and carefully wipes her face with it as if she were using a powder puff*)

GENTLEMAN   (*Watching her stupidly*)   I do not understand.

DANCER (*She pulls up her stockings—tries to smooth the wrinkles out of her dress—then takes her long hair and, having braided it, winds it into a coil around her head. She pinches her cheeks, already crimson with sunburn. Then turning coquettishly to the* GENTLEMAN, *she says*)   There! Do I not look better? How do I look?

GENTLEMAN (*Bursting into a mad guffaw*)   You look terrible! You are hideous!

DANCER   You lie! I am beautiful. Everyone knows I am beautiful. You yourself have said so. It is you who are hideous. You are jealous of me. I will not give you any water.

GENTLEMAN   You will get no water. You are frightful. What is it you would do—dance for him? (*Mockingly*) Dance! Dance, Salome! I will be the orchestra. He will be the gallery. We will both applaud you madly.

(*He leans on one elbow and watches her, chuckling to himself*)

DANCER (*Turning from him furiously and crawling on her knees over to the* SAILOR, *calls in her most seductive voice*)   Sailor! Sailor! (*He does not seem to hear—she takes his arm and shakes it gently— he turns around and stares wonderingly at her*) Listen to me, Sailor. What is your name—your first name? (*She smiles enticingly at him. He does not answer*) You will not tell me then? You are angry at me, are you not? I cannot blame you. I have called you bad names. I am sorry, very sorry. (*Indicating the* GENTLEMAN, *who has ceased to notice them and is staring at the horizon with blinking eyes*) It was he who put such ideas into my head. He does not like you. Neither did I, but I see now that you are the better of the two. I hate him! He has said dreadful things which I cannot forgive. (*Putting her hand on his shoulder she bends forward with her golden hair almost in his lap and smiles up into his face*) I like you, Sailor. You are big and strong. We are going to be great friends, are we not? (*The Negro is hardly looking at her. He is watching the sharks*) Surely you will not refuse me a little sip of your water?

SAILOR   I have no water.

DANCER   Oh, why will you keep up this suberfuge? Am I not offering you price enough? (*Putting her arm around his neck and half whispering in his ear*) Do you not understand? I will love you, Sailor! Noblemen and millionaires and all degrees of gentlemen have loved me, have fought for me. I have never loved any of them as I will love you. Look in my eyes, Sailor, look in my eyes! (*Compelled in spite of himself by something in her voice, the Negro gazes deep into her eyes. For a second his nostrils dilate—he draws in his breath with a hissing sound—his body grows tense and it seems as if he is about to sweep her into his arms. Then his expression grows apathetic again. He turns to the sharks*) Oh, will you never understand? Are you so stupid that you do not know what I mean? Look! I am offering myself to you! I am kneeling before you—I who always had men kneel to me! I am offering my body to you—my body that men have called so beautiful. I have promised to love you—a Negro sailor—if you will give me one small drink of water. Is that not humiliation enough that

you must keep me waiting so? (*Raising her voice*)
Answer me! Answer me! Will you give me that
water?

SAILOR (*Without even turning to look at her*)   I have
no water.

DANCER (*Shaking with fury*)   Great God, have I
abased myself for this? Have I humbled myself before this black animal only to be spurned like a
wench of the streets? It is too much! You lie, you
dirty slave! You have water. You have stolen my
share of the water. (*In a frenzy she clutches the
SAILOR about the throat with both hands*) Give it
to me! Give it to me!

SAILOR (*Takes her hands from his neck and pushes her
roughly away. She falls face downward in the middle of the raft*)   Let me alone! I have no water.

GENTLEMAN (*Aroused from the stupor he has been in*)
What is it? I was dreaming I was sitting before
great tumblers of ice water. They were just beyond
my reach. I tried and tried to get one of them. It
was horrible. But what has happened here? What
is the matter?

(*No one answers him. The Negro is watching the
sharks again. The DANCER is lying in a huddled heap,
moaning to herself. Suddenly she jumps to her feet. All
her former weakness seems quite gone. She stands swaying a little with the roll of the raft. Her eyes have a
terrible glare in them. They seem bursting out of her
head. She mutters incoherently to herself. The last
string has snapped. She is mad*)

DANCER (*Smoothing her dress over her hips and looking
before her as if in a mirror*)   Quick, Marie! You
are so slow tonight. I will be late. Did you not hear

the bell? I am the next on. Did he send any flowers tonight, Marie? Good, he will be in a stage box. I will smile at him, the poor old fool. He will marry me some day and I will be a duchess. Think of that, Marie—a real duchess! Yes, yes, I am coming! You need not hold the curtain.

(She drops her head on her breast and mutters to herself. The GENTLEMAN *has been watching her, at first in astonishment, then in a sort of crazy appreciation. When she stops talking he claps his hands)*

GENTLEMAN   Go on! Go on! It is as good as a play.

(He bursts into cackling laughter)

DANCER   They are laughing. It cannot be at me. How hot it is! How the footlights glare! I shall be glad to get away tonight. I am very thirsty. *(Passing her hand across her eyes)* There he is in the box—the poor old duke. I will wave to him. *(She waves her hand in the air)* He is kind to me. It is a pity he is so old. What song is it I am to sing? Oh yes. *(She sings the last few lines of some music hall ballad in a harsh cracked voice. The Negro turns and looks at her wonderingly. The* GENTLEMAN *claps his hands)* They are applauding. I must dance for them! *(She commences to dance on the swaying surface of the raft, half-stumbling every now and then. Her hair falls down. She is like some ghastly marionette jerked by invisible wires. She dances faster and faster. He arms and legs fly grotesquely around as if beyond control)* Oh, how hot it is! *(She grasps the front of her bodice in both hands and rips it over her shoulders. It hangs down in back. She is almost naked to the waist. Her breasts are withered and shrunken by starva-*

tion. She kicks first one foot and then the other frenziedly in the air) Oh, it is hot! I am stifling. Bring me a drink of water! I am choking!

(*She falls back on the raft. A shudder runs over her whole body. A little crimson foam appears on her lips. Her eyes glaze. The wild stare leaves them. She is dead*)

GENTLEMAN (*Laughing insanely and clapping his hands*) Bravo! Bravo! Give us some more! (*There is no answer. A great stillness hangs over everything. The heat waves rising from the raft near the woman's body seem like her soul departing into the great unknown. A look of fear appears on the GENTLEMAN's face. The Negro wears a strange expression. One might say he looks relieved, even glad, as if some perplexing problem has been solved for him*) She does not answer me. She must be sick. (*He crawls over to her*) She has fainted. (*He puts his hand on her left breast—then bends and rests his ear over her heart. His face grows livid in spite of the sunburn*) My God! She is dead! Poor girl! Poor girl!

(*He whimpers weakly to himself, mechanically running her long golden hair through his fingers with a caressing gesture. He is startled when he hears the Negro's voice*)

SAILOR   Is she dead?

GENTLEMAN   Yes. She is dead, poor girl. Her heart no longer beats.

SAILOR   She is better off. She does not suffer now. One of us had to die. (*After a pause*) It is lucky for us she is dead.

GENTLEMAN   What do you mean? What good can her death do us?

SAILOR   We will live now.

(*He takes his* SAILOR's *knife from its sheath and sharpens it on the sole of his shoe. While he is doing this he sings—a happy Negro melody that mocks the great silence*)

GENTLEMAN (*In hushed, frightened tones*)   I do not understand.

SAILOR (*His swollen lips parting in a grin as he points with his knife to the body of the* DANCER)   We shall eat. We shall drink.

GENTLEMAN (*For a moment struck dumb with loathing —then in tones of anguished horror*)   No! No! No! Good God, not that!

(*With a swift movement he grasps the* DANCER's *body with both hands and, making a tremendous effort, pushes it into the water. There is a swift rush of waiting fins. The sea near the raft is churned into foam. The* DANCER's *body disappears in a swirling eddy; then all is quiet again. A black stain appears on the surface of the water.*

The SAILOR, *who has jumped forward to save the body, gives a harsh cry of disappointed rage and, knife in hand, springs on the* GENTLEMAN *and drives the knife in his breast. The* GENTLEMAN *rises to his feet with a shriek of agony. As he falls backward into the sea, one of his clutching hands fastens itself in the neck of the* SAILOR's *jersey. The* SAILOR *tries to force the hand away, stumbles, loses his balance, and plunges headlong after him. There is a great splash. The waiting fins rush in. The water is lashed into foam. The* SAILOR's *black head appears for a moment, his features distorted with terror, his lips torn with a howl of despair. Then he is drawn under.*

The black stain on the water widens. The fins circle no longer. The raft floats in the midst of a vast silence. The sun glares down like a great angry eye of God. The eerie heat waves float upward in the still air like the souls of the drowned. On the raft a diamond necklace lies glittering in the blazing sunshine)

Curtain

THE WEB

A Play in One Act

CHARACTERS

Rose Thomas

Steve, a "Cadet"

Tim Moran, a Yeggman

A Policeman

Two Plain-Clothes Men

SCENE—*A squalid bedroom on the top floor of a rooming house on the Lower East Side, New York. The wallpaper is dirty and torn in places, showing the plaster beneath. There is an open window in back looking out on a fire escape on which a bottle of milk can be seen. On the right is a door leading to the hallway. On the left a washstand with a bowl and pitcher, and some meager articles of a woman's toilet set scattered on it. Above the washstand a cracked mirror hangs from a nail in the wall. In the middle of the room stand a rickety table and a chair. In the left-hand corner near the window is a bed in which a baby is lying asleep. A gas jet near the mirror furnishes the only light.*

ROSE THOMAS, *a dark-haired young woman looking thirty but really only twenty-two, is discovered sitting on the chair smoking a cheap Virginia cigarette. An empty beer bottle and a dirty glass stand on the table beside her. Her hat, a gaudy cheap affair with a scraggy imitation plume, is also on the table.* ROSE *is dressed in the tawdry extreme of fashion. She has earrings in her ears, bracelets on both wrists, and a quantity of rings —none of them genuine. Her face is that of a person in an advanced stage of consumption—deathly pale with hollows under the eyes, which are wild and feverish. Her attitude is one of the deepest dejection. When she glances over at the bed, however, her expression grows tenderly maternal. From time to time she coughs—a harsh, hacking cough that shakes her whole body. After these spells she raises her handkerchief to her lips, then glances at it fearfully.*

The time is in the early hours of a rainy summer night. The monotonous sound of the rain falling on the flags of the court below is heard.

ROSE (*Listening to the rain—throws the cigarette wearily on the table*) Gawd! What a night! (*Laughing bitterly*) What a chance I got! (*She has a sudden fit of coughing; then gets up and goes over to the bed and bending down gently kisses the sleeping child on the forehead. She turns away with a sob and murmurs*) What a life! Poor kid!

(*She goes over to the mirror and makes up her eyes and cheeks. The effect is ghastly. Her blackened eyes look enormous and the dabs of rouge on each cheek serve to heighten her aspect of feverish illness. Just as she has completed her toilet and is putting on her hat in front of the mirror, the door is flung open and* STEVE *lurches in and bolts the door after him. He has very evidently been drinking. In appearance he is a typical "cadet," flashily dressed, rat-eyed, weak of mouth, undersized, and showing on his face the effects of drink and drugs*)

ROSE (*Hurriedly putting her hat down on the washstand—half frightened*) Hello, Steve.

STEVE (*Looking her up and down with a sneer*) Yuh're a fine-lookin' mess! (*He walks over and sits down in the chair*) Yuh look like a dead one. Put on some paint and cheer up! Yuh give me the willies standin' there like a ghost.

ROSE (*Rushes over to the mirror and plasters on more rouge—then turns around*) Look, Steve! Ain't that better?

STEVE Better? Naw, but it'll do. (*Seeing the empty beer bottle*) Gimme a drink!

ROSE Yuh know there ain't any. That's the bottle yuh brought up last night.

STEVE (*With peevish anger*) Yuh lie! I'll bet yuh got some burried around here some place. Yuh're always holdin' out on me and yuh got to quit it, see?

ROSE I never hold out on yuh and yuh know it. That's all the thanks I get. (*Angrily*) What'ud yuh do if I was like Bessie with your friend Jack? Then yuh might have some chance to kick. She's got enough salted to leave him any time she wants to—and he knows it and sticks to her like glue. Yuh don't notice him runnin' after every doll he sees like some guys I know. He's afraid of losin' her—while *you* don't care.

STEVE (*Flattered—in a conciliating tone*) Aw, shut up! Yuh make me sick with dat line of bull. Who said I was chasin' any dolls? (*Then venomously*) I'm not so sure Jack is wise to Bessie holdin' out on him; but I'll tell him, and if he isn't wise to it, Bessie'll be in for a good beatin'.

ROSE Aw, don't do that! What'cha got against her? She ain't done nothin' to you, has she?

STEVE Naw; but she oughta be learned a lesson, dat's all. She oughta be on the level with him. Us guys has got to stand together. What'ud we do if all youse dolls got holdin' out on the side?

ROSE (*Dejectedly*) Don't ask me. I dunno. It's a bum game all round.

(*She has a fit of horrible coughing*)

STEVE (*His nerves shattered*) Dammit! Stop that
    barkin'. It goes right trou me. Git some medicine
    for it, why don't yuh?

ROSE (*Wiping her lips with her handkerchief*) I did
    but it ain't no good.

STEVE Then git somethin' else. I told yuh months ago
    to go and see a doctor. Did yuh?

ROSE (*Nervously, after a pause*) No.

STEVE Well den, yuh can't blame me. It's up to you.

ROSE (*Speaking eagerly and beseechingly, almost in
    tears*) Listen, Steve! Let me stay in tonight and go
    to the doc's. I'm sick. (*Pointing to her breast*)I got
    pains here and it seems as if I was on fire inside.
    Sometimes I git dizzy and everythin' goes round
    and round. Anyway, it's rainin' and my shoes are
    full of holes. There won't be no one out tonight,
    and even if there was they're all afraid of me on ac-
    count of this cough. Gimme a couple of dollars
    and let me go to the doc's and git some medicine.
    Please, Steve, for Gawd's sake! I'll make it up to
    yuh when I'm well. I'll be makin' lots of coin then
    and yuh kin have it all. (*Goes off into a paroxysm
    of coughing*) I'm so sick!

STEVE (*In indignant amazement*) A couple of beans!
    What'd yuh think I am—the mint?

ROSE But yuh had lots of coin this mornin'. Didn't I
    give yuh all I had?

STEVE (*Sullenly*) Well, I ain't got it now, see? I got
    into a game at Tony's place and they cleaned me.
    I ain't got a nick. (*With sudden anger*) And I
    wouldn't give it to yuh if I had it. D'yuh think I'm
    a simp to be gittin' yuh protection and keepin' the

bulls from runnin' yuh in when all yuh do is to
stick at home and play dead? If yuh want any coin
git out and make it. That's all I got to say.

ROSE (*Furiously*) So that's all yuh got to say, is it?
Well, I'll hand yuh a tip right here. I'm gittin' sick
of givin' yuh my roll and gittin' nothin' but abuse
in retoin. Yuh're half drunk now. And yuh been
hittin' the pipe too; I kin tell by the way your eyes
look. D'yuh think I'm goin' to stand for a guy
that's always full of booze and hop? Not so yuh
could notice it! There's too many others I kin get.

STEVE (*His eyes narrow and his voice becomes loud and
threatening*) Can that chatter, d'yuh hear me?
If yuh ever t'row me down—look out! I'll get yuh!

ROSE (*In a frenzy*) Get me? Wha'd I care? D'yuh think
I'm so stuck on this life I wanta go on livin'? Kill
me! Wha'd I care?

STEVE (*Jumps up from the table and raises his hand as
if to strike her. He shouts*) Fur Chris' sake, shut
up!

(*The baby, awakened by the loud voices, commences
to cry*)

ROSE (*Her anger gone in a flash*) Sssshhh! There, we
woke her up. Keep still, Steve. I'll go out, yuh
needn't worry. Jest don't make so much noise,
that's all.

(*She goes over to the bed and cuddles the child. It
soon falls asleep again. She begins to cough, and rising
to her feet walks away from the bed keeping her face
turned away from the baby*)

STEVE (*Who has been watching her with a malignant
sneer*) Yuh'll have to take that kid out of the
bed. I gotta git some sleep.

ROSE   But, Steve, where'll I put her? There's no place else.

STEVE   On the floor—any place. Wha'd I care where yuh put it?

ROSE   (*Supplicatingly*) Aw please, Steve! Be a good guy! She won't bother yuh none. She's fast asleep. Yuh got three-quarters of the bed to lie on. Let her stay there.

STEVE   Nix! Yuh heard what I said, didn't yuh? Git busy, then. Git her out of there.

ROSE   (*With cold fury*) I won't do it.

STEVE   Yuh won't, eh? Den I will.

   (*He makes a move toward the bed*)

ROSE   (*Standing between him and the bed in a resolute attitude, speaks slowly and threateningly*) I've stood about enough from you. Don't yuh dare touch her or I'll—

STEVE   (*Blusteringly, a bit shaken in his coward soul however*) What'll yuh do? Don't try and bluff me. And now we're talkin' about it I wanta tell yuh that kid has got to go. I've stood fur it as long as I kin with its bawlin' and whinin'. Yuh gotta git rid of it, that's all. Give it to some orphan asylum. They'll take good care of it. I know what I'm talkin' about cause I was brung up in one myself. (*With a sneer*) What'd *you* want with a kid? (ROSE *winces*) A fine mother *you* are and dis is a swell dump to bring up a family in.

ROSE   Please, Steve, for the love of Gawd lemme keep her! She's all I got to live for. If yuh take her away I'll die. I'll kill myself.

STEVE   (*Contemptuously*) Dat's what they all say. But she's got to go. All yuh do now is fuss over dat kid,

comin' home every ten minutes to see if it's hungry or somethin'! Dat's why we're broke all the
time. I've stood fur it long enough.

ROSE (*On her knees—weeping*) Please, Steve, for
Gawd's sake lemme keep her!

STEVE (*Coldly*) Stop dat blubberin'. It won't do no
good. I give yuh a week. If yuh don't git dat brat
outa here in a week, den I will.

ROSE What'd'yuh mean? What'll yuh do?

STEVE I'll have yuh pinched and sent to the Island.
The kid'll be took away from yuh then.

ROSE (*In anguish*) Yuh're jest tryin' to scare me, ain't
yuh, Steve? They wouldn't do that, would they?

STEVE Yuh'll soon know whether dey would or not.

ROSE But yuh wouldn't have me pinched, would yuh,
Steve? Yuh wouldn't do me dirt like that?

STEVE I wouldn't, wouldn't I? Yuh jest wait and see!

ROSE Aw, Steve, I always been good to *you*.

STEVE Git dat kid outa here or I'll put yuh in the
cooler as sure as hell!

ROSE (*Maddened, rushing at him with outstretched
hands*) Yuh dirty dog!

(*There is a struggle during which the table is overturned. Finally* STEVE *frees himself and hits her in the
face with his fist, knocking her down. At the same instant the door from the hallway is forced open and* TIM
MORAN *pushes his way in. He is short and thick-set, with
a bullet head, close-cropped black hair, a bull neck, and
small blue eyes close together. Although distinctly a
criminal type his face is in part redeemed by its look of
manliness. He is dressed in dark ill-fitting clothes, and
has an automatic revolver in his hand which he keeps
pointed at* STEVE)

TIM (*Pointing to the door, speaks to* STEVE *with cold contempt*) Git outa here, yuh lousy skunk, and stay out! (*As* STEVE'S *hand goes to his hip*) Take yer hand away from that gat or I'll fill yuh full of holes. (STEVE *is cowed and obeys*) Now git out and don't come back. If you bother this goil again I'll fix yuh and fix yuh right. D'yuh get me?

STEVE (*Snarling, and slinking toward door*) Yuh think yuh're some smart, dontcha, buttin' in dis way on a guy? It ain't none of your business. She's my goil.

TIM D'yuh think I'm goin' to stand by and let yuh beat her up jest cause she wants to keep her kid? D'yuh think I'm as low as you are, yuh dirty mutt? Git outa here before I croak yuh.

STEVE (*Standing in the doorway and looking back*) Yuh got the drop on me now; but I'll get yuh, yuh wait and see! (*To* ROSE) And *you* too.

(*He goes out and can be heard descending the stairs.* ROSE *hurries over to the door and tries to lock it, but the lock is shattered, so she puts the chair against it to keep it shut. She then goes over to the baby, who has been whimpering unnoticed during the quarrel, and soothes her to sleep again.* TIM, *looking embarrassed, puts the revolver back in his pocket, and picking up the table sets it to rights again and sits on the edge of it.* ROSE *looks up at him from the bed, half bewildered at seeing him still there. Then she breaks into convulsive sobbing*)

TIM (*Making a clumsy attempt at consolation*) There, there, Kid, cut the cryin'. He won't bother yuh no more. I know his kind. He's got a streak of yellow a yard wide, and beatin' up women is all he's game for. But he won't hurt *you* no more—not if I know it.

ROSE   Yuh don't know him. When he's full of booze
and hop he's liable to do anythin'. I don't care
what he does to me. I might as well be dead anyway. But there's the kid. I got to look after her.
And (*Looking at him gratefully*) I don't want you
to git in no mixups on account of me. I ain't worth
it.

TIM (*Quickly*)   Nix on that stuff about your not bein'
worth it!

ROSE (*Smiling*)   Thanks. And I'm mighty glad yuh
came in when yuh did. Gawd knows what he'd'a
done to the kid and me not able to stop him.

TIM   Don't yuh worry about my gettin' into no mix-ups.
I c'n take care of myself.

ROSE   How did yuh happen to blow in when yuh did?
There usually ain't no one around in this dump at
this time of the night.

TIM   I got the room next to yuh. I heard every word
the both of yuh said—tonight and every other night
since I come here a week ago. I know the way he's
treated yuh. I'd'a butted in sooner only I didn't
want to mix in other people's business. But tonight
when he started in about the kid there I couldn't
stand fur it no longer. I was jest wantin' to hand
him a call and I let him have it. Why d'yuh stand
fur him anyway? Why don't yuh take the kid and
beat it away from him?

ROSE (*Despondently*)   It's easy to say: "Why don't I
beat it?" I can't.

TIM   Wha'd'yuh mean? Why can't yuh?

ROSE   I never have enough coin to make a good break
and git out of town. He takes it all away from me.
And if I went to some other part of this burg he'd

find me and kill me. Even if he didn't kill me he'd
have me pinched and where'ud the kid be then?
(*Grimly*) Oh, he's got me where he wants me all
right, all right.

TIM   I don't get yuh. How could he have yuh pinched
if yuh ain't done nothin'?

ROSE   Oh, he's got a drag somewhere. He squares it
with the cops so they don't hold me up for walkin'
the streets. Yuh ought to be wise enough to know
all of his kind stand in. If he tipped them off to do
it they'd pinch me before I'd gone a block. Then
it'ud be the Island fur mine.

TIM   Then why don't yuh cut this life and be on the
level? Why don't yuh git a job some place? He
couldn't touch yuh then.

ROSE   (*Scornfully*) Oh, couldn't he? D'yuh suppose
they'd keep me any place if they knew what I was?
And d'yuh suppose he wouldn't tell them or have
someone else tell them? Yuh don't know the game
I'm up against. (*Bitterly*) I've tried that job thing.
I've looked fur decent work and I've starved at it.
A year after I first hit this town I quit and tried to
be on the level. I got a job at housework—workin'
twelve hours a day for twenty-five dollars a month.
And I worked like a dog, too, and never left the
house I was so scared of seein' someone who knew
me. But what was the use? One night they have a
guy to dinner who's seen me some place when I
was on the town. He tells the lady—his duty he
said it was—and she fires me right off the reel. I
tried the same thing a lot of times. But there was
always someone who'd drag me back. And then I
quit tryin'. There didn't seem to be no use. They—

all the good people—they got me where I am and they're goin' to keep me there. Reform? Take it from me it can't be done. They won't let yuh do it, and that's Gawd's truth.

TIM Give it another trial anyway. Yuh never know your luck. Yuh might be able to stick this time.

ROSE (*Wearily*) Talk is cheap. Yuh don't know what yuh're talkin' about. What job c'n I git? What am I fit fur? Housework is the only thing I know about and I don't know much about that. Where else could I make enough to live on? That's the trouble with all us girls. Most all of us ud like to come back but we jest can't and that's all there's to it. We can't work out of this life because we don't know how to work. We was never taught how. (*She shakes with a horrible fit of coughing, wipes her lips, and smiles pitifully*)Who d'yuh think would take a chance on hiring me the way I look and with this cough? Besides, there's the kid. (*Sarcastically*) Yuh may not know it but people ain't strong for hirin' girls with babies—especially when the girls ain't married.

TIM But yuh could send the kid away some place.

ROSE (*Fiercely*) No. She's all I got. I won't give her up.

(*She coughs again*)

TIM (*Kindly*) That's a bad cough yuh got, Kid. I heard yuh tellin' him tonight yuh hadn't seen a doctor. (*Putting a hand in his pocket*) I'll stake yuh and yuh c'n run around and see one now.

ROSE Thanks jest the same but it ain't no use. I lied to Steve. I went to a doc about a month ago. He told me I had the "con" and had it bad. (*With grim humor*) He said the only hope fur me was to git out in the country, sleep in the open air, and eat a lot of good food. He might jest as well 'uv told me to go to Heaven and I told him so. Then he said I could go out to some dump where yuh don't have to pay nothin', but he said I'd have to leave the kid behind. I told him I'd rather die than do that, and he said I'd have to be careful or the kid 'ud catch it from me. And I have been careful. (*She sobs*) I don't even kiss her on the mouth no more.

TIM   Yuh sure are up against it, Kid. (*He appears deeply moved*) Gee, I thought I was in bad, but yuh got me skinned to death.

ROSE (*Interested*)   You in bad? Yuh don't look it.

TIM   Listen! Yuh talk about tryin' to be good and not bein' able to— Well, I been up against the same thing. When I was a kid I was sent to the reform school fur stealin'; and it wasn't my fault. I was mixed up with a gang older than me and wasn't wise to what I was doin'. They made me the goat; and in the reform school they made a crook outa me. When I come out I tried to be straight and hold down a job, but as soon as anyone got wise I'd been in a reform school they canned me same as they did you. Then I stole again—to keep from starvin'. They got me and this time I went to the coop fur five years. Then I give up. I seen it was no use. When I got out again I got in with a gang of yeggmen and learned how to be a yegg—and I've been one ever since. I've spent most of my life in jail but I'm free now.

ROSE   What are yuh goin' to do?

TIM (*Fiercely*) What am I goin' to do? They made a yegg outa me! Let 'em look out!

ROSE When did yuh get out?

TIM (*Suspiciously*) What's it to you? (*Then suddenly*) Nix, I didn't mean that. Yuh're a good kid and maybe yuh c'n help me.

ROSE I'd sure like to.

TIM Then listen! (*Looking at her fixedly*) Yuh swear yuh won't squeal on me?

ROSE I won't, so help me Gawd!

TIM Well, I'm Tim Moran. I jest broke out two weeks ago.

ROSE (*Staring at him with a fascinated wonder*) You! Tim Moran! The guy that robbed that bank a week ago! The guy they're all lookin' fur!

TIM Sssshhh! Yuh never c'n tell who's got an ear glued to the wall in a dump like this.

ROSE (*Lowering her voice*) I read about yuh in the papers.

(*She looks at him as if she were half afraid*)

TIM Yuh're not afraid of me, are yuh? I ain't the kind of crook Steve is, yuh know.

ROSE (*Calmly*) No, I ain't afraid of yuh, Tim; but I'm afraid they may find yuh here and take yuh away again. (*Anxiously*) D'yuh think Steve knew yuh? He'd squeal sure if he did—to git the reward.

TIM No, I could tell by his eyes he didn't know me.

ROSE How long have yuh been here?

TIM A week—ever since I cracked that safe. I wanted to give the noise time to blow over. I ain't left that room except when I had to git a bite to eat, and then I got enough fur a couple of days. But when I come in tonight I seen a guy on the corner give me a long look. He looked bad to me and I wanta git out of here before they git wise.

ROSE   Yuh think he was a cop?

TIM   Yes, I got a hunch. He looked bad to me.

ROSE (*Wonderingly*)   And yuh come in here tonight knowin' he was liable to spot yuh! Yuh took that chance fur me when yuh didn't even know me! (*Impulsively going over to him and taking his hand, which he tries to hold back*) Gee, yuh're a regular guy, all right.

TIM (*In great confusion*)   Aw, that's nothin'. Anyone would'a done it.

ROSE   No one would'a done it in your place. (*A slight noise is heard from the hallway.* ROSE *looks around startled and speaks hurriedly almost in a whisper*) Supposin' that guy was a cop? Supposin' he had a hunch who you was? How're yuh goin' to make a getaway? Can't I help yuh outa this? Can't I do somethin' fur yuh?

TIM (*Points to the window*)   That's a fire escape, ain't it?

ROSE   Yes.

TIM   Where does it lead to?

ROSE   Down to the yard and up to the roof.

TIM   To hell with the yard. I'll try the roofs if it comes to a showdown. I'll stick in here with you so's if they come I c'n make a quick getaway. Yuh tell 'em yuh don't know anything about me, see? Give 'em a bum steer if you kin. Try and hold 'em so's I c'n get a good start.

ROSE (*Resolutely*)   I'll hold 'em as long as I c'n, don't worry. I'll tell 'em I seen yuh goin' downstairs an hour ago.

TIM   Good Kid!

(They are standing in the middle of the room with their backs to the window. STEVE'S *face appears peering around the edge of the window frame. He is crouched on the fire escape outside. His eyes glare with hatred as he watches the two persons in the room.* ROSE *starts to cough, is frightened by the noise she makes, and holds her handkerchief over her mouth to stifle the sound)*

TIM   Sssshhh! Poor Kid! *(He turns to her and speaks rapidly in low tones)* Here, Kid. *(He takes a large roll of money out of his pocket and forces it into her hand—as she starts to remonstrate)* Shut up! I ain't got time to listen to your beefin'. Take it. It ain't much but it's all I got with me. I don't need it. There's plenty more waitin' fur me outside. This'll be enough to git you and the kid out of town away from that dirty coward. *(STEVE'S face is convulsed with fury)* Go some place out in the mountains and git rid of that cough.

ROSE *(Sobbing)*   I can't take it. Yuh been too good to me already. Yuh don't know how rotten I am.

TIM   *(Suddenly taking her in his arms and kissing her roughly)* That's how rotten I think yuh are. Yuh're the whitest kid I've ever met, see?

(They look into each other's eyes. All the hardness of ROSE'S *expression has vanished. Her face is soft, transfigured by a new emotion.* STEVE *moves his hand into the room. He holds a revolver which he tries to aim at* TIM *but he is afraid to fire)*

ROSE *(Throwing her arms around his neck)*   Tim, Tim, yuh been too good to me.

TIM   *(Kissing her again)*   Lemme know where yuh are and when it's safe I'll come to yuh. *(He releases*

her and takes a small folded paper from pocket)
This'll find me. (She takes it, her eyes full of happy
tears) Maybe after a time we c'n start over again—
together! (A sound like the creaking of a floor
board is heard from the hallway) What's that?
(They both stand looking fixedly at the door. STEVE
noiselessly disappears from the window) Gee, Kid,
I got a feelin' in my bones they're after me. It's
only a hunch but it's never gone wrong yet. (He
pulls a cap out of his pocket and puts it on) I'm
goin' to blow.

ROSE (Goes over to the door and listens)   Sounds as if
somebody was sneakin' up the stairs. (She tiptoes
quickly over to him and kisses him) Go, go while
yuh got a chance. Don't let 'em git yuh? I love yuh,
Tim.

TIM   Good-bye, Kid. I'll come as soon as I c'n.

(He kisses her again and goes quickly to the window.
STEVE stretches his hand around the side of the window
and fires, the muzzle of the gun almost on TIM's chest.
There is a loud report and a little smoke. TIM staggers
back and falls on the floor. STEVE throws the gun into
the room, then quietly pulls down the window and disappears. The child in the bed wakes up and cries feebly)

ROSE (Rushes to TIM and kneels beside him, holding his
     head on her breast)   Tim! Tim! Speak to me,
     Tim!

(She kisses him frantically)

TIM (His eyes glazing)   Good Kid—mountains—git
     rid of that cough.

(He dies)

ROSE (Letting his head fall back on the floor, she sinks
     to a sitting position beside him. The money is still

clutched in her right hand. She stares straight be-
fore her and repeats in tones of horrible monotony)
Dead. Oh Gawd, Gawd, Gawd!

(*The sound of people running up the stairs in the*
hall is heard. A voice shouts: "Must be in here." The
door is pushed open and three men enter. One is a
POLICEMAN *in uniform and the other two are evidently*
PLAIN-CLOTHES MEN. *The landlady and several roomers*
stand in the doorway looking in with frightened faces)

POLICEMAN (*Goes to* ROSE *and, taking her arm, hauls*
her to her feet) Come, get up outa that!

(*The two* PLAIN-CLOTHES MEN *take one look at the*
dead man and both exclaim together: "Tim Moran!")

FIRST PLAIN-CLOTHES MAN   I told yuh it was him I seen
comin' in here tonight. I never forget a face.

SECOND PLAIN-CLOTHES MAN (*Picking the revolver off*
the floor and examining it)   I didn't think he'd be
fool enough to stick around here. (*Turning sud-*
denly to ROSE) What did yuh croak him for? (*Iron-*
ically) A little love spat, eh? (*He sees the roll of*
money in her hand and grabs her quickly by the
wrist) Pipe the roll! Little sister here attends to
business, all right. Gave him a frisk before we had
a chance to get here. (*To* ROSE *in loud, rough*
tones) Why did yuh kill him? It was for this coin,
wasn't it?

(*During the detective's remarks* ROSE *gradually real-*
izes the position she is in. Her expression becomes one
of amazed pain as she sees they think she is guilty of the
murder. She speaks brokenly, trying to hold herself in
control)

ROSE   Honest to Gawd, I didn't do it. He gave me this
money. Someone shot him from the window.

(*Then quite simply, as if that explained it all away*) Why, I loved him.

SECOND PLAIN-CLOTHES MAN   Stop that noise! Wha'd'-yuh take us for—boobs? The window ain't even open and the glass ain't broken. He gave yuh the money, eh? And then shot himself, I suppose? Aw say, Kid, wha'd'yuh take us for?

ROSE (*Losing all control, frenziedly breaks from the* POLICEMAN'S *grasp and throws herself beside the body*) Tim! Tim! For the love of Gawd speak to them. Tell 'em I didn't do it, Tim! Tell 'em yuh gave that money to me. Yuh know what yuh said —"Take the kid into the mountains and git rid of that cough." Tell 'em yuh said that, Tim! Speak to 'em! Tell 'em I loved yuh, Tim—that I wanted to help yuh git away. Tell 'em yuh kissed me. They think I shot yuh. They don't know I loved yuh. For the love of Gawd speak to 'em. (*Weeping and sobbing bitterly*) Oh Gawd, why don't yuh speak, why don't yuh speak?

FIRST PLAIN-CLOTHES MAN (*Sneeringly*) That's good stuff but it won't get yuh anything. (*Turning to his two companions*) Looks to me as if this doll was full of coke or something. You two better take her to the station and make a report. I'll stay here and keep cases on the room. I'm sick of listenin' to that sob stuff.

ROSE (*The* POLICEMAN *taps her on the shoulder and she rises to her feet with a spring, wildly protesting*) But I tell yuh I didn't do it! It was from the window. Can't yuh believe me? I swear I—

(*She stops, appalled by the unbelieving sneers of the policemen, by the white faces in the doorway gazing at* her with fascinated horror. She reads her own guilt in every eye. She realizes the futility of all protest, the maddening hopelessness of it all. The child is still crying. She notices it for the first time and goes over to the bed to soothe it. The POLICEMAN keeps a tight hold of one of her arms. She speaks words of tenderness to the child in dull, mechanical tones. It stops crying. All are looking at her in silence with a trace of compassionate pity on their faces. ROSE seems in a trance. Her eyes are like the eyes of a blind woman. She seems to be aware of something in the room which none of the others can see—perhaps the personification of the ironic life force that has crushed her)

FIRST PLAIN-CLOTHES MAN   Your kid?

ROSE (To the unseen presence in the room)   Yes. I suppose yuh'll take her too?

FIRST PLAIN-CLOTHES MAN (Misunderstanding her, good-naturedly)   I'll take care of her for the time bein'.

ROSE (To the air)   That's right. Make a good job of me. (Suddenly she stretches both arms above her head and cries bitterly, mournfully, out of the depths of her desolation) Gawd! Gawd! Why d'yuh hate me so?

POLICEMAN (Shocked)   Here, here, no rough talk like that. Come along now!

(ROSE leans against him weakly and he supports her to the door, where the group of horrified lodgers silently make way for them. The SECOND PLAIN-CLOTHES MAN follows them. A moment later ROSE's hollow cough echoes in the dark hallway. The child wakes up and cries fitfully. The FIRST PLAIN-CLOTHES MAN goes over to the bed and cuddles her on his lap with elephantine playfulness)

C

CHILD (*Feebly*) Maamaaaa!

FIRST PLAIN-CLOTHES MAN Mama's gone. I'm your mama now.

Curtain

WARNINGS

A Play in One Act

CHARACTERS

James Knapp, wireless operator of the S.S. Empress

Mary Knapp, his wife

Charles, aged fifteen ⎫
Dolly,   "   fourteen ⎪
Lizzie,   "   eleven   ⎬ their children
Sue,   "   eight   ⎪
A baby,   "   one year ⎭

Captain Hardwick of the Empress

Mason, First Officer of the Empress

Dick Whitney, wireless operator of the S.S. Duchess of the same line

Scene I

The dining room of JAMES KNAPP'S *flat in the Bronx. To the left is a door opening into the main hall; farther back a chair, and then a heavy green curtain which screens off an alcove probably used as a bedroom. To the right, a doorway leading into the kitchen, another chair, and a window, with some plants in pots on the sill, which opens on a court. Hanging in front of the window is a gilt cage in which a canary chirps sleepily. The walls of the room are papered an impossible green and the floor is covered with a worn carpet of nearly the same color. Several gaudy Sunday-supplement pictures in cheap gilt frames are hung at spaced intervals around the walls. The dining table with its flowered cover is pushed back against the middle wall to allow more space for free passage between the kitchen and the front part of the flat. On the wall above the table is a mantelpiece on the middle of which a black marble clock ticks mournfully. The clock is flanked on both sides by a formidable display of family photographs. Above the mantel hangs a "Home Sweet Home" motto in a black frame. A lamp of the Welsbach type, fixed on the chandelier which hangs from the middle of the ceiling, floods the small room with bright light. It is about half-past eight of an October evening. The time is the present.*

MRS. KNAPP *is discovered sitting at the end of the*

table near the kitchen. She is a pale, thin, peevish-look-
ing woman of about forty, made prematurely old by the
thousand worries of a penny-pinching existence. Her
originally fine constitution has been broken down by
the bearing of many children in conditions under which
every new arrival meant a new mouth crying for its
share of the already inadequate supply of life's neces-
sities. Her brown hair, thickly streaked with gray, is
drawn back tightly over her ears into a knot at the back
of her head. Her thin-lipped mouth droops sorrowfully
at the corners, and her faded blue eyes have an expres-
sion of fretful weariness. She wears a solid gray wrap-
per and black carpet slippers. When she speaks, her
voice is plaintively querulous and without authority.

Two of the children, LIZZIE *and* SUE, *are seated on*
her left facing the family photos. They are both bent
over the table with curly blond heads close together.
Under LIZZIE's *guidance* SUE *is attempting to write*
something on the pad before her. Both are dressed in
clean-looking dark clothes with black shoes and stock-
ings.

LIZZIE   That's not the way to make a "g." Give *me* the
    pencil and *I'll* show you.
    (*She tries to take the pencil away from* SUE)
SUE (*Resisting and commencing to cry*)   I don' wanta
    give you the pencil. Mama-a! Make her stop!
MRS. KNAPP (*Wearily*)   For goodness' sake stop that
    racket, Sue! Give her the pencil, Lizzie! You ought
    to be ashamed to fight with your little sister—and
    you so much older than her. I declare, a body can't

have a moment's peace in this house with you children all the time wranglin' and fightin'.

SUE (*Bawling louder than ever*)   Mama-a! She won't
give it to me!

MRS. KNAPP (*With an attempt at firmness*)   Lizzie!
Did you hear what I said? Give her that pencil this
instant!

LIZZIE (*Not impressed*)   I wanta show her how to
make a "g" and she won't let me. Make her stop,
Mama!

SUE (*Screaming*)   I did make a "g"! I did make a "g"!

LIZZIE   Ooo! Listen to her tellin' lies, Mama. She didn't
make a "g" at all. She don't know how.

SUE   I do! Gimme that pencil.

LIZZIE   You don't. I won't give it to you.

MRS. KNAPP (*Aggravated into action, she gets quickly
from her chair and gives* LIZZIE *a ringing box on
the ear*)   There, you naughty child! That will
teach you to do what I say. Give me that pencil.
(*She snatches it from* LIZZIE's *hand and gives it to*
SUE)   There's the pencil! For goodness sake hush
up your cryin'!

(SUE *subsides into sobbing but* LIZZIE *puts her hand
over the smarting ear and starts to howl with all her
might*)

SUE (*Whimpering again as she discovers the point of
the pencil has been broken off*)   Look Mama! She
broke the pencil!

MRS. KNAPP (*Distracted*)   Be still and I'll sharpen it for
you. (*Turning to* LIZZIE *and taking her on her lap*)
There! There! Stop cryin'! Mama didn't mean to
hurt you. (LIZZIE *only cries the harder*) Stop crying

and I'll give you a piece of candy. (LIZZIE's *anguish
vanishes in a flash*) Kiss Mama now and promise
not to be naughty any more!

LIZZIE (*Kissing her obediently*) I promise. Where's
the candy, Mama?

SUE (*No longer interested in pencils*) I wanta piece of
candy too.

MRS. KNAPP (*Goes to the kitchen and returns with two
sticky chunks of molasses candy*) Here, Lizzie!
Here, Sue! (SUE *manages with some effort to cram
the candy into her small mouth*) Neither one of
you said "thank you" (LIZZIE *dutifully mumbles
"Thanks" but* SUE *is beyond speech*) I declare I
don't know what I'll do with you children. You
never seem to learn manners. It's just as if you
were brought up on the streets—the way you act.
(*The clock strikes eight-thirty and* MRS. KNAPP
looks at it gratefully) There, children. It's half-past
eight and you must both go to bed right away.
Goodness knows I have a hard enough time gettin'
you up for school in the morning.

SUE (*Having eaten enough of her candy to allow of her
voicing a protest*) I don' wanta go to bed.

LIZZIE (*Sulking*) You said you'd let us stay up to see
Papa.

SUE I wanta see Papa.

MRS. KNAPP That will do. I won't listen to any more
of your talk. You've seen your father all afternoon.
That's only an excuse to stay up late. He went to
the doctor's and goodness knows when he'll be
back. I promised to let you sit up till half-past eight
and it's that now. Come now! Kiss me like two
good little girls and go straight to bed.

*(The two good little girls perform their kissing with
an ill grace and depart slowly for bed through the alcove)*

MRS. KNAPP   Mind you don't wake the baby with your
carryings-on or I'll tell your father to spank you
good. *(She has an afterthought)* And don't forget
your prayers!

*(She sinks back with a deep sigh of relief and, taking
up an evening paper from the table, commences to read.
She has hardly settled back comfortably when shouts
and the noise of running steps are heard from the stairs
in the hallway. Then a rattling tattoo of knocks shakes
the door and a girl's voice laughingly shouts through the
key hole: "Open up, Ma!")*

MRS. KNAPP   *(Going quickly to the door and unlocking
it)*   Hush up your noise for goodness sakes! Do
you want to wake up the baby? I never saw such
children. You haven't any feelin' for your mother
at all.

*(CHARLES and DOLLY push hurriedly into the room.
MRS. KNAPP locks the door again and resumes her seat
at the table. CHARLES is a gawky, skinny youth of fifteen
who has outgrown his clothes and whose arms and legs
seem to have outgrown him. His features are large and
irregular; his eyes small and watery-blue in color. When
he takes off his cap a mop of sandy hair falls over his
forehead. He is dressed in a shabby gray Norfolk suit.*

*Although extremely thin, DOLLY is rather pretty with
her dark eyes and her brown curls hanging over her
shoulders. She is dressed neatly in a dark blue frock with
black shoes and stockings and a black felt hat. Her ordi-
narily sallow city complexion is flushed from the run
upstairs)*

DOLLY (*Rushing over and kissing her mother—mischievously*) What do you think I saw, Ma?

CHARLIE (*In a loud voice—almost a shout*) What do you think I saw, Mom?

MRS. KNAPP For heaven's sake, Charlie, speak lower. Do you want the people in the next block to hear you? If you wake up the baby I shall certainly tell your father on you. Take off your hat when you're in the house! Whatever is the matter with you? Can't you remember anything? I'm really ashamed of you—the way you act.

CHARLIE (*Taking off his cap*) Aw, what's the matter, Mom? Gee, you've got an awful grouch on tonight.

MRS. KNAPP Never mind talkin' back to your mother, young man. Why shouldn't I be cranky with you bellowin' around here like a young bull? I just got the baby to sleep and if you wake her up with your noise heaven knows when I'll get any peace again.

DOLLY (*Interrupting her—with a laughing glance at* CHARLIE) You can't guess what I saw, Ma.

CHARLIE (*Sheepishly*) Aw, all right for you. Go ahead and tell her if you wanta. I don't care. I'll tell her what I saw too.

DOLLY You didn't see anything.

CHARLIE I did too.

DOLLY You didn't.

MRS. KNAPP For goodness sake stop your quarrelin'! First it's Lizzie and Sue and then it's you two. I never get time to even read a paper. What was it you saw, Dolly? Tell me if you're going to.

DOLLY—I saw Charlie and that red-headed Harris girl in the corner drug store. He was buying her ice cream soda with that quarter Pop gave him.

CHARLIE   I was no such thing.

DOLLY   Oh, what a lie! You know you were.

MRS. KNAPP   You ought to be ashamed of yourself, you big gump, you, goin' round with girls at your age and spendin' money on them. I'll tell your father how you spend the money he gives you and it'll be a long time before you get another cent.

CHARLIE   (*Sullenly*)   Aw, you needn't think I'm the only one. (*Pointing to* DOLLY) I saw her down in the hallway with that Dutch kid whose father runs the saloon in the next block. It was dark down there too. I could hardly see them. And he's cross-eyed!

DOLLY   He is not.

CHARLIE   Aw, g'wan, of course he is. He can't see straight or he'd never look at you.

DOLLY   He's better than you are.

CHARLIE   (*Losing control of his voice and shouting again*)   I'll hand him a punch in the eye the first time I see him. That's what I'll do to him, the Dutch boob. And I'll slap you in the nose too if you get too fresh.

(DOLLY *starts to cry*)

MRS. KNAPP   (*Rising up swiftly and giving him a crack over the ear with her open hand*)   That'll teach you, young man! Don't you dare to lay a hand on your sister or your father will whip you good.

CHARLIE   (*Backing away with his hand on his ear—in a whimper*)   Aw, what are you always pickin' on me for? Why don't you say something to her?

MRS. KNAPP   (*Turning to the still tearful* DOLLY)   And you, miss! Don't you let me hear of you bein' in any dark hallways with young men again or I'll

take you over my knee, so I will. The idea of such
a thing! I can't understand you at all. I never was
allowed out alone with anyone—not even with
your father, before I was engaged to be married to
him. I don't know what's come over you young
folks nowadays.

DOLLY   It—wasn't—dark.

MRS. KNAPP   It makes no difference. You heard what I
said. Don't let it happen again.

(DOLLY *wipes her eyes and makes a face at* CHARLIE)

CHARLIE   (*His tones loud with triumph*)   It was awful
dark. She's lyin' to you, Mom.

MRS. KNAPP   Hold your tongue! I've heard enough from
you. And don't yell at the top of your voice. You
don't have to shout. I'm not deaf.

CHARLIE   (*Lower*)   All right, Mom. But I've got into
the habit of talking loud since Pop's been home.
He don't seem to hear me when I talk low.

DOLLY   That's right, Ma. I was talking to him this
morning and when I got through he didn't know
half that I'd told him.

MRS. KNAPP   Your father has a bad cold and his head is
all stopped up. *He* says he hasn't got a cold but I
know better. I've been that way myself. But he
won't believe me. So he's gone to pay five dollars to
an ear specialist when all he needs is a dose of qui-
nine—says a wireless operator can't afford to take
chances. I told him a wireless operator couldn't
afford to pay five dollars for nothin'—specially
when he's got a wife and five children. (*Peevishly*)
I don't know what's come over your father. He
don't seem like the same man since this last trip

on the *Empress.* I think it must be that South
American climate that's affectin' him.

DOLLY   He's awful cross since he's been home this time.
He yells at Charlie and me for nothing.

MRS. KNAPP   He'd be all right if he could get another
job. But he's afraid if he gives up this one he won't
be able to get another. Your father ain't as young
as he used to be and they all want young men now.
He's got to keep on workin' or we'd never be able
to even pay the rent. Goodness knows his salary is
small enough. If it wasn't for your brother Jim
sendin' us a few dollars every month, and Charlie
earnin' five a week, and me washin', we'd never be
able to get along even *with* your father's salary. But
heaven knows what we'd do without it. We'd be
put out in the streets.

CHARLIE   Is that where Pop's gone tonight—to the
doctor's?

MRS. KNAPP   Yes, and I don't know what can be keepin'
him so long. He left after supper right after you
did. You'd think he'd spend his last night at home
when we won't see him again for three months.

CHARLIE   Shall I go out and see if I can see him?

MRS. KNAPP   Don't go makin' excuses to get out on the
street. You better go to bed if you wanta be up on
time in the morning—you too, Dolly.

DOLLY   I still got some of my lessons to finish.

(*There is a sound from the hallway of someone coming up the stairs with slow, heavy steps*)

MRS. KNAPP   Here your father comes now! Get into the
parlor, Dolly, if you wanta do your lessons. Don't
let him see you up so late. Keep the light shaded so

you won't wake up the baby. (*The steps stop before the door and a knock is heard*) Charlie, go
open that door. My feet are worn out from standin'
up all day.

(CHARLIE *opens the door and* JAMES KNAPP *enters. He
is a slight, stoop-shouldered, thin-faced man of about
fifty. When he takes off his derby hat he reveals a long
narrow head almost completely bald, with a thin line
of gray hair extending over his large ears around the
back of his head. His face has been tanned by the tropic
sun—but now it seems a sickly yellow in the white glare
of the lamp. His eyes are small, dark, and set close together; his nose stubby and of no particular shape; his
mouth large and weak. He is dressed in a faded brown
suit and unshined tan shoes. His expression must be
unusually depressed as he stands nervously fingering his
drooping gray mustache, for* MRS. KNAPP *looks at him
sharply for a moment, then gets up quickly and goes
over and kisses him*)

MRS. KNAPP (*Pulling out the armchair from the other
end of the table for him*)   Come! Sit down! You
look all worn out. You shouldn't walk so much.

KNAPP (*Sinking into the chair and speaking in a slow,
dull voice*)   I am a bit tired.

(*He stares at the flowered patterns of the table cover
for a moment—then sighs heavily*)

MRS. KNAPP   Whatever is the matter with you? You
look as if you'd lost your last friend.

KNAPP (*Pulling himself together and smiling feebly*)
I guess I've got the blues. I get to thinking about
how I've got to sail tomorrow on that long, lone-
some trip, and how I won't see any of you for three

months, and it sort of makes me feel bad. I wish
I could throw up this job. I wish I was young
enough to try something else.

CHARLIE (*Who is slouched down in a chair with his
hands in his pockets, speaks in his lowest, nicest
voice*) Aw, cheer up, Pop! It won't seem long.
I should think you'd be glad to get out of the cold
weather. Gee, I wish't I had a chance.

KNAPP (*Looking at him blankly*) Eh? What was that,
Charlie? I didn't hear what you said.

CHARLIE (*In his best bellow*) I said: Cheer up! It
won't seem long.

KNAPP (*Shaking his head sadly*) It's easy for you to
say that. You're young.

(*The shrill crying of a baby sounds from behind the
green curtain of the alcove.*)

MRS. KNAPP (*Turning on* CHARLIE *furiously*) There!
You've gone and done it with your big, loud
mouth. I told you to speak lower. (*Turning to her
husband*) James. I wish you'd do something to
make him behave. He don't mind what I say at all.
Look at him—sprawled all over the chair with his
long legs stretched out for everybody to trip over.
Is that the way to sit on a chair? Anybody'd think
you were brought up in a barn. I declare I'm
ashamed to have you go anywhere for fear you'd
disgrace me.

CHARLIE You needn't worry. There's no place for me
to go—and if there was, I wouldn't go there with
these clothes on. Why don't you ball out Pop? He
couldn't hear me, so I had to speak louder.

KNAPP (*With sudden irritation*) Of course I heard

you. But I wasn't paying any attention to what you said. I have other things to think about beside your chatter.

(CHARLIE *sulks back in his chair*)

MRS. KNAPP   That's right, James. I knew you'd have to tell him where he belongs. You'd think he owned the house the way he acts. (A *piercing wail comes from behind the curtain and* MRS. KNAPP *hurries there, saying*) Hush! Hush! I'm coming.

(*She can be heard soothing the baby.*)

CHARLIE (*Plucking up his courage now that his mother is out of the room*)   Say, Pop!

KNAPP   Well, Charlie, what is it?

CHARLIE   Please, can I have a new suit of clothes? Gee, I need 'em bad enough. This one is full of patches and holes and all the other kids down at the store laugh at me 'cause I ain't got long pants on and these don't fit me any more. Please, can I have a new suit, Pop?

KNAPP (A *look of pain crossing his features*)   I'm afraid not just now, boy. (CHARLIE *descends into the depths of gloom*) You see, I've had to go to this doctor about (*He hesitates*) the —er—trouble I've had with my stomach, and he's very expensive. But when I come back from this trip I'll surely buy you a fine new suit with long pants the very first thing I do. I promise it to you and you know I don't break my promises. Try and get along with that one until I get back.

CHARLIE (*Ruefully*)   All right, Pop. I'll try, but I'm afraid it's going to bust if I get any bigger.

KNAPP   That's a good boy. We haven't been having much luck lately and we've all got to stand for our share of doing without things. I may have to do without a lot—

(*He turns his face away to hide his emotion from* CHARLIE. *A sob shakes his shoulders.* CHARLIE *notices it and goes over clumsily and pats his father on the back*)

CHARLIE Gee Pop, what's the matter? I can get along without a suit all right. I wouldn't have asked you if I thought you was so blue.

KNAPP Never mind me, boy. I'm just not feeling well, that's all—something I must have eaten—or a touch of fever. (*He glances at the clock*) It's getting pretty late, Charlie, and you've got to be up early in the morning. Better go to bed. Your mother and I have a lot to talk about yet—things which wouldn't interest you.

CHARLIE All right, Pop. Good night. I'll see you in the morning before I go.

KNAPP Good night and—remember I'm trying to do the best I know how.

(CHARLIE *disappears behind the green curtain.* KNAPP *stares at the table, his head between his hands, his face full of suffering.* MRS. KNAPP *comes back into the room. The baby is safely asleep again*)

MRS. KNAPP You sent Charlie to bed, didn't you? (*He nods*) That's right. He stays up altogether too late nights. He's always prowlin' around the streets. I don't know what will become of him I'm sure. Dolly told me tonight she saw him buyin' soda for that red-headed Harris girl with the quarter you gave him. What do you think of that? And he says he saw her talkin' in the dark hallway downstairs with some German bartender's boy. What do you think of that?

KNAPP (*Mildly*)   Where's the hurt? They're only kids and they're got to have some fun.

MRS. KNAPP   Fun? I'm glad you call it fun. I think it's disgraceful.

KNAPP   Come, come, you exaggerate everything so. I see no harm in it. God knows I have enough to worry about without being bothered with children's pranks.

MRS. KNAPP (*Scornfully*)   You have worries? And what are they, I'd like to know? You sail away and have a fine time with nothin' to do but eat the best of food and talk to the pretty women in the First Class. Worries? I wish you'd stay home and change places with me—cookin', scrubbin', takin' care of the children, puttin' off the grocer and the butcher, doin' washin' and savin' every penny. You'd soon find out what worry meant then.

KNAPP (*Placatingly*)   I know you have to put up with a lot, Mary, and I wish I could do something to make it easier for you. (*Brokenly*) I don't know what's going to become of us—now.

MRS. KNAPP   Oh, we'll manage to get along as we have been doin', I expect.

KNAPP   But—Mary—something terrible has happened. I'm almost afraid to tell you.

MRS. KNAPP   What do you mean? You haven't lost your job, have you?

KNAPP   I went to see that ear specialist and—

(*His emotion chokes him; he stops to regain his composure*)

MRS. KNAPP   Yes?

KNAPP (*His voice breaking in spite of himself*)   He says

I'm losing my hearing—that I'm liable to go stone-deaf at any moment.

(*He lets his head fall on his arms with a sob*)

MRS. KNAPP (*Coming over and putting her arm around him*) There, Jim! Don't take on about it so. All those doctors make things worse than they really are. He's just trying to scare you so you'll keep comin' to see him. Why, you can hear just as well as I can.

KNAPP No, I've noticed how hard it's been for me to catch some of the messages lately. And since I've been home I've had a hard time of it now and then to understand the children. The doctor said I would probably be able to hear for a long time yet but I got to be prepared for a sudden shock which'll leave me stone-deaf.

MRS. KNAPP (*Quickly*) Does anyone on the ship know?

KNAPP Of course not. If they knew my hearing was going back on me I wouldn't hold my job a minute. (*His voice trembles*) But I've got to tell them now. I've got to give up.

MRS. KNAPP You didn't tell the specialist what you were, did you?

KNAPP No. I said I was a machinist.

MRS. KNAPP (*Getting up from her chair and speaking in a hard voice*) Then why have you got to tell them? If you don't tell them they'll never know. You say yourself the doctor told you your hearin' would hold out for a long time yet.

KNAPP He said "probably."

MRS. KNAPP (*An angry flush spreading over her face*)

Give up your job? Are you a fool? Are you such a
coward that a doctor can scare you like that?

KNAPP   I'm not afraid for myself. I'm not afraid of being deaf if I have to be. You don't understand. You
don't know the responsibility of a man in my job.

MRS. KNAPP   Responsibility? You've told me lots of
times there was so few messages to send and take
you wondered why they had a wireless. What's the
matter with you all of a sudden? You're not deaf
now and even if that lyin' doctor spoke the truth
you'll hear for a long time yet. He only told you
about that sudden stroke to keep you comin' to
him. I know the way they talk.

KNAPP   (*Protesting weakly*)   But it ain't right. I ought
to tell them and give up the job. Maybe I can get
work at something else.

MRS. KNAPP   (*Furiously*)   Right? And I suppose you
think it's right to loaf around here until we all get
out in the streets? God knows your salary is small
enough but without it we'd starve to death. Can't
you think of others besides yourself? How about
me and the children? What's goin' to buy them
clothes and food? I can't earn enough, and what
Charlie gets wouldn't keep *him* alive for a week.
Jim sends us a few dollars a month but he don't
get much and he ain't workin' regular. We owe
the grocer and the butcher now. If they found out
you wasn't workin' they wouldn't give us any more
credit. And the landlord? How long would he let
us stay here? You'll get other work? Remember the
last time you tried. We had to pawn everything we
had then and we was half-starved when you did
land this job. You had to go back to the same old

work, didn't you? They didn't want you at any tel-
egraph office, did they? You was too old and slow,
wasn't you? Well, you're older and slower than
ever now and that's the only other job you're fit
for. (*With bitter scorn*) You'll get another job!
(*She sits down and covers her face with her hands,
weeping bitterly*) And this is all the thanks I get
for slavin' and workin' my fingers off! What a
father for my poor children! Oh, why did I ever
marry such a man? It's been nothin' but worryin'
and sufferin' ever since.

KNAPP (*Who has been writhing under the lash of her
scorn, is tortured beyond endurance at her last re-
proaches*) For God's sake let me alone! I'll go!
I'll go! But this is going to be my last trip. I got to
do the right thing. (*He gets up and pushes aside
the green curtain*) Come on! I'm going to bed.

(*He leaves* MRS. KNAPP *alone. She lifts her tear-
stained face from her hands and sighs with relief as she
turns out the gas*)

SCENE II

A *section of the boat deck of the S. S. Empress just
abaft of the bridge. The deck slants sharply downward
in the direction of the bow. To the left are the officers'
cabins with several lighted port holes. Just in back of
them and in the middle of the deck is the wireless room
with its door wide open revealing* JAMES KNAPP *bent
over his instrument on the forward side of the compartment. His face is pale and set, and he is busy sending
out calls, pausing every now and then with a strained
expression as if he were vainly trying to catch some an-*

swer to his messages. Every time he taps on the key the snarl of the wireless sounds above the confused babble of frightened voices that rises from the promenade deck. To the right of the wireless room on the port side is a life raft. Still farther to the right is one of the funnels. The background is a tropic sky blazing with stars. The wires running up from the wireless room to the fore-mast may be seen dimly lined against the sky. The time is about eleven o'clock.

CAPTAIN HARDWICK enters hurriedly from the direction of the bridge and walks across to the door of the wireless room, where he stands looking in at KNAPP. He is a stocky man about fifty dressed in a simple blue uniform. His face is reddened by sun and wind—that is, all of it which is not hidden by his gray beard and mustache. He drums nervously on the door. KNAPP pretends not to see him and appears absorbed in his instrument.

CAPTAIN HARDWICK   No answer yet? (KNAPP *does not reply and the* CAPTAIN *leans over impatiently and shakes him by the shoulder*) I asked you if there was any answer yet?

KNAPP (*Looking at him furtively*)   I haven't heard a thing yet, sir.

CAPTAIN HARDWICK   Damnation? What in hell is the matter with them? Are they all asleep?

KNAPP   I'll try again, sir.

(*He taps on the key before him and the whine of the wireless shrills out discordantly*)

CAPTAIN HARDWICK (*Turning away with a muttered oath*)   Well, I've got to get back on the bridge. Let me know the moment you catch anyone.

KNAPP (*Who has been watching his lips move*) Yes, sir.

(*His tone is vague, as if he were guessing at the answer.*)

CAPTAIN HARDWICK Tell 'em we hit a derelict and are sinking. Make it as strong as you can. We need help and we need it right away.

KNAPP (*More vaguely than ever*) Yes, sir.

CAPTAIN HARDWICK You surely ought to get the *Verdari*. She can't be more than a hundred miles away if my reckoning is correct. (*Turning away again*) I've got to go. Keep sending until you get an answer.

KNAPP Yes, sir.

CAPTAIN HARDWICK (*Under his breath*) Damn your "yes, sirs." I believe you're frightened out of your wits. (*He walks quickly toward the bridge. Halfway across the deck he is met by* MASON, *a tall, cleanshaven, middle-aged man in uniform who hurries in from forward*) Well, Mason, how do things look below?

MASON Very bad, sir. I'm afraid the bulkhead can't hold out much longer. They're doing all they can to strengthen it but it don't look to me as if it would stand the pressure. I wouldn't give it more than half an hour—an hour at most, sir.

CAPTAIN HARDWICK She's listing pretty badly. Guess you're right, Mason. When that bulkhead goes it's only a question of five or ten minutes. Are the crew all ready to man the boats?

MASON Yes, sir.

CAPTAIN HARDWICK Good! Passengers all on deck and ready to leave?

MASON Yes, sir.

CAPTAIN HARDWICK Good! Lucky there's only a few of them or we'd be in a nice mess. Lucky it's a calm night too. There'll be no panic. (*There is a pause broken only by the confused sound of voices from below*) Damned funny we get no reply to our calls for help, eh? Don't you think so?

MASON Very funny, sir. The *Verdari* ought to be right around here about this time. There ought to be four or five vessels we could reach, I should think.

CAPTAIN HARDWICK Just what I told Knapp. The poor devil seems scared to death because he can't get an answer. All he says every time I ask him is (*Mimicking* KNAPP) "Haven't heard a thing yet, sir!"

MASON He's told me the same thing three or four times. I don't like the looks of it, sir. He appears to act queer to me.

CAPTAIN HARDWICK You're right. He has been strange all during the trip—didn't seem to want to speak to anyone. I thought he must be sick. Think it's drink?

MASON No, sir. I never saw him touch a drop—even on shore.

CAPTAIN HARDWICK Let's see what he's got to say now. By God, we've got to get a message in soon or there'll be the devil to pay.

(*They both go over to the wireless room where* KNAPP *is frenziedly sending out call after call. The* CAPTAIN *goes into the compartment and stands beside* KNAPP. MASON *remains outside the door.* KNAPP *looks up and sees them. He glances fearfully from one to the other*) Caught the *Verdari* yet?

KNAPP (*In the uncertain tone he had used before*)   I
   haven't heard a thing yet, sir.

CAPTAIN HARDWICK   Are you sure there's nothing wrong
   with this machine of yours?

KNAPP (*Bewilderedly*)   No, sir. Not a single answer,
   sir. I can't account for it, sir.

CAPTAIN HARDWICK (*Angrily*)   I know that. You've
   told me often enough. Answer my question?
   (KNAPP *looks at him with puzzled eyes; then turns
   to the key of his instrument. The* CAPTAIN *grabs
   him by the shoulder*) Did you hear what I said?
   Dammit, answer my question.

KNAPP (*His lips trembling*)   No, sir.

CAPTAIN HARDWICK (*Furiously*)   What?

MASON (*Interposing*)   Excuse me, sir, but something's
   wrong with the man. I don't think he heard what
   you said.

CAPTAIN HARDWICK   The coward is frightened silly—
   that's what's the matter. (*Bending down he shouts
   against the receivers which* KNAPP *has over both his
   ears*) Say something, can't you? Are you deaf?

(KNAPP *shrinks away from him, his face ashy with
fear, but does not answer*)

MASON   Maybe it's those things on his ears, sir.

CAPTAIN HARDWICK (*Taking hold of the metal loops
   that go over* KNAPP's *head and jerking the receivers
   off his ears*) Now! Answer me! What in hell's
   the matter with you? (*Then, his voice softening a
   bit*) If you're sick, why don't you say so?

KNAPP (*Looking at him helplessly for a moment—then
   hiding his face in his arms and weeping hysterically*) Oh my God! It's come! (*The* CAPTAIN *and*

MASON *look at each other in amazement as* KNAPP
blurts out between his sobs) I wasn't sure. I was
hoping against hope. I can't hear a word you say.
I can't hear anything. It's happened just as the
doctor said it might. (*Looking up at the* CAPTAIN
and clasping and unclasping his hands piteously)
Oh, I should have told you, sir, before we started
—but we're so poor and I couldn't get another job.
I was just going to make this one more trip. I
wanted to give up the job this time but she
wouldn't let me. She said I wanted them to starve
—and Charlie asked me for a suit. (*His sobs stifle
him*) Oh God, who would have dreamt this could
have happened—at such a time. I thought it would
be all right—just this trip. I'm not a bad man,
Captain. And now I'm deaf—stone-deaf. I can't
hear what you say. I'm deaf! Oh my God! My
God!

(*He flings his arms on the instrument in front of him
and hides his face on them, sobbing bitterly*)

CAPTAIN HARDWICK (*Turning to* MASON)   Well, I'll be
damned! What do you make of this?

MASON   I guess what he says is true, sir. He's gone deaf.
That's why we've had no answer to our calls.

CAPTAIN HARDWICK (*Fuming helplessly*)   What in hell
can we do? I must know they're coming for us before I send the boats away. (*He thinks a moment.
Suddenly his face lights up and he strikes his fist
into his open palm*) By God, I've got it. You know
Dick Whitney? (MASON *nods*) Operator of the
the First Cabin—run and get him. (MASON *runs*
Duchess—been laid up in Bahia with fever—came
on board there—going home on vacation—he's in

down the deck toward the bridge) Hurry, for God's sake! (MASON *is gone.* CAPTAIN HARDWICK *turns to* KNAPP, *and lifting him by the arms helps him out of the cabin and sits him down on the life raft. He pats him roughly on the back*) Brace up! Poor beggar!

(KNAPP *continues to sob brokenly.* MASON *reappears followed by* DICK WHITNEY, *a thin, sallow-faced young fellow of about twenty-five, wearing a light sack suit. He shows the effect of his recent battle with tropical fever but he walks over to the wireless room confidently enough and takes his seat before the instrument*)

CAPTAIN HARDWICK Get someone quick, Whitney. Tell 'em we're just about to launch the boats.

WHITNEY (*Who has put the receivers over his ears*) They're calling us now, sir. (*He sends an answering call—a pause*) It's the *Verdari*.

CAPTAIN HARDWICK Good! I knew she ought to be near us.

WHITNEY Operator says they're coming full speed— ought to reach us before daylight—wants to know if we can't keep up till then.

CAPTAIN HARDWICK No. Tell them the bulkhead is almost gone. We're due to sink within an hour at most. (*To* MASON) Better go down and see how things are below.

(MASON *leaves hurriedly*)

WHITNEY All right, sir.

(*He taps on the key—the wail of the wireless sounds again—then a pause*)

CAPTAIN HARDWICK What do they say now?

WHITNEY (*With a slight smile*) "Hard luck."

CAPTAIN HARDWICK (*Exploding*) Damn their sympathy!

WHITNEY The operator says he's been trying to communicate with us for a long time. He got our message all right but we never seemed to get his. (*The* CAPTAIN *glances at* KNAPP, *who is still sitting on the life raft with his face hidden in his hands*) He says he got a call from one of the Fruit Company's boats. She's rushing to help us too. He wants to know if we've heard anything from her.

CAPTAIN HARDWICK No. (*He looks at* KNAPP *again, then speaks dryly*) Tell him our receiving apparatus has been out of order.

WHITNEY (*Looks up in surprise—then sends the message. There is a pause*) He asks if we're sure it was a derelict we struck—says the *Verdari* sighted one about where we are now yesterday and he sent out warnings to all vessels he could reach—says he tried to get us especially because he knew we passed this way; but if our receiving end was bad that explains it.

CAPTAIN HARDWICK (*Staring at* KNAPP) By God!

WHITNEY Anything more you want to say, sir?

CAPTAIN HARDWICK (*Mechanically*) Tell them to hurry, that's all. (*Suddenly in a burst of rage he strides toward* KNAPP *and raises his fist as if to strike him.* MASON *comes in from astern and steps in between them.* CAPTAIN HARDWICK *glares at him for a moment—then recovers himself*) You're right, Mason. I won't touch him; but that miserable, cowardly shrimp has lost my ship for me. (*His face plainly shows how much this loss means to him.* MASON *does not understand what he means.*

CAPTAIN HARDWICK *turns to the wireless room again, where young* WHITNEY *is sitting expectantly awaiting orders*) Say, Whitney! Write out that last message from the *Verdari* about her sending out warnings of that derelict yesterday—warnings which we didn't get. Put down how the operator on the *Verdari* tried especially to warn us because he knew we would pass this way.

(MASON *now understands and turns from* KNAPP *with a glance full of scorn.* WHITNEY *writes rapidly on the report pad near him and hands the sheet to the* CAPTAIN, *who walks over to* KNAPP *and, shaking him, holds the message out.* KNAPP *takes it in a trembling hand*)

MASON   I've got all the men up from below, sir. The bulkhead's ready to go any minute. Shall I get some of the boats away, sir?

CAPTAIN HARDWICK   Yes. (MASON *starts astern*) Wait a moment. I'm coming with you. Come on, Whitney. You can't do any good there any longer. (*He stops in front of* KNAPP *as he walks toward the stern.* KNAPP *is staring at the paper in his hand with wild eyes and pale, twitching features.* CAPTAIN HARDWICK *motions to him to follow them. They go off to right.* KNAPP *sits still with the sheet of paper in his hand. The creaking of blocks is heard and* MASON'S *voice shouting orders*)

KNAPP (*In a hoarse whisper*)   God! It's my fault then! It's my fault! (*He staggers weakly to his feet*) What if the ship is lost! (*He looks astern where they are lowering the boats—his face is convulsed with horror—he gives a bitter cry of despair*) O-o-h! They're lowering the boats! She is lost! She is lost! (*He stumbles across the deck into the wire-*

less room, pulls out a drawer and takes out a re-
volver, which he presses against his temple) She is
lost!

(*There is a sharp report and* KNAPP *falls forward on*
his face on the floor before his instrument. His body
twitches for a moment, then is still. The operator WHIT-
NEY *comes running in from the right, calling, "Knapp!*
They're waiting for you." He gives one horrified glance
at the body in the room; says, "Good God!" in a stupe-
fied tone, and then, seized with sudden terror, rushes
astern again)

Curtain

FOG

A Play in One Act

CHARACTERS

A Poet

A Man of Business

A Polish Peasant Woman

A Dead Child

The Third Officer of a Steamer

Sailors from the Steamer

Scene—*The lifeboat of a passenger steamer is drifting helplessly off the Grand Banks of Newfoundland. A dense fog lies heavily upon the still sea. There is no wind and the long swells of the ocean are barely perceptible. The surface of the water is shadowy and unreal in its perfect calmness. A menacing silence, like the genius of the fog, broods over everything.*

Three figures in the boat are darkly outlined against the gray background of vapor. Two are seated close together on the thwarts in the middle. The other is huddled stiffly at one end. None of their faces can be distinguished.

Day is just about to break, and as the action progresses, the vague twilight of dawn creeps over the sea. This, in turn, is succeeded by as bright a semblance of daylight as can sift through the thick screen of fog.

MAN'S VOICE (*Appallingly brisk and breezy under the circumstances*) Brrr! I wish daylight would come. I'm beginning to feel pretty chilly. How about you? (*He receives no answer and raises his voice, the fear of solitude suddenly alive within him*) Hello there! You havn't gone to sleep, have you?

ANOTHER MAN'S VOICE (*More refined than the first, clear and unobtrusively melancholy*) No, I'm not asleep.

D

FIRST VOICE (*Complacently reassured*) Thought you
    might have dozed off. I did a while ago—eyes re-
    fused to stay open any longer—couldn't imagine
    where I was when I woke up—had forgotten all
    about the damned wreck.

SECOND VOICE   You are fortunate to be able to sleep.
    I wish I could go to sleep and forget—all this—

FIRST VOICE   Oh, come now! You mustn't keep think-
    ing about it. That won't do any good. Brace up!
    We're sure to get out of this mess all right. I've
    figured it all out. You know how long a time it was
    between the time we hit the derelict—it was a der-
    elict we hit, wasn't it?

SECOND VOICE   I believe so.

FIRST VOICE   Well, the wireless was going all the time,
    if you remember, and one of the officers told me
    we had lots of answers from ships saying they were
    on the way to help us. One of them is sure to pick
    us up.

SECOND VOICE   In this fog?

FIRST VOICE   Oh, this'll all go away as soon as the sun
    goes up. I've seen plenty like it at my country place
    on the Connecticut shore, maybe not as thick as
    this one but nearly as bad, and when the sun came
    up they always disappeared before the morning
    was over.

SECOND VOICE   You forget we are now near the Grand
    Banks, the home of fog.

FIRST VOICE (*With a laugh that is a bit troubled*) I
    must say you aren't a very cheerful companion.
    Why don't you look at the bright side? (*A pause
    during which he is evidently thinking over what*

the other man has told him) The Grand Banks?
Hmm, well, I refuse to be scared.

SECOND VOICE   I have no intention of making our situation seem worse than it really is. I have every hope that we will eventually be rescued, but it's better not to expect too much. It only makes disappointment more bitter when it comes.

FIRST VOICE   I suppose you're right, but I can't help being optimistic.

SECOND VOICE   You remember how downcast you were yesterday when we failed to hear any sound of a ship? Today is liable to be the same unless this fog lifts. So don't hope for too much.

FIRST VOICE   You're forgetting the fact that there was no sun yesterday. That kind of weather can't last forever.

SECOND VOICE (*Dryly*)   Perhaps we could not see the sun on account of the fog.

FIRST VOICE (*After a pause*)   I'll admit I did feel pretty dismal yesterday—after that terrible thing happened.

SECOND VOICE (*Softly*)   You mean after the child died?

FIRST VOICE (*Gloomily*)   Yes. I thought that woman would never stop crying. Ugh! It was awful—her cries, and the fog, and not another sound anywhere.

SECOND VOICE   It was the most horrible thing I have ever seen or even heard of. I never dreamed anything could be so full of tragedy.

FIRST VOICE   It was enough to give anyone the blues, that's sure. Besides, my clothes were wet and I was freezing cold and you can imagine how merry I felt. (*Grumbling*) Not that they're any dryer now but somehow I feel warmer.

SECOND VOICE (*After a long pause*)   So you think the child's death was a terrible thing?

FIRST VOICE (*In astonishment*)   Of course. Why? Don't you?

SECOND VOICE   No.

FIRST VOICE   But you said just a minute ago that—

SECOND VOICE   I was speaking of the grief and despair of the mother. But death was kind to the child. It saved him many a long year of sordid drudgery.

FIRST VOICE   I don't know as I agree with you there. Everyone has a chance in this world; but we've all got to work hard, of course. That's the way I figure it out.

SECOND VOICE   What chance had that poor child? Naturally sickly and weak from underfeeding, transplanted to the stinking room of a tenement or the filthy hovel of a mining village, what glowing opportunities did life hold out that death should not be regarded as a blessing for him? I mean if he possessed the ordinary amount of ability and intelligence—considering him as the average child of ignorant Polish immigrants. Surely his prospects of ever becoming anything but a beast of burden were not bright, were they?

FIRST VOICE   Well, no, of course not, but—

SECOND VOICE   If you could bring him back to life would you do so? Could you conscientiously drag him away from that fine sleep of his to face what he would have to face? Leaving the joy you would give his mother out of the question, would you do it for him individually?

FIRST VOICE (*Doubtfully*) Perhaps not, looking at it from that standpoint.

SECOND VOICE There is no other standpoint. The child was diseased at birth, stricken with a hereditary ill that only the most vital men are able to shake off.

FIRST VOICE You mean?

SECOND VOICE I mean poverty—the most deadly and prevalent of all diseases.

FIRST VOICE (*Amused*) Oh, that's it, eh? Well, it seems to be a pretty necessary sickness and you'll hardly find a cure for it. I see you're a bit of a reformer.

SECOND VOICE Oh no. But there are times when the frightful injustice of it all sickens me with life in general.

FIRST VOICE I find life pretty good. I don't know as I'd change it even if I could.

SECOND VOICE Spoken like a successful man. For I'm sure you are a successful man, are you not? I mean in a worldly way.

FIRST VOICE (*Flattered*) Yes, you might call me so, I guess. I've made my little pile but it was no easy time getting it, let me tell you.

SECOND VOICE You had some advantages, did you not? Education and plenty to eat, and a clean home, and so forth?

FIRST VOICE I went to high school and of course had the other things you mentioned. My people were not exactly what you could call poor but they were certainly not rich. Why do you ask?

SECOND VOICE Do you think you would be as successful and satisfied with life if you had started with handicaps like those which that poor dead child would have had to contend with if he had lived?

FIRST VOICE (*Impatiently*)   Oh, I don't know! What's the use of talking about what might have happened? I'm not responsible for the way the world is run.

SECOND VOICE   But supposing you are responsible?

FIRST VOICE   What!

SECOND VOICE   I mean supposing we—the self-satisfied, successful members of society—are responsible for the injustice visited upon the heads of our less fortunate "brothers-in-Christ" because of our shameful indifference to it. We see misery all around us and we do not care. We do nothing to prevent it. Are we not then, in part at least, responsible for it? Have you ever thought of that?

FIRST VOICE (*In tones of annoyance*)   No, and I'm not going to start in thinking about it now.

SECOND VOICE (*Quietly*)   I see. It's a case of what is Hecuba to you that you should weep for her.

FIRST VOICE (*Blankly*)   Hecuba? Oh, you mean the woman. You can't accuse me of any heartlessness there. I never felt so sorry for anyone in my life. Why, I was actually crying myself at one time, I felt so sorry for her. By the way, she hasn't made a sound since it got dark last evening. Is she asleep? Can you see her? You're nearer to her than I am.

(*It is becoming gradually lighter although the fog is as thick as ever. The faces of the two men in the boat can be dimly distinguished—one round, jowly, and clean-shaven; the other oval with big dark eyes and a black mustache and black hair pushed back from his high forehead. The huddled figure at the end of the boat is clearly that of a woman. One arm is flung over*

her face, concealing it. In the other she clutches some-
thing like a bundle of white clothes)

DARK MAN (*He of the Second Voice, who is seated on
the thwart nearer to the woman—turning round
and peering in her direction*) She is very still.
She must be asleep. I hope so, poor woman!

OTHER MAN Yes, a little sleep will do her a world of
good.

DARK MAN She still holds the body of the child close
to her breast. (*He returns to his former position
facing the* OTHER MAN) I suppose you—

OTHER MAN (*Exultingly*) Excuse my interrupting you,
but have you noticed how light it's getting? It
didn't strike me until you turned around just now.
I can see your face plainly and a few minutes ago
I couldn't tell whether you were a blond or bru-
nette.

DARK MAN Now if this fog would only lift—

OTHER MAN It's going to lift. You wait and see. You'll
find my optimism is justified. But what was it you
started to say?

DARK MAN I was saying that I supposed you had never
seen this woman on board.

OTHER MAN No. I was in the smoking room playing
bridge most of the time. I'm not much of a sailor—
don't care much about the water—just went over to
Europe because the wife and the girls insisted. I
was bored to death—made an excuse to get away as
soon as I could. No, sir, you can't teach an old dog
new tricks. I'm a businessman pure and simple and
the farther I get away from that business the more
dissatisfied I am. I've built that business up from
nothing and it's sort of like a child of mine. It gives

me pleasure to watch over it and when I'm away I'm uneasy. I don't like to leave it in strange hands. As for traveling, little old New York in the U.S.A. is good enough for me. (*He pauses impressively, waiting for some word of approval for his sterling patriotic principles. The* DARK MAN *is silent and he of the U.S.A. continues, a bit disconcerted*) But you asked me if I had seen the woman. I don't think so, because I never went down into the steerage. I know some of the first-class passengers did but I wasn't curious. It's a filthy sort of hole, isn't it?

DARK MAN   It's not so bad. I spent quite a good deal of my time down there.

BUSINESSMAN (*For he of the jowly, fat face and the bald spot is such by his own confession. Chuckling*) In your role of reformer?

DARK MAN   No. Simply because I found the people in the steerage more interesting to talk to than the second-class passengers. I am not a reformer—at least not in the professional sense.

BUSINESSMAN   Do you mind my asking what particular line you are in?

DARK MAN   I am a writer.

BUSINESSMAN   I thought it was something of the kind. I knew you weren't in business when I heard those socialistic ideas of yours. (*Condescendingly*) Beautiful idea—socialism—but too impractical—never come about—just a dream.

DARK MAN   I'm not a socialist—especially—just a humanist, that is all.

BUSINESSMAN   What particular kind of writing do you do?

DARK MAN   I write poetry.

BUSINESSMAN (*In a tone indicating that in his mind poets and harmless lunatics have more than one point in common*)   Oh, I see. Well, there's not much money in that, is there?

POET   No.

BUSINESSMAN (*After a long pause*)   I don't know about you but I'm beginning to feel hungry. Is that box of crackers near you? (*The* POET *reaches in under a thwart and pulls out a box of sea biscuits. The* BUSINESSMAN *takes a handful and munches greedily*)   Never thought hardtack could taste so good. Aren't you going to have any?

POET   No. I am not hungry. The thought of that poor woman takes all my hunger away. I used to watch her every day down in the steerage playing with her little son who is now dead. I think he must have been the only child she ever had, the look on her face was so wonderfully tender as she bent over him. What will her life be now that death has robbed her of the only recompense for her slavery? It seems such needless cruelty. Why was I not taken instead?—I, who have no family or friends to weep, and am not afraid to die.

BUSINESSMAN (*His mouth full*)   You take things to heart too much. That's just like a poet. She'll forget all about it—probably sooner than you will. One forgets everything in time. What a devil of a world it would be if we didn't. (*He takes another handful of sea biscuits and continues his munching. The* POET *turns away from him in disgust*) Funny thing when you come to think of it—I mean how we happened to come together in this boat. It's a mystery to me how she ever got in here. And then, how is it there's no oars in this boat and still there's plenty of food? You remember there was no lack of lifeboats, and after the women and children were taken off I was ordered into one and we were rowed away. The damned thing must have gotten smashed somehow, for it leaked like a sieve and in spite of our bailing we were soon dumped in the water. I heard the noise of voices near us and tried to swim to one of the other boats, but I must have got twisted in the fog, for when I did find a boat—and let me tell you I was pretty nearly "all in" about then—it was this one and you and she were in it. Now what I want to know is—

POET   It is easily explained. Did you ever become so sick of disappointment and weary of life in general that death appeared to you the only way out?

BUSINESSMAN   Hardly. But what has that to do—

POET   Listen and you will see. That is the way I felt— sick and weary of soul and longing for sleep. When the ship struck the derelict it seemed to me providential. Here was the solution I had been looking for. I would go down with the ship, and that small part of the world which knew me would think my death an accident.

BUSINESSMAN   (*Forgetting to eat in his amazement*) You mean to say you were going to commit—

POET   I was going to die, yes. So I hid in the steerage fearing that some of the ship's officers would insist on saving my life in spite of me. Finally, when everyone had gone, I came out and walked around the main deck. I heard the sound of voices come from a dark corner and discovered that this woman

and her child had been left behind. How that happened I don't know. Probably she hid because she
was afraid the child would be crushed by the terror-stricken immigrants. At any rate there she was
and I decided she was so happy in her love for her
child that it would be wrong to let her die. I
looked around and found this lifeboat had been
lowered down to the main deck and left hanging
there. The oars had been taken out—probably for
extra rowers in some other boat. I persuaded the
woman to climb in and then went up to the boat
deck and lowered the boat the rest of the way to
the water. This was not much of a task, for the
steamer was settling lower in the water every minute.
I then slid down one of the ropes to the boat and,
cutting both of the lines that held her, pushed off.
There was a faint breeze which blew us slowly
away from the sinking ship until she was hidden
in the fog. The suspense of waiting for her to go
down was terrible. Even as it was we were nearly
swamped by the waves when the steamer took her
final plunge.

BUSINESSMAN (*Edges away from the* POET, *firmly convinced that his convictions regarding the similarity
of poets and madmen are based upon fact*)   I
hope you've abandoned that suicide idea.

POET   I have—absolutely. I think all that happened to
me is an omen sent by the gods to convince me
my past unhappiness is past and my fortune will
change for the better.

BUSINESSMAN   That's the way to talk! Superstition is
a good thing sometimes.

POET   But if I had known the sufferings that poor

woman was to undergo as a result of my reckless
life-saving, I would have let her go down with the
ship and gone myself.

BUSINESSMAN Don't think of it any longer. You
couldn't help that. I wonder what it was the child
died of? I thought it was asleep when I heard it
choke and cough—and the next minute *she* commenced to scream. I won't forget those screams for
the rest of my life.

POET The child was naturally frail and delicate and I
suppose the fright he received and the exposure
combined to bring on some kind of convulsion.
He was dead when I went over to see what was the
matter.

BUSINESSMAN (*Peering upward through the fog*) It's
getting considerably lighter. It must be about time
for the sun to rise—if we're going to have any sun.

POET (*Sadly*) It was just about this time yesterday
morning when the poor little fellow died.

BUSINESSMAN (*Looks apprehensively toward the huddled figure in the end of the boat. Now that it is
lighter, what appeared before like a bundle of
white clothes can be seen to be a child four or five
years old with a thin, sallow face and long black
curls. The body is rigid, wrapped in a white shawl,
and the eyes are open and glassy*) Let's not talk
any more about it. She might wake up and start
screaming again—and I can't stand that.

POET She does not understand English.

BUSINESSMAN (*Shaking his head*) She'd know we were
talking about the kid just the same. Mothers have
an instinct when it comes to that. I've seen that
proved in my own family more than once.

POET Have you ever lost any of your children?

BUSINESSMAN No. Thank God!

POET You may well thank God, even if people do, as you claimed a while ago, forget so easily.

BUSINESSMAN You're not married, are you?

POET No.

BUSINESSMAN I didn't think you were. (*Jocularly*) You people with artistic temperaments run more to affinities than to wives. I suppose you've lots of those?

POET (*Does not hear or will not notice this question. He is staring through the fog and speaks in excited tones*) Did you hear that?

BUSINESSMAN Hear what?

POET Just now when you were talking. I thought I heard a sound like a steamer's whistle.

(*They both listen intently. After a second or so the sound comes again, faint and far-off, wailing over the water*)

BUSINESSMAN (*Wildly elated*) By God, it is a steamer!

POET It sounded nearer that time. She must be coming this way.

BUSINESSMAN Oh, if only this rotten fog would lift for a minute!

POET Let's hope it will. We run as much risk of being run down as we do of being saved while this continues. They couldn't see us twenty feet away in this.

BUSINESSMAN (*Nervously*) Can't we yell or make some kind of a noise?

POET They couldn't hear us now. We can try when they get close to us. (*A pause during which they hear the steamer whistle again*) How cold the air is! Or is it my imagination?

BUSINESSMAN   No, I notice it too. I've been freezing to death for the last five minutes. I wish we had the oars so we could row and keep warm.

POET   Sssh! Do you hear that?

BUSINESSMAN   What? The whistle? I heard it a moment ago.

POET   No. This is a sound like running water. There! Don't you hear it now?

(A *noise as of water falling over rocks comes clearly through the fog*)

BUSINESSMAN   Yes, I hear it. What can it be? There isn't any water out here except what's under us. (*With a shiver*) Brrr, but it's chilly!

POET   That poor woman will be frozen when she wakes up.

(*He takes off his ulster, and walking carefully to the end of the boat, covers the form of the sleeping woman with it*)

BUSINESSMAN   It sounds louder every minute but I can't see anything. Damn this fog!

(*The noise of the falling water grows more and more distinct. At regular intervals the steamer's whistle blows and that, too, seems to be drawing nearer*)

POET (*Still bent over the sleeping woman*)   Perhaps it may be land but I hardly think we could have drifted that far.

BUSINESSMAN (*In terrified tones*)   Good God, what's that?

(*The* POET *turns quickly around. Something huge and white is looming up through the fog directly beside the boat. The boat drifts up to it sideways and strikes*

against it with a slight jar. The BUSINESSMAN *shrinks
away as far along the thwart as he can get, causing the
boat to tip a little to one side. The spattering splash of
falling water sounds from all around them*)

POET (*Looking at the white mass towering above them*)
An iceberg! (*Turning to the* BUSINESSMAN) Steady
there! You will be in the water in a minute if
you're not careful. There is nothing to be frightened over. Lucky for us it's calm or we would be
smashed to pieces.

BUSINESSMAN (*Reassured by finding out that what he
took for some horrible phantom of the sea is an
ice and water reality, he moves over to the center of his thwart and remarks sarcastically*)   As it
is we'll only freeze to death. Is that what you
mean?

POET (*Thumping his hands against his sides*)   It *is*
cold. I wonder how big the berg is. Help me try
to push the boat away from it.

(*They push against the side of the berg. The boat
moves away a little but drifts right back again*)

BUSINESSMAN   Ouch! My hands are freezing.

POET   No use wasting effort on that. The boat is too
heavy and you can get no grip on the ice. (*A blast
of the steamer's whistle shrills through the fog. It
sounds very close to them*) Oh God, I never
thought of that.

(*He sits down dejectedly opposite the* BUSINESSMAN)

BUSINESSMAN   Never thought of what?

POET (*Excitedly*)   The steamer, man, the steamer!
Think of the danger she is in. If she were ever to
hit this mass of ice she would sink before they could
lower a boat.

BUSINESSMAN   Can't we do something? We'll yell to them when they get nearer.

POET   Oh my God, man, don't do that. This may be one of the rescue ships come to pick up the survivors from our boat, and if they heard any shouts they would think they were cries for help and come right in this direction. Not a sound if you have any regard for the lives of those on board.

BUSINESSMAN   (*Almost whimpering*)   But if we don't let them know we're here they are liable to pass by us and never know it.

POET   (*Sternly*)   We can die but we cannot risk the lives of others to save our own.

(*The* BUSINESSMAN *does not reply to this but a look of sullen stubbornness comes over his face. There is a long pause. The silence is suddenly shattered by a deafening blast from the steamer's whistle*)

POET   God! She must be right on top of us.

(*They both start to their feet and stand straining their eyes to catch some glimpse of the approaching vessel through the blinding mist. The stillness is so intense that the throb of the engines can be plainly heard. This sound slowly recedes and the next whistle indicates by its lack of volume that the steamer has passed and is proceeding on her way*)

BUSINESSMAN   (*Furiously*)   She's going away. I'm not going to be left here to die on account of your damn-fool ideas.

(*He turns in the direction he supposes the steamer to be and raises his hands to his mouth, shaping them like a megaphone*)

POET   (*Jumping over and forcing his hand over the* BUSINESSMAN'S *mouth in time to stifle his call for*

help)   You damned coward! I might have known
what to expect.

(*The* BUSINESSMAN *struggles to free himself, rocking
the boat from side to side with his futile twistings, but
he is finally forced down to a sitting position on the
thwart. The* POET *then releases him. He opens his
mouth as if to shout but the* POET *stands over him with
his right fist drawn back threateningly and the* BUSINESS-
MAN *thinks better of it*)

BUSINESSMAN (*Snarling*)   I'll get even with you, you
loafer, if we ever get on shore.

(*The* POET *pays no attention to this threat but sits
down opposite him. They hear the whistle again, seem-
ingly no farther away than before. The* BUSINESSMAN
*stirs uneasily. A rending, tearing crash cracks through
the silence, followed a moment later by a tremendous
splash. Great drops of water fall in the rocking boat*)

BUSINESSMAN (*Trembling with terror*)   She must have
hit it after all.

POET   No. That can't be it. I don't hear any shouts.
(*Suddenly smiling with relief as he guesses what
has happened*) I know what it is. The berg is melting and breaking up. That was a piece that fell in
the water.

BUSINESSMAN   It almost landed on us. (*He becomes
panic-stricken at this thought and jumps to his
feet*) I'm not going to stand this any longer. We'll
be crushed like flies. I'll take a chance and swim
for it. You can stay here and be killed if you want
to. (*Insane with fear of this new menace he puts
one foot on the gunwale of the boat and is about
to throw himself into the water when the* POET
grabs him by the arm and pulls him back) Let me

go! This is all right for you. You want to die. Do
you want to kill me too, you murderer?

(*He hides his face in his hands and weeps like a fat
child in a fit of temper*)

POET You fool! You could not swim for five minutes
in this icy water. (*More kindly*) Come! Be sensible!
Act like a man!

(*The* BUSINESSMAN *shakes with a combination of sigh
and sob. The whistle blows again and seems once more
to be in their immediate vicinity. The* BUSINESSMAN
*takes a new lease on life at this favorable sign and raises
his head*)

BUSINESSMAN She seems to be getting quite near us
again.

POET Yes, and a moment ago I heard something like
oars creaking in the oarlocks and striking the
water.

BUSINESSMAN (*Hopefully*) Maybe they've lowered a
boat.

(*Even as he is speaking the curtain of fog suddenly
lifts. The sun has just risen over the horizon rim, and
the berg behind them, its surface carved and fretted by
the streams of water from the melting ice, its whiteness
vivid above the blue-gray water, seems like the façade
of some huge Viking temple*)

POET (*He and the* BUSINESSMAN, *their backs turned to
the berg, are looking at something over the water
as if they could hardly believe their good fortune*)
There's the steamer now and she can hardly be
more than a quarter of a mile away. What luck!

BUSINESSMAN And there's the boat you heard. Look!
They were rowing straight toward us.

POET (*Half to himself, with a puzzled expression*) I

wonder how they knew we were here.

VOICE FROM OVER THE WATER   Hello there!

BUSINESSMAN (*Waving frantically*)   Hello!

VOICE (*Nearer—the creak of the oars can be clearly heard*)   Are you people off the *Starland?*

BUSINESSMAN   Yes.

(*With the return of his courage he has regained all his self-assured urbanity. He tries to pull his clothes into some semblance of their former immaculateness, and his round face with its imposing double chin assumes an expression of importance. The* POET's *face is drawn and melancholy as if he were uncertain of the outcome of this unexpected return to life*)

BUSINESSMAN (*Turning to the* POET *with a smile*)   You see, my optimism was justified after all. (*Growing confused before the* POET's *steady glance*) I wish you'd—er—forget all about the little unpleasantness between us. I must confess I was a bit—er—rattled and didn't exactly know what I was doing.

(*He holds out his hand uncertainly. The* POET *takes it with a quiet smile*)

POET (*Simply*)   I had forgotten all about it.

BUSINESSMAN   Thank you.

(*The voice that hailed them is heard giving some orders. The sound of the oars ceases and a moment later a lifeboat similar to the one they are in, but manned by a full crew of sailors, comes alongside of them. A young man in uniform, evidently the Third Officer of the ship, is in the stern steering*)

BUSINESSMAN (*Breezily*)   Hello! You certainly are a welcome sight.

OFFICER (*Looking up at the towering side of the berg*)   You picked out a funny island to land on. What

made you cling so close to this berg? Cold, wasn't
it?

POET   We drifted into it in the fog and having no oars
could not get away. It was about the same time we
first heard your whistle.

OFFICER (*Nodding toward the woman's figure*)   Woman
sick?

POET   She has been asleep, poor woman.

OFFICER   Where's the kid?

POET   In her arms. (*Then, wonderingly*) But how did
you know—?

OFFICER   We'd never have found you but for that.
Why didn't you give us a shout or make some kind
of a racket?

BUSINESSMAN (*Eagerly*)   We were afraid you would
come in our direction and hit this iceberg.

OFFICER   But we might have passed you and never had
an inkling—

BUSINESSMAN (*Impressively*)   In a case of that kind
one has to take chances.

(*The* POET *smiles quietly. The* OFFICER *looks surprised*)

OFFICER   That was very fine of you, I must say. Most
people would only have thought of themselves. As
it was, if it hadn't been for the kid crying we would
have missed you. I was on the bridge with the
First Officer. We had been warned about this berg,
and when the fog came up we slowed down until
we were barely creeping, and stopped altogether
every now and then. It was during one of these
stops, when everything was still, we heard the crying, and I said to the First Officer: "Sounds like a
kid bawling, doesn't it?" And he thought it did too.

It kept getting plainer and plainer until there was
no chance for a mistake—weird too it sounded
with everything so quiet and the fog so heavy. I
said to him again: "It's a kid sure enough, but how
in the devil did it get out here?" And then we both
remembered we had been ordered to keep a look-
out for any of the survivors of the *Starland* who
hadn't been picked up yet, and the First Officer
said: "It's probably some of the poor devils from
the *Starland*," and told me to have a boat lowered.
I grabbed a compass and jumped in. We could
hear the kid crying all the time, couldn't we, boys?
(*He turns to the crew, who all answer:* "Yes, sir")
That's how I was able to shape such a direct course
for you. I was steering by the sound. It stopped just
as the fog rose.

(*During the* OFFICER's *story the* BUSINESSMAN *has been
looking at him with an expression of annoyed stupe-
faction on his face. He is unable to decide whether the*
OFFICER *is fooling or not and turns to the* POET *for enlightenment. But the latter, after listening to the* OF-
FICER's *explanation with intense interest, goes quickly
to the side of the woman and, removing his ulster from
over her shoulders, attempts to awaken her*)

OFFICER (*Noticing what he is doing*) That's right.
    Better wake her up. The steamer will be ready to
    pick us up in a minute, and she must be stiff with
    the cold. (*He turns to one of his crew*) Make a
    line fast to this boat and we'll tow her back to the
    ship.

(*The sailor springs into the* Starland's *boat with a
coil of rope in his hand*)

POET (*Failing to awaken the woman he feels for her*

pulse and then bends down to listen for a heart beat, his ear against her breast. He straightens up finally and stands looking down at the two bodies and speaks to himself half aloud) Poor happy woman.

(*The* OFFICER *and the* BUSINESSMAN *are watching him*)

OFFICER (*Sharply*) Well?

POET (*Softly*) The woman is dead.

BUSINESSMAN Dead!

(*He casts a horrified glance at the still figures in the end of the boat—then clambers clumsily into the other boat and stands beside the officer*)

OFFICER Too bad! But the child is all right, of course?

POET The child has been dead for twenty-four hours. He died at dawn yesterday.

(*It is the* OFFICER'*s turn to be bewildered. He stares at the* POET *pityingly and then turns to the* BUSINESS-MAN)

OFFICER (*Indicating the* POET *with a nod of his head*) A bit out of his head, isn't he? Exposure affects a lot of them that way.

BUSINESSMAN (*Solemnly*) He told you the exact truth of the matter.

OFFICER (*Concluding he has two madmen to deal with instead of one*) Of course. (*To the sailor who has made fast the towing rope*) All fast? (*The sailor jumps into his own boat with a brisk "Aye, aye, sir." The* OFFICER *turns to the* POET) Coming in here or going to stay where you are?

POET (*Gently*) I think I will stay with the dead.

(*He is sitting opposite the two rigid figures, looking*

*at their still white faces with eyes full of a great long-
ing)*

OFFICER (*Mutters*) Cheerful beggar! (*He faces the
    crew*) Give way all.

(*The oars take the water and the two boats glide
swiftly away from the iceberg.*

*The fresh morning breeze ripples over the water
bringing back to the attentive ear some words of the*
MAN OF BUSINESS *spoken argumentatively, but in the
decided accents of one who is rarely acknowledged to
be wrong*)

BUSINESSMAN —the exact truth. So you see that, if you
    will pardon my saying so, Officer, what you have
    just finished telling us is almost unbelievable.

Curtain

RECKLESSNESS

A Play in One Act

CHARACTERS

Arthur Baldwin

Mildred, his wife

Fred Burgess, their chauffeur

Gene, Mrs. Baldwin's maid

Mary, a housemaid

SCENE—*The library of Arthur Baldwin's summer home in the Catskills, New York. On the left a door and two large French windows open on the veranda. A book-case covers the space of wall between the two windows. In the corner is a square wicker worktable. The far side of the room also looks out on the veranda. Two French windows are on each side of a rolltop desk that stands against the wall. Near the desk there is a small tele-phone such as is used on estates to connect the house with the outbuildings; on top of the desk a Bell tele-phone and a small pile of letters. In the right back-ground is a divan, then a door leading to the hallway, and a long bookcase. A heavy oak table stands in the center of the room. On it are several magazines and books, an ash receiver, cigar box, etc., and an electric reading lamp wired from the chandelier above. Two Morris chairs are within reading reach of the lamp, and several light rocking chairs are placed about the room. The walls are of light wainscoting. The floor is of polished hard wood with a large darkish-colored rug covering the greater part. Several pictures of a sporting nature, principally of racing automobiles, are hung on the walls in the spaces between windows and book-cases.*

The room is the typical sitting room of a moderately

*wealthy man who has but little taste and is but little
worried by its absence. On this warm August night,
with the door and all the windows thrown open, and
only the reading lamp burning, it presents a cool and
comfortable appearance.*

*It's about eight o'clock in the evening. The time is
the present.*

MRS. BALDWIN *is discovered lying back in one of the
Morris chairs with an unopened book in her lap. She
is holding her head on one side in an attitude of
strained attention as if she were waiting for someone or
something. In appearance she is a tall, strikingly volup-
tuous-looking young woman of about twenty-eight. Her
hair is reddish-gold, almost a red, and her large eyes are
of that dark grayish-blue color which is called violet.
She is very pale—a clear transparent pallor that serves
to accentuate the crimson of the full lips of her rather
large mouth. She is dressed in a low-cut evening gown
of a gray that matches her eyes. Her shoulders, neck and
arms are beautiful.*

MRS. BALDWIN (*Rousing herself with a sigh of vexation,
goes to the wall on the right and pushes an electric
button near the bookcase. After a moment a maid
enters*)   I won't wait any longer, Mary. He evidently isn't coming. You may clear the table. I
won't eat anything now. I'll have something after
a while.

MARY   Very well, ma'am.

(*She goes out*)

MRS. BALDWIN (*Looks around quickly to make sure she
is alone, then locks the door to the hallway and,*

*going to the door on the left opening on the ve-
randah, calls in a low voice)* Fred.

*(She beckons with her hand to someone who is evi-
dently waiting outside. A moment later* FRED BURGESS
*comes quickly into the room. He throws a furtive glance
around him—then, reassured, takes* MRS. BALDWIN *in his
arms and kisses her passionately on the lips. In appearance he is a tall, clean-shaven, dark-complected young
fellow of twenty-five or so with clear-cut, regular features, big brown eyes and black curly hair. He is dressed
in a gray chauffeur's uniform with black puttees around
the calves of his legs)*

MRS. BALDWIN *(Putting her arms about his neck and
    kissing him again and again)* Oh, Fred! Fred! I
    love you so much!

FRED Ssh! Someone might hear you.

MRS. BALDWIN There's no one around. They're all in
    back having dinner. You've had your's? *(He nods)*
    They won't expect you then. There's nothing to
    fear. I've locked the door. *(He is reassured)* But
    you do love me, don't you, Fred? *(He kisses her
    smilingly)* Oh, I know! I know! But say so! I love
    to hear it.

FRED *(Stroking her hair caressingly with one hand)*
    Of course I love you. You know I do, Mildred.

*(*MRS. BALDWIN's *maid* GENE *appears noiselessly in the
doorway from the veranda. They are looking raptly into
each other's eyes, and do not notice her. She glares at
them for a moment, vindictive hatred shining in her
black eyes. Then she disappears as quietly as she came)*

MRS. BALDWIN *(Brokenly)* I can't stand this life much
    longer, Fred. These last two weeks while he has

been away have been heaven to me, but when I think of his coming back tonight—I—I could kill him!

FRED (*Worried by this sudden outbreak*)   You mustn't feel so badly about it. You—we have got to make the best of it, that's all.

MRS. BALDWIN (*Reproachfully*)   You take it very easily. Think of me.

FRED (*Releasing her and walking nervously up and down the room*)   You know, Mildred, I'd like to do something. But how can I help matters? I haven't any money. We can't go away together yet.

MRS. BALDWIN   But I can get money—all the money we need.

FRED (*Scornfully*)   His money!

MRS. BALDWIN   I have my jewels. I can sell those.

FRED   He gave you those jewels.

MRS. BALDWIN   Oh, why are you so hard on me? (*She sinks down in one of the Morris chairs. He comes over and stands before her*)   Why won't you let me help a little?

FRED   I don't want to touch any of his money. (*Kneeling beside her he puts one arm around her—then with sudden passion*)   I want you! God, how I want you! But I can't do that! (*He leans over and kisses her bare neck. She gives a long shuddering gasp, her white fingers closing and unclosing in his dark curls. He gets suddenly to his feet*)   We'll have to wait and love when we can for a while. I promise you it won't be long. I worked my way this far and I don't intend to stop here. As soon as I've passed those engineering examinations—and I will

pass them—we'll go away together. I won't be anybody's servant then.

(*He glances down at his livery in disgust*)

MRS. BALDWIN (*Pleading tearfully*) Fred dearest,
please take me away now—tonight—before he
comes. What difference does the money make as
long as I have you?

FRED (*With a harsh laugh*) You don't know what
you're talking about. You'd never stand it. Being
poor doesn't mean anything to you. You've never
been poor. Well, I have, and I know. It's hell,
that's what it is. You've been used to having everything, and when you found out you were tied to
a servant who could give you nothing, you'd soon
get tired. And I'd be the last one to blame you for
it. I'm working out and I don't want to go back
and drag you with me.

MRS. BALDWIN You don't realize how much I love you
or you wouldn't talk like that. I'd rather die of starvation with you than live the way I'm living now.

FRED (*Shaking his head skeptically*) You don't know
what starvation means. Besides, how do you know
he'll get a divorce? He might keep you bound to
him in name for years—just for spite.

MRS. BALDWIN No. I'm sure he isn't as mean as all
that. To do him justice, he's been kind to me—in
his way. He has looked upon me as his plaything,
the slave of his pleasure, a pretty toy to be exhib-
ited that others might envy him his ownership. But
he's given me everything I've ever asked for without a word—more than I ever asked for. He hasn't
ever known what the word "husband" ought to

mean but he's been a very considerate "owner."
Let us give him credit for that. I don't think—
(*She hesitates*)

FRED   Go on! Go on! I expect to hear you love him
next.

MRS. BALDWIN (*Smiling*)   Don't misunderstand me. I
simply can't think him the devil in human form
you would make him out to be. (*Grimly*) I love
him? It was my kind parents who loved his money.
He is so much older than I am and we have nothing in common. Well, I simply don't love him—
there's an end to it. And so—being his wife—I hate
him! (*Her voice is like a snarl as she says these
last words—there is a pause*) But what is your
plan?

FRED   When the time comes I shall go to him frankly
and tell him we love each other. I shall offer to go
quietly away with you without any fuss or scandal.
If he's the man you think him—and I don't agree
with you on that point—he'll get a divorce so
secretly it will never even get into the papers. He'll
save his own name and yours. If he tries to be
nasty about it I know something that'll bring him
around. (MRS. BALDWIN *looks at him in astonishment*) Oh, I haven't been idle. His past is none
too spotless.

MRS. BALDWIN   What have you found out?

FRED   I can't tell you now. It's got nothing to do with
you anyway. It was a business deal.

MRS. BALDWIN   A business deal?

FRED   Yes. It happened a long time ago. (*Abruptly
changing the subject*) What can be keeping him?
What time did he say he'd be here?

MRS. BALDWIN   The telegram said "for dinner." (*Suddenly, with intense feeling*) Oh, if you knew the agony that telegram caused me! I knew it had to come but I kept hoping against hope that something would detain him. After the wire came and I knew he would be here, I kept thinking of how he would claim me—force his loathsome kisses on me. (FRED *groans in impotent rage*) I was filled with horror. That is why I asked you to take me away tonight—to save me that degradation. (*After a pause—her face brightening with hope*) It's getting late. Maybe he won't come after all. Fred, dear, we may have one more night together.

(*He bends over and kisses her. The faint throb of a powerful motor with muffler cut out is heard.* FRED *listens for a moment—then kisses* MRS. BALDWIN *hastily*)

FRED   There he is now! I know the sound of the car.

(*He rushes to the open door and disappears in the darkness*)

MRS. BALDWIN (*Springing tensely to her feet, runs over and unlocks the door to the hall and opens it*) Oh God! (*The noise of the motor sounds louder, then seems to grow fainter, and suddenly ceases altogether*) He's gone to the garage. They're meeting. Oh God!

(*She shrinks away from the door—then remains standing stiffly with one hand clenched on the table. Quick footsteps are heard on the gravel, then on the steps of the veranda. A moment later* ARTHUR BALDWIN *enters from the hall. He comes quickly over to her, takes both of her hands and kisses her. A shudder of disgust runs over her whole body.*

BALDWIN *is a stocky, undersized man of about fifty.*

E

His face is puffy and marked by dissipation, and his thick-lipped mouth seems perpetually curled in a smile of cynical scorn. His eyes are small with heavily drooping lids that hide their expression. He talks in rather a bored drawl and exhibits enthusiasm on but two subjects—his racing car and his wife—in the order named. He has on a motoring cap with goggles on it and a linen duster, which he takes off on entering the room and throws in a chair. He is rather foppishly dressed in a perfectly fitting dark gray suit of extreme cut)

BALDWIN (*Holding his wife at arm's length and throwing an ardent glance at her bare neck and shoulders*) As beautiful as ever, I see. Why, you're all togged out! (*With a half-sneer*) Is it to welcome the prodigal bridegroom?

MRS. BALDWIN (*Forcing a smile*) Of course!

BALDWIN And how has the fairest of the fair been while her lord has been on the broad highway?

MRS. BALDWIN Very well.

BALDWIN Time hang heavily on your hands in this rural paradise?

MRS. BALDWIN (*Nervously avoiding his eyes*) The limousine has been out of commission—Fred has had to send away for some new part or other. I was rather glad of the opportunity to rest up a bit. You know when you're here we're always on the go. How's the car?

BALDWIN (*Enthusiastically*) Great! (*He drops her hand and takes a cigar out of the box on the table*) I made eighty-six about a week ago. (*He lights the cigar*) Ran across eight straight miles of level road —let her out the limit. It's some car all right! (*His *enthusiasm suddenly vanishing—with a frown*) By the way, where's Fred?

MRS. BALDWIN (*Startled*)   Wasn't he at the garage?

BALDWIN   No. No one was there.

MRS. BALDWIN   He must have gone to dinner. We had all given you up. (*Anxiously*) Why do you want to see him?

BALDWIN   Because I was forgetting. The car isn't all right just now. I blew out a tire yesterday and went into a ditch—nothing serious. I backed out all right and everything seemed to be okay after I'd put on a new tire. She ran smoothly today until I hit the road up here about six o'clock. That's why I'm so late—had the devil of a time making this hill—or mountain I should say. Engine worked fine but something wrong with the steering gear. It was all I could do to hold the road—and you know I'm no slouch at driving. I nearly ran into boulders and trees innumerable. All the people at the summer camp down the line were looking at me—thought I was drunk I guess. I had to just creep up here. If I'd have gone fast your hubby would be draped around some pine tree right now. (*With a laugh*) Sorry! You'd look well in black. (MRS. BALDWIN *starts guiltily*) I think I'll have to have this house moved into the valley. It's too much of a climb and the roads are devilish. No car, even if it has ninety horsepower, can stand the gaff long. I've paid enough for tires on account of this road to have it macadamized ten times over. Eaten yet?

MRS. BALDWIN   No. I wasn't hungry enough to eat

alone. I'll have something light later on. And you?

BALDWIN　I had something on the way—knew I'd probably be too late up here.

MRS. BALDWIN　Shall I have them get you anything?

BALDWIN　No. I'm not hungry.

MRS. BALDWIN　Then if you don't mind I think I'll go upstairs and take off this dress. I'm rather tired to-night. I'll be with you again in a short time.

BALDWIN　Why the formality of asking? Have I been away as long as that? Make yourself comfortable, of course. (*With his cynical laugh*) I have only to humbly thank you for going to all this trouble. I assure you I appreciate it. You look more than charming.

MRS. BALDWIN　(*With a cold smile*) Thank you. (*Moving toward the door*)You will find the letters I did not forward on top of the desk.

(*She goes out*)

BALDWIN　(*Going to the desk and glancing over the letters*)　Humph! There's nothing much here except bills.

(*He throws them down and walks back to the table again.* GENE *enters from the hall and stands just inside the doorway, looking quickly around the room. Having assured herself that* BALDWIN *is alone, she comes farther into the room and waits nervously for him to speak to her. She is a slight, pretty young woman of twenty-one or so neatly dressed in a black ladies-maid costume. Her hair and eyes are black, her features small and regular, her complexion dark*)

BALDWIN　(*Glancing up and seeing her*)　Why, hello, Gene! As pretty as ever, I see.

GENE　Good evening, sir.

BALDWIN   Are you looking for Mrs. Baldwin? She just
went upstairs to change her dress.

GENE   No sir. I just left Mrs. Baldwin. She said she
wished to be alone—that I was to tell you she had
a headache but would be down later if she felt
better.

(*She pauses and clasps her hands nervously together*)

BALDWIN   (*Looking at her curiously*)   Anything you
wish to see me about?

GENE   (*A look of resolution coming into her face*)   Yes,
sir.

BALDWIN   (*Half-bored*)   All right; what is it? Oh, by
the way, before you begin can you tell me if Fred
has gone down to the village tonight or not?

GENE   I'm quite sure he's over at the garage, sir.

BALDWIN   I must phone to him about fixing the car—
if he can. Can't use it the way it is. But what is it
that's troubling you?

GENE   I hardly dare to tell you, sir.

BALDWIN   I love to comfort beauty in distress.

GENE   I know you'll be awful angry at me when you
hear it.

BALDWIN   You are foolish to think so. It's a love affair,
of course.

GENE   Yes, sir.

BALDWIN   Well, who is the fortunate party and what
has he done or not done?

GENE   Oh no, you're mistaken, sir. It isn't my love affair. It's someone else's.

BALDWIN   (*Impatiently*)   You're   very   mysterious.
Whose is it then?

GENE   It's Fred's, sir.

BALDWIN   But—I had rather an idea that you and Fred

were not altogether indifferent to each other. (*Sarcastically*) You don't mean to tell me the handsome young devil has jilted you?

GENE (*Her voice harsh with anger*)   He does not love me any more.

BALDWIN (*Mockingly*)   I shall have to chide him. His morals are really too corrupt for his station in life. My only advice to you is to find another sweetheart. There is nothing that consoles one so much for the loss of a lover as—another lover.

GENE (*Trembling with rage at his banter*)   I am well through with him. It's you and not me who ought to be concerned the most this time.

BALDWIN (*Frowning*)   I? And pray tell me why I should be interested in the amours of my chauffeur?

GENE (*A bit frightened*)   There's lots of things happened since you've been away.

BALDWIN (*Irritably*)   I am waiting for you to reveal in what way all this concerns me.

GENE   They've been together all the time you've been away—every day and (*Hesitating for a moment at the changed look on his face—then resolutely*) every night too. (*Vindictively*) I've watched them when they thought no one was around. I've heard their "I love yous" and their kisses. Oh, they thought they were so safe! But I'll teach him to throw me over the way he did. I'll pay her for all her looking down on me and stealing him away. She's a bad woman, is what I say! Let her keep to her husband like she ought to and not go meddling with other people—

BALDWIN (*Interrupting her in a cold, hard voice and holding himself in control by a mighty effort*) It isn't one of the servants? (GENE *shakes her head*) No. I forget you said she was married. One of the summer people near here? (GENE *shakes her head*) Someone in this house? (GENE *nods.* BALDWIN's *body grows tense. His heavy lids droop over his eyes, his mouth twitches. He speaks slowly as if the words came with difficulty*) Be careful! Think what you are saying! There is only one other person in this house. Do—you—mean to—say it is that person? (GENE *is too terrified to reply*) Answer me, do you hear? Answer me! Is that the person you refer to?

GENE (*In a frightened whisper*) Yes.

BALDWIN (*Springing at her and clutching her by the throat with both hands*) You lie! You lie! (*He forces her back over the edge of the table. She frantically tries to tear his hands away*) Tell me you lie, damn you, or I'll choke you to hell!

(*She gasps for breath and her face becomes a dark crimson.* BALDWIN *suddenly realizes what he is doing and takes his hands away.* GENE *falls half across the table, her breath coming in great shuddering sobs.* BALDWIN *stands silently beside her waiting until she can speak again. Finally he leads her to one of the Morris chairs and pushes her into it. He stands directly in front of her*)

BALDWIN You can speak again?

GENE (*Weakly*) Yes—no thanks to you.

BALDWIN You understand, don't you, that what you have said requires more proof than the mere statement of a jealous servant.

(*He pronounces the "servant" with a sneer of contempt*)

GENE   I've got proof, don't you worry, but I don't know whether I'll show it to you or not. A man that chokes women deserves to be made a fool of.

BALDWIN (*Stung by her scorn*)   You will show me, damn you, or—

(*He leans over as if to grab her by the throat again*)

GENE (*Shrinking back in the chair*)   Don't you dare touch me or I'll scream and tell them all about it. I'll prove it to you, but it isn't because I'm afraid of you or your threats but simply because I want to get even with her. (*She reaches in under her belt and pulls out a closely folded piece of paper*) Do you recognize her writing when you see it?

BALDWIN   Give it to me.

GENE (*Holding it away from him*)   Will you promise to tell her—them—just how you found out—after I'm gone? I'm leaving tomorrow morning. I'd like them to know it was me who spoiled their fun. Will you promise?

BALDWIN   Yes! Yes! Anything. Give it to me!

GENE   There! Take it.

BALDWIN (*He reads the letter slowly and a terrible expression comes over his pale, twitching features.* GENE *watches him with a smile of triumph. When he speaks his voice is ominously soft and subdued*)   What night was this she speaks of?

GENE   The night before last.

BALDWIN   She says she would come to him at half-past eleven. Did she mean to the garage?

GENE   Yes. When she thought we were all in bed in

the back part of the house she would slip down
and go out the front door. She kept on the grass
and in the shade of the trees so no one would notice her.

BALDWIN   You know all this?

GENE   I followed her on several different nights.

BALDWIN   You *must* hate her.

GENE   I loved Fred.

BALDWIN   Why was she so careless as to write this
note? Couldn't she have telephoned or told him?

GENE   The little garage telephone was out of order. It
was only fixed this morning. The Lynches were
here to dinner and she had no chance to speak to
him alone. She sent me to the garage to tell him
to come over. When he came she pretended to
give him some orders and dropped this at his feet.
I suspected something, so I was watching and saw
it all.

BALDWIN   How did you get hold of this?

GENE   Yesterday when he went to the village to see
if the new part for the limousine had come, I went
to the garage and found this in the inside pocket
of his other clothes.

BALDWIN   (*His eyes narrowing*)   He is very careless.

GENE   Oh, they knew you wouldn't be home until today and they felt safe. And I knew you wouldn't
believe me without proof.

BALDWIN   Do you think he has missed this?

GENE   No. (*With a sneer*) As you say, he is very careless in such matters. If he does miss it he'll think
he has forgotten where he hid it.

BALDWIN   (*After a pause—putting the note in his*

pocket)   You may go. Be sure you do leave in the morning, otherwise—

GENE   You needn't fret. I wouldn't stay another day if you paid me a million. (*She yawns heavily*) Oh, I'm glad that's off my mind. I'll sleep tonight. I haven't slept a bit, it seems, since you've been away. (*She goes slowly to the hall door—then turns around and looks at him curiously*) What are you going to do?

BALDWIN   Go! Go!

GENE (*With a mocking laugh*)   I wish you luck!

(*She goes out*)

BALDWIN (*Stares at the rug for a moment—then takes the note out of his pocket and reads it again. In a burst of rage he crumples it up in his hand and curses beneath his breath. His eyes wander to his auto coat and goggles in the chair, then to the garage telephone near his desk. They seem to suggest an idea to him—a way for vengeance. His face lights up with savage joy and he mutters fiercely to himself*)   The dirty cur! By God, I'll do it! (*He ponders for a moment, turning over his plan in his mind, then goes over and shuts the door to the hall and striding quickly to the garage telephone, takes off the receiver. After a pause he speaks, making his voice sound as if he were in a state of great anxiety*) Hello! Fred? You haven't touched the car yet? Good! Take it out immediately! Go to the village and get the doctor—any doctor. Mildred—Mrs. Baldwin has been taken very ill. Hemorrhage, I think—blood running from her mouth. She's unconscious—it's a matter of life and death. Drive

like hell, do you hear? Drive like hell! Her life's in
your hands. Turn the car loose! Drive like hell!
(*He hangs up the receiver and stands listening intently, with one hand on the desk. A minute later
the purr of an engine is heard. It grows to a roar as
the car rushes by on the driveway near the house—
then gradually fades in the distance.* BALDWIN's *thick
lips are narrowed taut in a cruel grin*) Drive to hell,
you b—rd!

(*The stage is darkened. Half to three-quarters of an
hour are supposed to intervene before the lights go up
again.*

BALDWIN *is discovered sitting in one of the Morris
chairs. He nervously pulls at the cigar he is smoking
and glances at the telephone on his desk. There is a
ring and goes quickly over to it. He answers in a very
low voice*)

BALDWIN Yes. This is Mr. Baldwin. What? Ran into
a boulder you say? He's dead? (*This last question
burst out exultingly—then in tones of mocking
compassion*) How horrible! They're bringing it up
here? That's right. How did you happen to find
him?—Quite by accident then?—Yes, come right
to the house. It *is* terrible—awful road— Knew
something of the kind would happen sometime—
ever so much obliged for your trouble.

(*He hangs up the receiver and opens the door into
the hallway—then pushes the electric bell button in the
wall. A moment later* MARY, *the housemaid, enters*)

MARY Yes, sir?

BALDWIN Where's Gene?

MARY She's gone to bed, sir. Shall I call her?

BALDWIN   No. You'll do just as well. Will you run up
    and tell Mrs. Baldwin I'd like very much to see
    her for a few minutes. Tell her it's something of
    importance or else I wouldn't disturb her.

MARY   Yes, sir.

(*She goes out.* BALDWIN *walks over and fixes the two
Morris chairs and lamp so that the light will fall on the
face of the person sitting in one while the other will be
in shadow. He then sits down in the shaded chair and
waits. A minute or so elapses before* MRS. BALDWIN *appears in the doorway. She walks over to him with an
expression of wondering curiosity not unmixed with
fear. She wears a light blue kimono and bedroom slippers of the same color. Her beautiful hair hangs down
her back in loose braid*)

MRS. BALDWIN   I'm sorry not to have come down be-
    fore but my head aches wretchedly. I sent Gene to
    tell you. Did she?

BALDWIN (*With curious emphasis*)   Yes. She told me.
    Sit down, my dear.

(*He points to the other Morris chair. She sits in it*)

MRS. BALDWIN (*After a pause in which she waits for him
    to begin and during which he is studying her closely
    from his position of vantage in the shadow*)   I
    really thought you had gone out again. That was
    one reason why I didn't come down. I heard the
    car go out and supposed of course it was you.

BALDWIN   No. It was Fred.

MRS. BALDWIN   You sent him to the village for some-
    thing?

BALDWIN   No, I simply told him there was something
    wrong with the steering gear—something I couldn't

discover. I told him to attend to it—if he could—
the first thing in the morning. It seems he has gone
me one better and is trying to locate the trouble tonight. (*With grim sarcasm*) Really, his zeal in my
service is astounding.

MRS. BALDWIN (*Trying to conceal her anxiety*) But
isn't it very dangerous to go over these roads at
night in a car that is practically disabled?

BALDWIN Fred is very careless—very, very careless in
some things. I shall have to teach him a lesson. He
is absolutely reckless (MRS. BALDWIN *shudders in
spite of herself*), especially with other people's prop-
erty. You are worrying about Fred; but I am bewailing my car, which he is liable to smash from
pure overzealousness. Chauffeurs—even overzealous
ones—are to be had for the asking, but cars like
mine are out of the ordinary.

MRS. BALDWIN (*Coldly*) Why do you talk like that?
You know you do not mean it.

BALDWIN I assure you I do—every word of it.

MRS. BALDWIN You said you wished to see me on something of importance?

BALDWIN (*Dryly*) Exactly, my dear. We are coming to
that. (*Then, softly*) I wanted to ask you, Mildred,
if you are perfectly happy up here.

MRS. BALDWIN (*Astonished*) Why—of course—what
makes you ask such a question?

BALDWIN Well, you know I have left you so much
alone this summer I feel rather conscience-stricken.
You must be bored to death on this mountain with
none of your old friends around. I was thinking it
might be a good plan for us to economize a bit by

letting Fred go and getting along with just my car. It would be quite possible then for you to go to some more fashionable resort where things would be livelier for you.

MRS. BALDWIN (*Eagerly*) I assure you I am quite contented where I am. Of course I miss you and feel a trifle lonely at times, but then I have the other car, and you know I enjoy motoring so much.

BALDWIN Do you? You never seemed to care very much about touring round with me.

MRS. BALDWIN You drive so dreadfully fast I am frightened to death.

BALDWIN Fred is a careful driver then?

MRS. BALDWIN Very careful.

BALDWIN You have no complaint to make against him?

MRS. BALDWIN None at all. I think he is the best chauffeur we have ever had.

BALDWIN Why, I am delighted to hear that. I had an idea he was reckless.

MRS. BALDWIN He is always very careful when he drives me. As for the rest of the help, they are the average with one exception. I think I shall discharge Gene. (BALDWIN *smiles*) She is getting so bold and insolent I can't put up with it any longer. As soon as I can get a new maid I shall let her go.

BALDWIN You may save yourself the trouble. She is going to leave tomorrow. She gave me notice of her departure when you sent her downstairs.

MRS. BALDWIN (*Flushing angrily*) It's just like her to act that way—another piece of her insolence. I suppose I'll have to make the best of it. It's good riddance at all events.

BALDWIN (*In the same soft, half-mocking voice he has*

used during the whole conversation with his wife)
Do you suppose Fred will stay with us when he
finds out?

MRS. BALDWIN (*Puzzled*) Finds out what? Why
shouldn't he stay?

BALDWIN   He is Gene's lover—or was.

MRS. BALDWIN (*Growing pale—violently*) That is a
lie!

BALDWIN (*As if astonished*) Why, my dear, as if it
mattered.

MRS. BALDWIN (*Forcing a laugh*) How silly of me! It
is my anger at Gene breaking out. But I am sure
you are mistaken. I know Gene was very much in
love with him but I do not think he ever noticed
her.

BALDWIN   Now *you* are mistaken. He may not care for
her at present but there was a time when—

MRS. BALDWIN (*Biting her lips*) I do not believe it.
That was servant's gossip you heard.

BALDWIN   It was not what I heard, my dear Mildred,
but what I saw with my own eyes.

MRS. BALDWIN (*In an agony of jealousy*) You—saw—
them?

BALDWIN (*Apparently oblivious of her agitation*) In a
very compromising position, to say the least. (MRS.
BALDWIN *winks back her tears of rage*) But that was
long ago. (MRS. BALDWIN *sighs as if relieved*) Besides, what have these servant intrigues to do with
us? (MRS. BALDWIN *tries to look indifferent*) I was
only joking about Fred leaving. In fact, from what
Gene said, Fred already has some other foolish
woman in love with him. Only this time it is no
maid, if you please, but the lady of the house her-

self who has lost her heart at the sight of his dark
curls. The fellow is ambitious.

MRS. BALDWIN (*Her face terror-stricken—her words fal-
tering on her lips*) Do—you—know—who—this
woman—is?

BALDWIN (*Watching her with grim amusement*) I
have one of her letters here. Would you care to
read it?

(*He takes her note from his pocket and gives it to
her*)

MRS. BALDWIN (*Taking it in her trembling hand and
smoothing it out. One glance and her face grows
crimson with shame. She seems to crumple up in
her chair. After a moment she throws her head
back defiantly and looks up at him—a pause*)
Well?

BALDWIN (*Dryly, his voice softly menacing*) Well?
You do not know how to play the game, my sweet
Mildred. If ever guilt was stamped on a face it was
on yours a moment ago.

MRS. BALDWIN (*Her eyes flashing*) Yes. I love him! I
acknowledge it.

BALDWIN You are better at affirming than denying. It
takes courage to proclaim oneself the mistress of
one's chauffeur—to play second fiddle to one's
maid!

MRS. BALDWIN (*In a fury*) You lie! He is a man and
not the beast you are.

BALDWIN (*Softly*) Be calm! You will awaken your
rival and she will listen and gloat!

MRS. BALDWIN (*Lowering her voice to a shrill whisper*)
Oh, it was she who stole that letter?

BALDWIN Exactly. You are a novice at the game, my
dear. Take the advice of a hardened old sinner—
in the years and loves to come never write any
more letters. Kisses come and kisses go, but letters
remain forever—and are often brought into court.

MRS. BALDWIN (*Relieved at the easy way he takes it*) I
cannot help this. I love him—that's all. (*Pause*)
What are you going to do?

BALDWIN It was to tell you that, I sent for you.

MRS. BALDWIN You will get a divorce?

BALDWIN No.

MRS. BALDWIN You will keep me tied to you when you
know I do not love you—when you know I love
someone else? (*In pleading tones*) You will not be
as hard on me as that, will you, Arthur? This is not
all my fault. You have never really loved me. We
are not the same age. (BALDWIN *winces*) We do
not look at things in the same light—we have nothing in common. It would be needless cruelty to
both of us to keep up this farce. You will not keep
me tied to you for mere spite, will you?

BALDWIN (*In his kindest tone*) No. What I intend to
do is to *let you* get a divorce. I will give you all the
evidence you need. Could I be fairer than that?

MRS. BALDWIN (*Staring at him as if she could not believe her ears*) You will do that? (*She rushes over
and kneels at his feet, kissing his hands and sobbing*) Oh, thank you! Thank you!

BALDWIN (*Looking down at her bowed head with a
cruel smile*) There! There! It is no more than
just. I realize that youth must have its day. You
should have trusted me.

MRS. BALDWIN (*Her voice thrilling with gratitude*)
How could I dream that you would be so kind?
I did not dare to hope that you would ever forgive
me—and he was certain you would think only of
revenge. Oh, how unjust we have been to you!
(*She takes one of his hands in hers and kisses it*)

BALDWIN   It is true neither of you have given me due
credit for being the man I am, or you would never
have acted as you did. I have known from the first
it must have been for money you married me—
(*With a twisted smile*) An old man like me. Tell
me the truth. Wasn't it?

MRS. BALDWIN (*Falteringly*)   Yes. I would not lie to
you now. My family forced me into it. You must
have realized that. I hardly knew you, but they were
nagging me night and day until I gave in. It was
anything to get away from home. Oh, I am sorry,
so sorry! Will you forgive me?

BALDWIN (*Evading her question*)   I have done my best
to make you happy. I have given you everything
you desired, have I not?

MRS. BALDWIN   You have been very good, very kind to
me. I have tried to love you but there has always
been a gulf separating us. I could never understand
you.

BALDWIN   I have trusted you, have I not—always and
in everything?

MRS. BALDWIN (*Slowly*)   Yes, but you have never loved
me. I have been just a plaything with which you
amused yourself—or so it has always seemed to me.
Perhaps I have been unjust to you—in that too.

BALDWIN   If I have regarded you as a plaything I was
only accepting the valuation your parents set upon

you when they sold you. But these things are over
and done and it is useless to discuss them. Let us
talk of the present. You love Fred?

MRS. BALDWIN Yes, I do.

BALDWIN I will not stand in your way. You shall have
him.

MRS. BALDWIN (*Getting up and putting her arms around
his neck*) Oh, I do love you now—you are so
good to me.

(*She kisses him on the lips. He does not move or
touch her in any way but looks at her coldly with half-
closed eyes, his thick lips curled in a sneering smile. In
sudden fear* MRS. BALDWIN *moves away from him with
a shudder. The noise of an automobile is faintly heard.*
BALDWIN *springs to his feet, his face transformed with
savage exultation*)

BALDWIN (*With a hard laugh*) Thanks for that Judas
kiss. I hear a machine coming. It is Fred, I know.
We will have him in and relieve his mind by telling him of our agreement.

(*The machine is heard coming slowly up the drive
toward the house*)

MRS. BALDWIN (*Frightened by* BALDWIN's *change of
manner*) It does not sound like your car.

BALDWIN It is Fred, I tell you. I know it is Fred. (*The
car stops before the house. The horn sounds.* BALD-
WIN *hurries to the door leading into the hall. Several persons can be heard coming up the steps to
the veranda. A door is opened and shut and the
hushed murmur of voices comes from the hallway*)
In here if you please—in here! (MRS. BALDWIN
*moves closer to the door, her face wan with the
terror of an unknown fear. Three men, one a chauf-*

*feur, the other two servants of some description,
enter carrying the dead man. Two are supporting
the shoulders and one the feet. A dark robe is
wrapped around the whole body. They hurriedly
place it on the divan to which* BALDWIN *points and
go out quickly, glad to be rid of their gruesome
task.* MRS. BALDWIN *is swaying weakly on her feet,
her eyes wildly staring at the figure on the divan.
Suddenly she gives a frantic cry, and rushing over,
pulls the covering from the dead man's head. The
livid countenance of* FRED *is revealed. Several crimson streaks run down his cheek from his clotted,
curly hair.* MRS. BALDWIN *shrieks and falls senseless
on the floor.* BALDWIN, *who has watched her with
the same cruel smile on his lips, goes slowly over
and pushes the button of the electric bell* MARY
appears) Help me to get Mrs. Baldwin to her
room.

(*He picks up the prostrate woman in his arms, and
with the assistance of the maid, carries her out to the
hallway. They can be heard stumbling up the stairs to
the floor above. A moment later* BALDWIN *reappears,
breathing heavily from his exertion, his pale face emo-
tionless and cold. He stands looking down at the dead
body on the divan—finally shrugs his shoulders disdain-
fully, comes over to the table, takes a cigar out of the
box and lights it. The maid rushes in, all out of breath
and flustered*)

MARY   Please go upstairs, sir. Mrs. Baldwin has come
to, and she ordered me out of the room. I think
she's gone mad, sir. She's pulling out all the
drawers looking for something. (*A dull report
sounds from upstairs. The maid gives a terrified*

gasp. BALDWIN *is startled for a moment and starts as if to run out to the hallway. Then his face hardens and he speaks to the trembling maid in even tones)* Mrs. Baldwin has just shot herself. You had better phone for the doctor, Mary.

Curtain

ABORTION

A Play in One Act

❀

CHARACTERS

Jack Townsend

John Townsend, his father

Mrs. Townsend, his mother

Lucy Townsend, his sister

Evelyn Sands, his fiancée

Donald (Bull) Herron, his roommate

Joe Murray, a machinist

Students of the University

SCENE—*The study of the suite of rooms occupied by* JACK TOWNSEND *and* DONALD HERRON *on the ground floor of a dormitory in a large eastern university of the United States. The left wall is composed almost entirely of a large bow window looking out on the campus, forming a window seat which is piled high with bright-colored cushions. In the middle of the far side, a door opening into a hallway of the dormitory. On either side of the door, leather-covered divans with leather cushions. In the right corner to the rear, a writing desk with an electric drop-light hanging over it. In the middle of the right wall, a fireplace. In the extreme right foreground, a door opening into a bedroom. In the center of the room, a table with an electric reading lamp wired from the chandelier above. Books, periodicals, pipes, cigarette boxes, ashtrays, etc., are also on the table. The walls of the room are hung with flags, class banners, framed photographs of baseball and football teams, college posters, etc. Two Morris chairs and several rockers are grouped about the table.*

It is about eight o'clock in the evening of a warm day in June. At first the windows on the left are gray with the dim glow of the dying twilight, but as the action progresses this slowly disappears.

A sound of voices comes from the hall. The door in

the rear is opened and MRS. TOWNSEND *and* LUCY *enter, escorted by* HERRON. *Their figures can be vaguely made out in the dusk of the room.*

LUCY (*Feeling her way toward the table*)   Do put on the lights, Bull! I know I'm going to break my neck in a minute.

(MRS. TOWNSEND *remains standing by the doorway*)

HERRON (*Cheerfully*)   One minute, one minute! (*Striking his shin against the corner of the divan —wrathfully*) Oh—

(*He bites his tongue just in time*)

LUCY (*With a gurgling laugh*)   Say it! Say it!

HERRON (*Leaning over the divan and feeling on the wall for the electric switch—softly*)   Oh darn!

LUCY   Hypocrite! That isn't what you were going to say.

HERRON   Oh gosh, then. (*Finding the switch*) There! (*Turning on all the lights except the drop-light*) Let there be light!

LUCY (*She is a small, vivacious blond, nineteen years old, gushing with enthusiasm over everything and everybody. She wears an immense bouquet of flowers at the waist of her dark blue dress and carries a flag*) Don't stand there posing, Bull. (*She flings herself into one of the Morris chairs*) You look much more like a god of darkness than one of light.

MRS. TOWNSEND (*She is a sweet-faced, soft-spoken, gray-haired lady in her early fifties. She is dressed in dark gray. She turns to* LUCY *with smiling remonstrance*) Lucy! (*To* HERRON, *who clumsily arranges a cushion at the back of a rocking chair for her*)

Thank you, Donald. (HERRON *winces at the "Donald"*)

LUCY (*Contemptuously*) Donald!

HERRON (*Chuckling. He is a huge, swarthy six-footer with a bull neck and an omnipresent grin, slow to anger and to understanding but—an All-American tackle. His immense frame is decked out in white flannels which make him look gigantic*) I don't care much for the "Donald" myself.

LUCY And I still claim, Mother, that Donald, alias Bull, resembles Pluto more than any other divinity. It is true, judging from the pictures I have seen, that Pluto was not as fat (*As* HERRON *slouches into a sitting position on the divan*) nor as clumsy, but—

HERRON (*Grinning*) What have I done today? What have I done? Didn't I purchase candy and beautiful flowers? And now I reap nothing but abuse. I appeal to you, Mrs. Townsend. She is breaking me on the wheel.

LUCY Poor butterfly! (*Convulsed with laughter*) Ha ha ha! Poor, delicate, fragile butterfly!

HERRON There you go again! (*Appealingly*) You see, Mrs. Townsend? Every word of mine is turned to mockery.

(*He sighs explosively*)

MRS. TOWNSEND (*Smiling*) Never mind, Donald; you ought to hear the nice things she says behind your back.

LUCY (*Indignantly*) Mother!

HERRON I find it hard to believe.

LUCY Mother is fibbing so as not to hurt your feelings. (*With a roguish smile*) I never, never in all my life said a good word about you. You don't deserve it.

MRS. TOWNSEND   Why, Lucy, what a thing to say!

(*While she is speaking* JOE MURRAY *appears in the doorway to the rear. He is a slight, stoop-shouldered, narrow-chested young fellow of eighteen, with large, feverish black eyes, thin lips, pasty complexion, and the sunken cheeks of a tuberculosis victim. He wears a shabby dark suit. He peers blinkingly around the room and knocks, but they do not hear him*)

LUCY   (*Glancing toward the door and seeing him*) Someone to see you, Bull.

HERRON   (*Turning to* MURRAY)   Anything you want?

MURRAY   (*Aggressively*)   I wanna see Townsend, Jack Townsend.

HERRON   He's not here.

MURRAY   D'yuh know when he'll be in?

HERRON   Any minute; but I advise you not to wait. He won't have any time for you tonight. If you want to leave a message I'll give it to him.

MURRAY   (*Truculently*)   He'll find time for me all right.

HERRON   (*Staring at him*)   You think so? Suit yourself. (*Pointedly*) You can wait for him *outside*.

(MURRAY'S *face pales with rage. He starts to say something, then turns abruptly and disappears into the hallway*)

HERRON   Pleasant little man!

LUCY   Don't you know who it was?

HERRON   Never saw him before; probably some fresh "townie" who thinks Jack's indebted to him because he recovered a stolen baseball bat or something, and wants to put the acid on him for a dollar or two. Jack's such a good-natured slob—

LUCY (*With a giggle*)   Listen to who is talking.

MRS. TOWNSEND (*Proudly*)   Jack always has been so good-hearted.

HERRON (*With a smile*)   He's only stingy with base hits. Great game he pitched today. Star players usually fall down when they're captains of teams and it's their last year in college; but not old Jack —only three hits off him.

MRS. TOWNSEND   This game we saw today decides the championship, doesn't it?

LUCY   Certainly, Mother. You don't suppose I'd have yelled my whole voice away if it wasn't, do you? I can hardly speak.

MRS. TOWNSEND (*With a sly wink at* HERRON)   I hadn't noticed that, Lucy.

(HERRON *shakes with suppressed mirth*)

LUCY (*Pouting*)   Oh, Mother, how unkind!

MRS. TOWNSEND   I must confess I'm not much of a fan— Is that what you call it? I do not understand the game and if it wasn't for Jack playing I'm afraid I would find it rather wearisome.

HERRON   Jack is the big man of the college tonight, all right. The president is a mere nonentity beside him. Add to our list of athletic heroes one Jack Townsend, captain and pitcher.

MRS. TOWNSEND   How they carried him around the field after the game!

LUCY   And cheered him!

HERRON   You bet we did. I had a hold of one leg. But I agree with you, Mrs. Townsend. If Jack didn't play I wouldn't take much interest in baseball myself. (*Enthusiastically*)   Football is the real game.

LUCY   Of course you'd say that.

MRS. TOWNSEND   That's beyond me, too. I've heard it's
    so rough, that so many players are injured. When
    John first entered college his father and I made
    him promise not to go in for it on any account.

HERRON   (*Regretfully*) You spoiled a fine player.
    (*There is a noise of voices from the hall*) Speaking
    of the—hm—angel.

(EVELYN SANDS *enters followed by* JACK TOWNSEND.
EVELYN *is a tall, dark-haired, beautiful girl about twenty
years old. Her eyes are large and brown; her mouth full-
lipped, resolute; her figure lithe and graceful. She is
dressed simply but stylishly in white.* JACK *is a well-
built handsome young fellow about twenty-two years old,
with blond hair brushed straight back from the forehead, intelligent blue eyes, a good-natured, self-indul-
gent mouth and ruddy, tanned complexion. He has the
easy, confident air of one who has, through his prowess
in athletics, become a figure of note in college circles
and is accustomed to the deference of those around
him. He wears a dark coat, white soft shirt with a
bright-colored tie, flannel trousers and white tennis
shoes*)

LUCY   Hail to the hero!

(EVELYN *comes over and sits on the arm of* LUCY'S
chair. JACK *stands beside his mother*)

MRS. TOWNSEND   (*Smiling fondly up at him*) Where is
    your father?

JACK   Right outside, talking to Professor Simmons.
    After dinner, as we were following you out of the
    Inn, we ran into the Prof and he walked down with
    us. Did you think we were lost?

LUCY   (*With a mischievous glance at* EVELYN) We

thought you might have forestalled the forthcoming happy event by eloping.

(EVELYN *blushes*)

JACK (*Laughing*) With Father for chaperon?

LUCY Well, don't you dare do it! I'd never forgive you spoiling my chance to wear my gown. I'm going to be just the most stunning bridesmaid. Am I not, Mother?

MRS. TOWNSEND Of course, dear. (*To* JACK) Why didn't you ask the professor to come in?

JACK I did, Mother, but he's on his way somewhere or other.

HERRON By the way, Jack, there was a "townie" in here asking to see you a few minutes ago.

JACK (*Starting nervously*) A "townie"? Did he give any name?

HERRON No. A fresh little shrimp; said he'd wait. Wasn't he outside?

JACK (*Visibly uneasy*) I didn't see anyone.

HERRON He'll be back probably; and look out for a touch.

(*The singing of a distant quartet sounds faintly from the campus*)

LUCY (*Springing up*) I hear them singing on the campus. I'm going out. Bull, when does the big P'rade start?

HERRON Pretty soon; you can hear the clans gathering now.

LUCY I'm going to march beside them all the way to the lake.

MRS. TOWNSEND The lake?

LUCY There's going to be a canoe carnival, and bonfires, and dancing, and everything, Mother. You've simply got to come, all of you, in honor of hero Jack.

JACK (*Embarrassed*)   Come, come, Sis, praise from you is rare indeed.

HERRON (*Emphatically*)   Indeed!

LUCY (*Archly, to* HERRON)   Indeed?

MRS. TOWNSEND (*Getting quickly from her chair—with a girlish laugh*)   I'm going with you. I'll show you young people I can celebrate with the best of you.

JACK   Are you sure it isn't too much for you, Mother?

MRS. TOWNSEND (*Her face flushed with excitement*) Nonsense, Jack!

JACK (*Putting his arm around her affectionately*)   Dear old Mother—young Mother, I should say.

LUCY   Come on, everybody!

JACK   You people go on ahead and I'll catch up with you.

(MRS. TOWNSEND *goes out*)

LUCY (*To* HERRON)   Come on, Jumbo.

HERRON (*Groaning*)   Jumbo! And Bull! Lucy thinks I'm a menagerie.

(*He and* LUCY *go out.* EVELYN *starts to follow them but* JACK *stops her and takes her in his arms*)

JACK   We won't be alone again for ages.

(*He kisses her*)

EVELYN (*Smiling up into his face*)   I'm so proud of you, Jack dear.

JACK (*Laughingly puts his fingers across her lips*) Ssshhh! You'll give me an awful attack of exaggerated ego if you go on talking like that.

EVELYN   But it's true, dear.

JACK   Then for the good of my soul don't tell me.

Praise from Sis is wonder enough for one day.

EVELYN (*Moving a few steps away from him*) I wish I could tell you how proud I felt when I sat in the grandstand and watched you. (*With a laugh*) It was a horrid sort of selfish pride, too, for I couldn't help saying to myself from time to time: "He loves me, *me!* He belongs to *me!*" And I thought of how jealous all the girls around me who were singing his praises would be if they knew.

JACK (*His face suddenly grows serious, as if at some painful memory*) Please, Evelyn! You make me feel so mean—and contemptible when you talk like that.

EVELYN (*Astonished*) Mean? Contemptible? How foolish you are, Jack. (*Excitedly*) I felt like standing on my seat and shouting to all of them: "What right have you to think of him? He is *mine, mine!*" (*Laughing at her own enthusiasm, adds in a matter-of-fact tone*) Or will be in three months.

JACK (*His voice thrilling with emotion*) In three months! (*Jokingly*) Do you know those three months are going to seem like three years?

EVELYN (*Gaily*) Three centuries; but I was telling you how splendid you were this afternoon.

JACK (*Protestingly*) Ssshhh, Evelyn!

(*He tries to put his arms around her*)

EVELYN (*Backing away and avoiding him*) You were so cool, so brave. It struck me as symbolic of the way you would always play, in the game of life— fairly, squarely, strengthening those around you, refusing to weaken at critical moments, advancing others by sacrifices, fighting the good fight for the cause, the team, and always, always, whether van-

F

quished or victor, reserving a hearty, honest cheer for the other side. (*Breaking off breathlessly*) Oh, Jack dear, I loved you so!

JACK (*A strong note of pain in his voice, he puts his hands over his ears, and forces a laugh*)   I won't listen any longer. I positively refuse.

EVELYN (*Smiling*)   It's all over. I'm through. I simply had to tell you.

(*She holds out both hands to him. He draws her into his arms and kisses her*)

JACK (*With deep feeling*)   I shall try—with all my strength—in the future, Evelyn—to live as you have said and become worthy of you. Today was nothing. One does one's best for the sake of the game, for the love of the struggle. Our best happened to be luckier, more skillful, perhaps, than the other fellow's—that's all.

EVELYN   It's so like you to say that. You're a dear.

(*She kisses him.* JACK's *father,* JOHN TOWNSEND, *appears in the doorway. He is a tall, kindly old man of sixty or so with a quantity of white hair. He is erect, well-preserved, energetic, dressed immaculately but soberly. He laughs and shakes a finger at* EVELYN)

TOWNSEND   Caught in the act. (EVELYN *smiles and blushes*) Evelyn, they're waiting for you outside and Lucy threatens to come in and drag you out if my persuasive powers have no effect. They want to make a start for the Steps and see the P'rade form. It's due to start shortly.

(*While he is speaking he comes forward, puts his straw hat on the table and sits down in one of the Morris chairs*)

EVELYN (*Eagerly*)   I wouldn't miss it for worlds. (*She*

goes to the door; then turns and looks at JACK *ir-resolutely*) Aren't you coming with us, both of you?

(JACK *looks at his father uncertainly*)

TOWNSEND We'll join you there; or, better still— (*To* JACK)˙ The P'rade passes right by here, doesn't it? They always used to in the old days.

JACK Yes, Dad.

TOWNSEND Then you go ahead with the others, Eve-lyn, and since Lucy tells me you're going to follow the P'rade, we'll be able to join you when you pass by. (*Explanatively*) I've seen and taken part in so many of these affairs that their novelty has sort of worn off for me; and Jack—if they were to dis-cover the hero of the day at this stage of the game he wouldn't have a rag to his back, eh, Jack?

JACK (*Smiling*) I'm black and blue all over from their fond caresses this afternoon.

EVELYN (*Gaily*) I'm off, then. (*Looking at* JACK) You'll surely join us when we pass?

JACK Sure thing.

EVELYN (*Waving her hand*) Bye-bye.

(*She goes out.* JACK *sits down near his father*)

TOWNSEND (*He takes out a cigar and lights it.* JACK *watches him uneasily as if he foresees what his father is going to say and dreads it.* TOWNSEND *avoids his eyes. There is an uncomfortable silence. Then* TOWNSEND *begins vaguely*) It certainly re-moves the burden of the years from my shoulders to come out to the old college in the spring and live the old days over in memory and hobnob with some of the old-timers who were young-timers with me. It becomes more difficult every year, I find. All the old landmarks are disappearing one by one.

JACK (*Perfunctorily*) Yes, even in my time there have been great changes.

TOWNSEND (*Very palpably talking to gain time*) It gives me a painful heart-throb every time I come back and look for some old place and find it renovated or torn down.

JACK (*Shortly*) I can well understand that.

TOWNSEND You don't realize what this college comes to mean to you in after years; how it becomes inseparably woven into the memories of one's lost youth until the two become identical.

JACK (*Impatiently*) Yes, I suppose so.

TOWNSEND (*More and more vaguely*) Happiest days of my life, of anyone's life—

JACK (*Abruptly*) Come to the point, Dad.

TOWNSEND (*Confused*) What? Eh?

JACK (*Firmly*) You didn't send Evelyn away in order that you might wax reminiscent; you know that, Dad.

TOWNSEND (*Heaving a sigh of relief*) You are quite right, I did not; but what I ought to speak about is such a deuced painful subject for both of us that I hardly dare speak of it—especially on your day of triumph when I should be the last one to bring up any unpleasantness.

JACK (*Kindly*) Never mind that, Dad.

TOWNSEND You see, I didn't know when I'd have another opportunity of seeing you without arousing your mother's suspicions.

JACK I understand.

TOWNSEND And the thing has caused me much worry,

I simply had to hear from your own lips that everything was all right.

JACK Then I will set your mind at rest immediately.
Everything *is* all right.

TOWNSEND (*Fervently*) Thank God for that! Why
haven't you written to me?

JACK Until a few days ago I had nothing new to tell
you.

TOWNSEND When was the operation performed?

JACK Last Monday.

TOWNSEND And you've heard from her since?

JACK I received a short note from her that night. It
was all over and everything was all right, she said.
She told me I needn't worry any longer.

TOWNSEND That was five days ago. You haven't had
any word since then?

JACK No.

TOWNSEND That's a favorable sign. If any further complications had cropped up she would surely have
let you know, wouldn't she?

JACK Yes, I think she would. I imagine she's frightened to death and doesn't want any more to do
with me. I'm sure I hope so. And then, you see, I
never answered her letter or telephoned.

TOWNSEND (*Gravely*) You were wrong there, my boy.

JACK (*Excitedly*) I know it, I know it, Dad; but I had
just received a letter from Evelyn telling me she
was coming out for Commencement Week and
the game, and— Oh, when I thought of her the
other affair seemed so horrible and loathsome, I
swore I'd never speak or write again. When I was
certain she was in no danger I judged it best for

both of us to break off once and for all.

TOWNSEND Listen, my boy, are you sure—you know one's vanity blinds one in such cases—are you sure, absolutely sure, you were the father of this child which would have been born to her?

JACK (*Emphatically*) Yes, I am certain of it, as certain as one can possibly be. (*Wildly*) Oh, I wish to God I had grounds for some suspicion of the sort. What a salve it would be for my conscience! But no, no! To even think such is an insult to a sweet girl. (*Defiantly*) For she is a sweet, lovely girl in spite of everything, and if I had loved her the least particle, if I had not been in love with Evelyn, I should certainly have married her.

TOWNSEND Hm—if you did not love this girl, why did you—why, in the first place—?

JACK (*Leaning toward his father and fixing his eyes upon him searchingly*) Why? Why? Who knows why or who, that does know, has the courage to confess it, even to himself. Be frank, Dad! Judging from several anecdotes which your friend Professor Simmons has let slip about your four years here, you were no St. Anthony. Turn your mind back to those days and then answer your own question: Why, in the first place?

TOWNSEND (*Staring at the floor in moody retrospection —a pause*) We've retained a large portion of the original mud in our make-up. That's the only answer I can think of.

JACK (*Ironically*) That's it! Do you suppose it was the same man who loves Evelyn who did this other thing? No, a thousands time no, such an idea is abhorrent. It was the male beast who ran gibbering through the forest after its female thousands of years ago.

TOWNSEND Come, Jack, that is pure evasion. You are responsible for the Mr. Hyde in you as well as for the Dr. Jekyll. Restraint—

JACK (*Scornfully*) Restraint? Ah, yes, everybody preaches it but who practices it? And could they if they wanted to? Some impulses are stronger than we are, have proved themselves so throughout the world's history. Is it not rather our ideals of conduct, of Right and Wrong, our ethics, which are unnatural and monstrously distorted? Is society not suffering from a case of the evil eye which sees evil where there is none? Isn't it our moral laws which force me into evasions like the one which you have just found fault with?

TOWNSEND You're delving too deep for me, my boy. Save your radical arguments for the younger generation. I cannot see them in the same light you do (*Grumblingly*) and if I could, I wouldn't. What I cannot understand is how you happened to get in with this young woman in the first place. You'll pardon me, Jack, but it seems to me to show a lack of judgment on your part, and—er—good taste.

JACK (*Shrugging his shoulders*) Such things usually are errors in taste.

TOWNSEND This young woman was hardly of the class you have been accustomed to associate with, I presume.

JACK She is a working girl, a stenographer.

HERRON Has she any immediate relations who would be liable to discover the unfortunate termination of your (*Sarcastically*) love affair?

JACK   Her father is dead. Her mother is a silly woman
who would be the last to suspect anything. She has
two sisters, both youngsters under ten, and one
brother about eighteen, a machinist or something
of the sort who is only home for weekends.

TOWNSEND   And she and her brother support the others?

JACK (*Avoiding his father's eyes*)   So I believe.

TOWNSEND (*His expression stern and accusing; he starts
to say something but restrains himself*)   Ah.

JACK (*Glancing at his father*)   Yes, yes, I know it,
Dad. I have played the scoundrel all the way
through. I realize that now. Why couldn't I have
felt this way before, at the start? Then this would
never have happened. But at that time the whole
thing seemed just a pleasant game we were playing;
its serious aspects appeared remote, unreal. I never
gave them a thought. I have paid for it since then,
I want you to believe that. I have had my glance
into the abyss. In loss of confidence and self-respect,
in bitter self-abasement I have paid, and I am sure
the result of it all will be to make me a better man,
a man more worthy to be Evelyn's husband.

TOWNSEND (*Huskily*)   God grant it, my boy. (*He gets
to his feet*) I want to thank you for the confidence
you placed in your father by making a frank appeal
to me when you got in this trouble. It shows you
regard me not only as a father but as a friend; and
that is the way I would have it.

JACK   You have always urged me to come to you and
be frank about everything; and I always have and
always will. I had to have the money and I thought
I owed it to you to be open and above board and

not start in deceiving you at this late day. I couldn't get it in any other way very well. Two hundred dollars is quite a sum for a college student to raise at a moment's notice.

TOWNSEND (*Restored to good humor*) The wages of sin are rather exorbitant.

JACK He was the only doctor I could find who would do that sort of thing. He knew I was a college student and probably made inquiries about your financial rating—and there you are. There was nothing for me to do but grin and pay. But as I said in my letter, this money is a loan. It would be unfair for me to make you shoulder my—mistakes.

TOWNSEND (*Cheerfully*) Let's forget all about it. (*He holds out his hand to* JACK, *who clasps it heartily*) All's well that ends well. You've learned your lesson. (*The sound of a college cheer comes faintly through the open window*) And now shall we join the others? That cheer wakens the old fever in me. I want to follow the band and get singed by the Roman candles.

(*He picks his straw hat from the table*)

JACK (*Eagerly*) Yes, let's do that.

(*They are going toward the door in the rear when* JOE MURRAY *appears in the doorway.* JACK *cannot repress an exclamation of alarm and his face grows pale*)

MURRAY (*Fixing his eyes on* JACK *with an expression of furious hatred*) Look here, Townsend, I gotta see yuh for a minute.

JACK (*Unwillingly*) All right, Murray. You join the others, Dad, and I'll catch you in a few minutes.

(TOWNSEND, *struck by the change in his son's voice,
looks questioningly at him, asking an explanation.* JACK
turns away from him)

JACK   Come in, Murray, and have a seat.

(TOWNSEND *goes out.* MURRAY *slouches to the middle
of the room but does not sit down. His fingers fumble
nervously at the buttons of his coat. He notices this and
plunges his hands into his coat pockets. He seems en-
deavoring to restrain the hatred and rage which the
spasmodic working of his features show to be boiling
within him*)

JACK (*He appears occupied in arranging the things on
     the table*)   Well?

MURRAY (*Chokingly*)   Well!

(*He can go no further*)

JACK (*Coldly, without looking at him*)   Anything I
     can do for you?

MURRAY (*In strangled tones*)   Anything you can do
     for *me!*

JACK (*Hurriedly*)   Yes. I'm in rather a hurry and if it's
     nothing very important I'd be just as well pleased
     if you'd come some other time.

MURRAY   Important? *You* mayn't think so. It's not im-
     portant to *you*, yuh—

(*He is stopped by a fit of violent coughing which
racks his thin body*)

JACK (*Irritably*)   You've come here looking for trou-
     ble, Murray. You better wait until you've cooled
     off. (*Then, more kindly*)   What is it you want to
     say to me? Out with it!

MURRAY (*Wiping his mouth on his coat sleeve—an-
     grily*)   I'll out with it, damn yuh! Standing there so
     cool—dressed in swell clothes—and all these other

goils— (*Choking*) and Nellie—and Nellie—

JACK (*Leaning toward him*) Yes—Nellie?

MURRAY (*Sobbing*) She's dead. (*In a transport of rage*) You killed her, yuh dirty murderer!

JACK (*Dully, as if he did not understand*) Dead? No, no, you don't mean that. She wrote to me everything was all right. Dead?

(*As he speaks he backs away from* MURRAY *in horror and stumbles against one of the Morris chairs. He sits down in it mechanically*)

MURRAY (*Shrilly*) She's dead—Nellie, my sister—she's dead.

JACK (*Half to himself*) No, it's impossible. (*Fiercely*) It's a lie! What scheme is this of yours? You're trying to frighten me.

MURRAY (*Raging*) She's dead, I tell yuh, dead! She died this morning.

JACK (*Forced to believe*) She died this morning? (*In a dazed voice*) But why didn't she—I didn't know —(*Stares straight before him*) God!

MURRAY Why didn't she let yuh know, yuh mean? She wrote to yuh, she told me she did; and yuh knew she was sick and never answered it. She might'a lived if she thought yuh cared, if she heard from yuh; but she knew yuh were trying to git rid of her.

JACK (*In agony*) Stop, for God's sake! I know I should have written. I meant to write but—

MURRAY She kept sayin': "I wanta die. I don't wanta live!" (*Furiously*) But I'll fix yuh! I'll make yuh pay.

JACK (*Startled, he turns to him quickly*) What do you mean?

MURRAY Don't give me any of that. Yuh know what I mean. Yuh know how she died. (*Fiercely*) Yuh know who killed her.

JACK (*His voice trembling—not looking at* MURRAY) How she died? Killed her? I don't understand—

MURRAY Yuh lie! She was murdered and yuh know it.

JACK (*Horror-struck*) Murdered?

MURRAY Yes, and *you* murdered her.

JACK (*Shuddering*) I? What? I murdered? Are you crazy?

MURRAY You and your dirty skunk of a doctor.

JACK (*Sinking back in his chair with a groan*) Ooh!

MURRAY (*With fierce scorn*) Yuh thought yuh was safe, didn't yuh, with me away from home? Yuh c'd go out and pitch the championship game— and she lyin' dead! Yuh c'd ruin her and throw her down and no one say a word because yuh're a swell college guy and captain of the team, and she ain't good enough for yuh to marry. She's goin' to have a kid, *your* kid, and because yuh're too rotten to act like a man, yuh send her to a faker of a doctor to be killed; and she does what yuh say because she loves yuh; and yuh don't even think enough of her to answer her letter (*Sobbing*) when she's dyin' on account of *you!*

JACK (*Speaking with difficulty*) She—told you—all this?

MURRAY Not a word! (*Proudly*) She died game; she wasn't no coward. I tried every way I knew how to git her to tell me but she wouldn't. Not a word outa her against you. (*Choking with angry sobs*) And *you*—and *you*—yuh dirty coward!—playin' ball!

JACK (*Dully*) I did what I thought was best for her.

MURRAY Yuh sneaked out like a coward because yuh
thought she wasn't good enough. (*With a sneer*)
Yuh think yuh c'n get away with that stuff and
then marry some goil of your own kind, I s'pose—
some goil like I seen yuh come in with tonight.
(*Vindictively*) But yuh won't; not if I have to go
to hell for it!

(*A pause. JACK is silent, breathing hard. His eyes are
haunted, full of despair, as he vainly seeks to escape
from the remorse which is torturing him. The faint
sound of a college cheer, then of the band, comes from
the open window. From this point to the end these
sounds are continuous, the band only being silenced to
permit the giving of the cheer, and as the action progresses they become more and more distinct*)

MURRAY (*Continuing in the same vindictive tones*)
I've always hated yuh since yuh come to the house.
I've always hated all your kind. Yuh come here to
school and yuh think yuh c'n do as yuh please with
us town people. Yuh treat us like servants, an' what
are *you*, I'd like to know? A lot of lazy no-good
dudes spongin' on your old men; and the goils, our
goils, think yuh're grand!

(*JACK is staring at the floor, his head bowed, and does
not seem to hear him*)

MURRAY I knew somethin' would happen. I told Nellie to look out, and she laughed. When the old
lady sent for me and I come home and saw Nellie
and she wouldn't leave me go for a doctor, I had
a hunch what was wrong. She wouldn't say nothin'
but I got our doc, not the one *you* sent her to, and
he told me just what I thought and said she was

goin' to die. (*Raging*) If I'd seen yuh that minute I'd killed yuh. I knew it was *you* but I couldn't prove it. Then one of the kids got scared and told me Nellie'd sent her to your doc for medicine when she first took sick. I bought a gun and the kid showed me where he was. I shoved the gun in his face and he owned up and told me about you. He offered me money, lots of it, to keep my mouth shut, and I took it—the money he'd got from you —blood money! (*With a savage grin*) An' I'll keep my mouth shut—maybe!

JACK (His eyes lighting up with a gleam of hope, he *turns eagerly to* MURRAY) Listen, Murray! This affair is unspeakably horrible, and I am—everything you say; but I want you—you must believe I honestly thought I was acting for the best in having the operation performed. That it has turned out so tragically is terrible. You cannot realize how I am suffering. I feel as if I were what you called me—a murderer. (*Brokenly*) It is horrible, horrible! The thought of it will torture me all my life.

MURRAY That don't bring her back to life. Yuh're too late!

JACK (*Frenziedly*) Too late! What do you mean? You haven't told anyone? You haven't—

MURRAY When I left his office I went home and—she was dead. Then I come up here lookin' for *you*. I wanted to kill yuh, but—I been thinkin'—yuh're not worth gittin' hung for. (*With a cruel grin*) I c'n see a better way of fixin' yuh—one that'll get yuh right.

JACK (*Half to himself*) You haven't told anyone?

MURRAY What's the difference? There's plenty of
time. *I* know.

JACK (*Trying to steady his voice, which is trembling
with apprehension*) Murray, for your own sake,
for your dead sister's good name, for your family's
sake, you must keep this thing quiet. I do not plead
for myself. I am willing to have you punish me individually in any way you see fit; but there are
others, innocent ones, who will suffer.

MURRAY She was innocent, too, before you—

JACK (*Interrupting him*) My mother and father, my
sister, Ev—(*Bites back the name*) This would kill
my mother if she knew. They are innocent. Do not
revenge yourself on them.

MURRAY (*Inflexibly*) You killed my sister.

JACK Why will you keep saying that? You know it was
an accident; that I would gladly have given my
own life rather than have it happen. And you must
keep silent. I will do anything you want, I tell you!
(*He goes close to* MURRAY) You say the doctor
gave you money? I'll give you ten times as much
as he did. (MURRAY'*s face grows livid*) I'll see that
you get so much a year for the rest of your life. My
father is rich. We'll get you a good position, do
everything you wish. (*Breaking down*) Only do
not punish the innocent.

MURRAY (*Slowly*) You want—to pay me—for Nellie!
(*With a terrible cry of rage he pulls a revolver from
the pocket of his coat. Before he can pull the trigger*
JACK *seizes his wrist. There is a short struggle.* JACK
*takes the revolver away from him and lays it on the
table.* MURRAY *has a violent attack of coughing. He re-*

covers and is slinking toward the door when JACK *suddenly picks up the revolver from the table and holds it out to him*)

JACK (*Steadily*)   Here, take it! I was a fool to stop you. Let the thing end with me and leave the innocent alone.

MURRAY (*Malevolently*)   It's too good for yuh. (*He has edged stealthily nearer and nearer the door and with a final spring gains the safety of the hallway. He shouts back*) I'm goin' to the p'lice station. D'yuh hear, yuh dirty ba - rd! To the p'lice station!

(*His quick footsteps can be heard as he runs out.* JACK *makes a movement as if to follow him but stops and sits down heavily by the table, laying the revolver on it. He hears the band and the cheers of the paraders, who have evidently just invaded that section of the campus. He hurries to the windows, closes them and pulls down the shades. The band is playing a march song and the students are singing.* JACK *groans and hides his face in his hands. The parade is about to pass by his windows. The glare of the red fire glows dully on the right. Several students crowd in the doorway from the hall*)

ONE STUDENT   He's not here.

ANOTHER STUDENT   He ran away.

(*All go out laughing and shouting. The band stops playing.* JACK *comes out from the bedroom, his face drawn with agony. The cheerleader's voice can be heard shouting:* "He ran away but if we give him a cheer, he'll hear us. A long cheer for Townsend, fellows! Hip! Hip!" JACK *staggers toward the window, crying brokenly:* "No! No! For God's sake!" *The first part of the cheer booms out. He reels to the table and sees the revolver lying there. He snatches it up and presses it to his temple. The report is drowned by the cheering. He falls forward on his face, twitches, is still*)

THE STUDENTS (*Winding up the nine long rahs*) Rah! Rah! Rah! Townsend! Townsend! Townsend! (*The band strikes up "For He's a Jolly Good Fellow." The students commence to sing. The parade moves off again.* EVELYN *appears in the doorway to the rear*)

EVELYN Jack! It's all right now, dear. You can come out of hiding. (*She blinks for a moment, blinded by the light; then comes into the room and sees the body—in terror*) Jack! What's the matter?

(*She rushes over and kneels beside him; then faints as she sees the blood on his temples, the revolver still clutched in his right hand. She falls on the floor beside him*)

THE STUDENTS (*Their voices growing gradually fainter*) "For he's a jolly good fellow, which nobody can deny."

Curtain

THE
MOVIE MAN

A Comedy in One Act

✻

CHARACTERS

Henry (Hen) Rogers, Representative of
    Earth Motion Picture Company
Al Devlin, photographer for the same company
Pancho Gomez, Commander-in-Chief
    of the Constitutionalist Army
Luis Virella, General of a Division
Anita Fernandez
A Sentry

SCENE—*The main room of a house in the suburb of a large town in northern Mexico. To the left, a white-washed wall of adobe with a small black crucifix hanging from a nail. In the rear wall, a doorway opening on the street. On either side of the doorway, an open window. On the right side of the room, another door which is closed. On the wall above it, a faded lithograph of the Virgin. In the left-hand corner several Mauser carbines are stacked, and bandoleers of cartridges are thrown on the dirt floor beside them. In the right-hand corner several saddles are lying. Near the door, another saddle. In the middle of the room, a rickety table with a pen, paper and ink on it. Three or four stiff cane-bottomed chairs are placed about the table.*

HEN ROGERS *and* AL DEVLIN *are sitting by the table. Both are smoking pipes. Both are dressed in khaki shirts, riding breeches, puttees, etc. Their wide-brimmed Stetson hats are on the table beside them.* ROGERS *is tall, blond, clean-shaven, in his early thirties.* DEVLIN *is short, dark, with a good-natured irregular face, middle-aged.*

A sentry in a filthy, ragged olive-drab uniform lolls in the doorway leaning on his rifle. He wears the wide sombrero of the Mexican peon, and is barefooted. He is smoking a cigarette and watching the two Americans with an expression of bored indifference.

It is in the early hours of a sultry tropic night.

DEVLIN (*Singing in a cracked falsetto*) Mexico, my nice cool Mexico!

ROGERS (*Mopping the perspiration from his forehead with a bandana handkerchief*) Have a heart, Al, have a heart, and kill the canary-bird stuff. If you see anything to be merry over in this flea-bitten cluster of shanties, you got something on me.

DEVLIN (*Chuckling*) Lovely little spot to spend the summer!

ROGERS (*Dryly*) Ideal is the word. And speaking of fleas, on the level, I never knew what a poor dog has to put up with until I hit this one-horse country.

DEVLIN They don't bother me any.

ROGERS No, they've got some class, you gotta hand it to them.

DEVLIN Is *that* so?

ROGERS "Discretion is the better part of valor"—any well-bred Mexican flea is hep to that. Those are the first words in the Mexican Constitution, and every man and beast in this country swears by them. If they didn't we'd have been in Mexico City months ago, and right now I'd be down at Manhattan Beach in God's Country with a large mint julep, full of ice—

DEVLIN (*With a groan*) Help! Help! I'm a nut!

ROGERS When this cruel war is over and on the films I'm going to quit the picture business and go way up north, marry an Esquimau, and start housekeeping on an exclusive, refined, accordion-pleated, little iceberg.

DEVLIN (*Whistling shrilly to the sentry, who grabs his rifle in alarm*) Boy, page an iceberg for Mr. Rogers!

THE SENTRY (*With lazy scorn*) Muy loco!

ROGERS What's that he said, Al? Look it up in your little book. It sounded almost like real talk.

DEVLIN (*With a laugh*) I don't have to look that up. He means we're crazy.

ROGERS (*To the sentry—approvingly*) You said something then, Mike. We sure are as nutty as a fruitcake or we wouldn't be here. Phew, but it's hot! (*After a short pause—musingly*) Say, Al, did you ever notice the happy, contented expression on a polar bear's face?

DEVLIN (*Laughing*) Basta! Basta!

(*The sentry instinctively springs to attention, then lapses into indifference again as he realizes it is only the crazy American speaking*)

ROGERS Say, you're getting to be a regular talker of spigoty! Slip me the answer to that word *basta*, will you? I hear friend General pulling it all the time; and just to show you what a fine little guesser I am, I'll bet you a case-note it means when.

DEVLIN Come across with that peso. It doesn't mean when; it means enough.

ROGERS Same thing. I knew it—I never yet heard him say it when I was pouring him out a drink.

DEVLIN You owe me a peso, don't forget it.

ROGERS (*Grumblingly*) I'm not liable to with you around. (*An excited babble of voices is heard from the door on the right*) Listen to those boobs, will you! What do you suppose they're framing up in there?

DEVLIN   Who is it—Gomez?

ROGERS   Yes. He and all his little generals are having some sort of a confab. I'll bet you that smack back again he's going to try and capture the town to-morrow.

DEVLIN   What's this you're springing on me—inside information?

ROGERS   Nope; but this afternoon I gave him that case of Scotch I promised him when he signed our contract, and he's feeling some brave this evening.

DEVLIN   Say, Hen, about that contract, I forgot to tell you, you wanta hand a call to this Gomez guy. He is playing the game. You remember the other day when they were going after that fort on the outskirts?

ROGERS   Sure—good stuff—plenty of real live action that day.

DEVLIN   (*Indignantly*)   It was good stuff all right, but I missed all the first part of it on account of that simp General Virella. He was just waving his sword and ordering 'em to charge when I came up. "Here, you!" I said to him. "Wait a minute. Can't you see I'm not ready for you yet?" And what do you think that greaser said to me? You know he speaks good English. He says: "Shall my glorious soldiers be massacred waiting for your machine?" And away he runs with all his yellow-bellies after him. What d'you know about that?

ROGERS   (*Frowning*)   He's a fresh guy, that Virella. I'll have Gomez stick him back in the rear after this. He's a mean little worm, too. He's the one who's nagged Gomez into croaking old Fernandez.

DEVLIN   What! Are they going to shoot Fernandez?

ROGERS   At sunrise tomorrow they stand him against the wall and—curtain.

DEVLIN   It's a damn shame—just because they can't get any more coin out of him. He's a good fellow —Fernandez. Went to school in the States— Cornell or some place. Can't you get him off?

ROGERS   Nix. Virella has a grudge against him and Gomez needs Virella. Anyway, I've got no license to butt in on their little scraps. Besides, it'll make a great picture. Be sure and get it.

DEVLIN   I'll be there. Say, have them hold it till a little later, will you? The light isn't any good so early.

ROGERS   How'll eight o'clock do?

DEVLIN   Great!

ROGERS   All right, I'll tell Gomez to postpone it till then. (A *shrill voice is heard shouting* "Viva" *from the room on the right*) That's Virella, now. I'd like to take just one swing at that guy. They'd carry him home in a white-pine kimono. (*Another cheer from the room next door*) Full of booze and patriotism! Gee, I wish I was a war correspondent. I'd send in a little notice like this: "The courage and spirits of the troops were never better. A train-load of rum arrived today. We will be in Mexico City in two weeks."

DEVLIN   (*Picking his hat from the table, he gets to his feet*) I think I'll take a look around and see what's doing.

ROGERS   Oho! I've got your number all right!

DEVLIN   (*Laughing*)   What do you mean: got my number?

ROGERS   Have a care, little one, have a care! Some one of these Mexican dolls you're googooing at will carve her initials on your back with the bread knife some one of these days.

DEVLIN   I should fret!

ROGERS   (*Disgustedly*) What you can see in these skirts has got me beat. They're so homely the mules shy at them.

DEVLIN   Is *that* so? Well, let me tell you, there's some class to some of the dames down here. You ought to have seen the bear I lamped this afternoon. Some queen, take it from me.

ROGERS   Load that noise in one of the cannons and fire it off!

DEVLIN   On the level, Hen, she had the swellest lamps I've ever seen on a dame; and a figure—my boy! my boy!

ROGERS   Captain Sweeney of the Marines, please listen! And I suppose you copped her and dated her up?

DEVLIN   Nothing like it, Hen. She was doing a sob act on one of the benches in that little park out here, and I asked her in my best Spanish what was the matter. Phew! Talk about the icy onceover! She looked at me as if I was a wet dog. I turned and beat it like a little man.

ROGERS   You were wise, for once. She'd have operated on you with her stiletto in another second. I wouldn't trust one of these dolls as far as I could hit Walter Johnson's fast one.

DEVLIN   But what d'you suppose she was doing a weep about?

ROGERS   (*Dryly*) Maybe one of her husbands got killed in the war.

DEVLIN   What sweet thoughts you have! S'long, Hen.
       Don't forget to have Gomez postpone that shoot-
       ing thing.

(*He goes to the door in the rear*)

ROGERS   I won't; and you come back early—if you're
       still alive. I want you to scratch my back before
       I hit the hay. I'd have to be a contortionist or a
       centipede to follow this flea-game properly.

DEVLIN   (*Laughing*)   They'll take your mind off your
       worries. Be good!

(*He passes the sentry and disappears in the darkness.
Another cheer is heard from the next room.* ROGERS
*grunts disgustedly and attempts to scratch the middle of
his back. The sentry's head falls forward on his chest as
he dozes in the doorway.*

ANITA FERNANDEZ *appears outside the door and creeps
stealthily by the sentry into the room. She is a beautiful
young Mexican girl with a mass of black hair and great
black eyes. She stumbles over the saddle by the door
and utters a little cry of pain. The sentry wakes up,
rushes over to her and grabs her furiously by the arm.
He drags her toward the door.* ROGERS *springs from his
chair and yells at the sentry*)

ROGERS   Hey, you, Mike, what are you doing? Let go
       of that dame!

(*The sentry scowls uncertainly at him.* ROGERS *makes
a threatening gesture and the sentry releases* ANITA *and
returns to his post by the doorway.* ANITA *sinks into a
chair by the table and, hiding her face in her hands,
commences to sob.* ROGERS *stands beside her not knowing what to do*)

ROGERS   What'll I say to her? (*Sees the English-Span-
       ish book of* DEVLIN's *on the table*) Here's Al's Span-

ish book. Let's see. (*Turning over the pages*) "What do you want?"—I wonder how you say it? Oh, here it is. (*He repeats the line to himself, then bends down to* ANITA) *Que quere, señorita?* (*He pronounces it "Kwi query, seenorita?" She raises her head and stares at him with a puzzled expression*) She doesn't make me at all—oh hell!

ANITA (*Haughtily*) Pleese to not swear, *señor.*

ROGERS (*Confused*) Excuse me—awfully sorry—tongue slipped. (*With a sigh of relief*) Thank Go—heavens, you speak English.

ANITA But most badly, *señor.*

ROGERS (*Sitting down across the table from her*) No, very good, just as good as mine. Who was it you wanted to see?

ANITA El Generalissimo Gomez.

ROGERS (*Shaking his head*) You better wait. He'll be all lit up like a torch tonight.

ANITA (*Mystified*) *Señor?*

ROGERS You know what I mean—he's soused, pickled, stewed, boiled—

ANITA (*In puzzled accents*) Es-stewed? Boiled? (*In horrified tones*) You mean he is cooking—the General? But no, *señor,* I onderstand Eenglish veree badly. For one year alone, I estudy in the convent in Nueva York—Noo York. Then *mi madre*—my mothair—die and I must come home to the house of my fathair becose I have more years —I am older than my sisters.

(*There is a ringing "Viva" from the next room.* ANITA *turns pale*)

ROGERS (*Making a motion with his hand as if he were taking a drink and nodding toward the room*)

You understand now? He's drinking, and—

ANITA (*Shuddering*)   Ah, he es drunk, no?

ROGERS   I'm afraid he will be before he leaves that room—if he isn't already.

ANITA (*The tears starting to her eyes*)   *Mi padre!*

ROGERS   You better wait until tomorrow to see him.

ANITA   Eet ees not possible. I must—tonight!

ROGERS (*Earnestly*)   Don't do it, kid! Don't you know Gomez is a bad guy—man—for a young girl to come and see at night—specially when he's drunk?

ANITA (*Flushing*)   I know, *si, señor,* but eet must be.

ROGERS   Won't you tell me why?

ANITA (*Her voice trembling*)   *Si,* I will tell you. Eet ees not long to tell, *señor.* You have heard—you know Ernesto Fernandez?

ROGERS   You mean the Fernandez who is going to be shot tomorrow morning?

ANITA (*Shuddering*)   *Si, señor,* he eet ess I mean. He ees my fathair.

ROGERS (*Astounded*)   Your father! Good God!

ANITA   I must see the General Gomez tonight to ask him to save my fathair.

ROGERS   He will not do it.

ANITA (*Faintly*)   You know that, *señor?*

ROGERS   Virella is with him—in there—now!

ANITA (*Terrified*)   Virella? He is the most bad enemy of my fathair.

ROGERS   You might buy Gomez off; pay him to set your father free. He'll do anything for money. Have you any money?

ANITA   Alas, no, *señor*; Gomez has taken from us everything.

ROGERS   Too bad, too bad! Hm— Well, you mustn't

stay here any longer. They're liable to come out any minute. Go home now, and I'll see what I can do with Gomez.

ANITA (*Resolutely*) *Gracias*, I thank you, *señor*; you are very kind—but I must see Gomez.

ROGERS (*Deliberately—looking steadily into her eyes*) Don't you know what Gomez will want—the price he will make you pay if he finds you here?

ANITA (*Closing her eyes and swaying weakly on her feet*) For the life—of my fathair—

(*She sobs softly*)

ROGERS (*Looking at her in admiration*) God!

ANITA (*Fiercely*) I would keel myself to save him!

ROGERS But even if he said he'd free your father you couldn't believe him. What is Gomez' word worth? No, you must let me fix this for you.

ANITA (*Doubtfully*) But you—Gomez ees veree powerful, *señor*—ess it possible for you to do?

ROGERS (*Decisively*) I'll save your old man if I have to start a revolution of my own to do it.

ANITA (*Her eyes shining with gratitude*) Ah, thank you, *señor*—but if you should fail?

ROGERS (*Emphatically*) I won't fail. You just watch me start something!

(*He has scarcely finished speaking when the door to the right is thrown open and* GOMEZ *and* VIRELLA *enter the room. They are both in a state of great excitement and show they have been drinking.* VIRELLA *is an undersized man with shifty, beady black eyes and a black mustache.* GOMEZ *is tall and heavily built, with a bloated, dissipated-looking face and a bristly black mustache. Both are dressed in new uniforms of olive-drab and wear military caps. Cartridge belts with automatic*

*revolvers in leather holsters are strapped about their
waists over their coats.*

ANITA *stares at them for a moment with horrified
loathing; then shrinks away into the far corner of the
room.* GOMEZ *turns to shout an "Adiós" to the officers
who are still carousing in the room he has just left; then
bangs the door shut behind him.* VIRELLA *sees* ANITA *and
walks toward her with a drunken leer on his flushed
face)*

VIRELLA   *Buenas noches, señorita.*

ROGERS   *(Steps forward and places himself in front of*
    VIRELLA, *whom he grasps by the shoulders and forci-
    bly turns in the direction of the door)*   Now beat
    it, snake-in-the-grass!

VIRELLA   *(Struggling to free himself)*   Pig of a Gringo!

ROGERS   General Gomez and I want to have a talk in
    private, don't we, Gomez?

    (He glances at GOMEZ *with a commanding air)*

GOMEZ   *(Uncertainly)*   *Por cierto, amigo,* if you like
    eet.

VIRELLA   *(Frothing at the mouth with rage)*   Dog! Pig!

ROGERS   *(Calmly)*   Those are hard words, my pet—and
    you hear what your General commands?

    (He turns to GOMEZ)

GOMEZ   *Si,* Virella, I command eet.

ROGERS   *(To* VIRELLA, *contemptuously)*   Now blow be-
    fore I crown you!

    (He draws back his fist threateningly. VIRELLA *shrinks
    away from him, salutes* GOMEZ *and slinks out of the
    door in the rear)*

GOMEZ   *(Forcing a laugh)*   Ees thees the way you treat
    my generals?

ROGERS You ought to shoot that little scorpion—before he shoots you.

GOMEZ (*Frowning*) Eet ees true, *amigo*, what you say, and pairhaps soon—but—now he ees to me necessary. (*He notices* ANITA *for the first time and turns to* ROGERS *with a chuckle*) Excuse me, *señorita!* (*He takes his cap off and makes her a gallant bow*) Ah, Señor Rogers, you are—how you call eet?— a man of—ladies, no? (*He walks over to* ANITA, *who shrinks back to the wall in terror*) Have you fear of me, *chiquita*? Of Gomez? But Pancho Gomez, he loav the ladies, that ees well known. Ask el señor Rogers.

(*He chucks her under the chin*)

ROGERS (*Stepping between them—quietly*) This young lady is *my* friend, Gomez.

GOMEZ (*Biting his lips*) I say in fun only. (*He walks back to the table and remarks sullenly to* ROGERS, *who is following him*) She ees *muy hermosa*, veree preety, your *señorita*.

ROGERS She is the daughter of Ernesto Fernandez.

GOMEZ (*Surprised*) *Que dice?* What you say?

ROGERS She's the daughter of the man you're going to have shot in the morning. She came to ask you—

GOMEZ (*Emphatically*) No, *hombre*, no! I know what you will say. I cannot do. Eet ees not possible! (ANITA *rushes forward and throws herself at his feet*) No, no, no, *señorita*, I must go.

(*He strides toward the door in the rear.* ANITA *lies where she has thrown herself, sobbing hopelessly*)

ROGERS One minute, Gomez! Where are you going?

GOMEZ To prepare the attack. Ah, I forget! I have not

tole you. (*Excitedly*) Tonight, *amigo*, we storm
the town. We catch them asleep, no? and before
they wake they are—(*He makes a motion across
his neck with his forefinger*) dead, how you call
eet?—as a nail. (*Proudly*) Eet ees a plan sublime,
most glorious—eet ees the plan of Gomez! In one
small week, *hombre*, we shall be in Mexico City.

ROGERS That Scotch is great stuff. One more drink and
old Napoleon would be a piker.

GOMEZ (*Puzzled*) What you say?

ROGERS Nothing, nothing. (*His face lighting up with
a ray of hope*) A night attack, eh?

GOMEZ *Si, hombre*, at twelve hours—twelve o'clock.

ROGERS (*Calmly*) Who said so?

GOMEZ I say it, I, Pancho Gomez!

ROGERS (*Emphatically*) Well, you just listen to me,
Gomez; I say you can't do it. There'll be no night
attack in this war when I'm around. (GOMEZ *is
stupefied*) How do you expect us to get pictures at
night? You didn't think of that, eh?

GOMEZ (*Bewildered*) But, *amigo*—

ROGERS Nix on the night attacks, do you get me?
(*Pulling a paper out of his pocket*) Here's a copy
of your contract giving us rights to all your fights—
all, do you hear, all! And we got one clause especially for night attacks. (*Reads*) "The party of the
second part hereby agrees to fight no battles at
night or on rainy days or at any time whatsoever
when the light is so poor as to make the taking of
motion pictures impracticable. Failure to comply
with these conditions will constitute a breach of
contract and free the party of the first part from all

G

the obligations entered into by this contract." (*He hands the contract to* GOMEZ) Here it is, black and white, English and Spanish both, with your signature at the bottom with mine. Read for yourself.

(GOMEZ *glances at the paper mechanically and hands it back*)

GOMEZ (*With a defiant snarl*) And if I say to hell, you! Then what you do, eh?

ROGERS (*Mimicking the* GENERAL's *tone*) Who buys and sends you most of your ammunition, eh? Who pays you and the other generals and the German in charge of your artillery—the only man who savvys how to use the guns right, eh? Who has promised to see that you get siege guns for Mexico City and twenty more machine guns with men, real men, to run them for you, eh? Your soldiers'll desert you if you don't pay them soon, and you know it. Well, who has agreed to loan you the money to give them their back pay, eh? And, above all, who has promised to help you become President when you reach Mexico City? (*Impressively*) We have—The Earth Motion Picture Company! Well, you break this contract and all that stops, see?—and goes to the other side.

GOMEZ (*Softly—fingering his revolver*) *Bueno;* but I can also have you shot, *hombre.*

ROGERS Nix on that rough stuff! You wouldn't dare. You've got to keep on the right side of the U.S.A. or your revolution isn't worth the powder to blow it to—Mexico.

GOMEZ (*Pleadingly*) But, *amigo,* permit eet this once. The plan is fine, the town will be ours, my soldiers will steal and no more grumble against Gomez.

Tomorrow I will shoot all the prisoners for your
pictures, I promise eet.

ROGERS (*Kindly*) I'd like to do you a favor, Gomez,
but I don't see my way to do this, unless—

GOMEZ (*With a smile*) Aha, tell me, *hombre*, your
price.

ROGERS (*Firmly*) The life of Ernesto Fernandez!

(ANITA *jumps to her feet and stretches out her arms
beseechingly to* GOMEZ. *He twirls his mustache thoughtfully for a moment*)

GOMEZ *Bueno*, my friend, I accept your terms. (*He
goes to the table and hurriedly scratches a few
lines which he hands to* ANITA) *Su padre de uste*—
your father, he ees free, *señorita*. For this thank my
fine friend Señor Rogers. (*He claps* ROGERS *jovially
on the back*) Now must I have shot the General
Virella, who will never forgive me your father
should live, *señorita*. Mexico ees too es-small for
those two *hombres*—both alive. (*He pulls a flask
from his pocket and offers it to* ROGERS, *who refuses
with a smile*) Señor Rogers—how you call eet?—
here ees looking at you! (*He drinks*) And now I
must to prepare the attack. (*He goes to the door;
then turns and remarks grandiloquently*) Should
anyone wish me, *señor*, tell them that een the hour
of battle, Pancho Gomez, like the immortal Juarez,
will ever be found at the head of his brave soldiers. *Adiós!*

(*He makes a sweeping bow and goes out past the
saluting sentry*)

ROGERS (*With a long whistle of amusement—turning
to* ANITA) Some bull! Honest, you've got to hand
it to that guy, at that.

ANITA And now I, too, must go—to my poor fathair.

ROGERS Can't I take you there? You know, there's lots of drunken soldiers around and—

ANITA No, no, *señor*, you are too kind. Eet ees but two steps to the carcel—the prison. Eet ees not necessary. (*Indicating the paper in her hand*) The name of Gomez is most sufficient. (*Holding out her hand to him with a shy smile*) *Muchísima gracias, señor*—with all my heart do I thank you. My fathair and I, we will be at the home tomorrow —eet ees the first hacienda beyond the hill—you will come, *señor*? As a brother, my father's son, shall you be to us!

ROGERS (*Holding her hand and looking into her eyes*) Only—a brother?

ANITA (*Drawing her hand away in confusion, she runs to the door; then turns*) *Quién sabe, señor?* Who knows?

(*She hurries out*)

ROGERS (*He does a few Spanish dance steps, snapping his fingers and humming. The sentry grins at him*) What are you grinning at, Mike?

SENTRY (*With a contemptuous smile he makes a gesture of turning a wheel near his head*) *Muy loco!*

ROGERS I got you the first time, Mike. Crazy is the right word. (*He commences to sing*) "Mexico, my bright-eyed Mexico."

(DEVLIN *appears in the doorway and scowls darkly at him*)

DEVLIN Kill it, kill it, you bone! (*He comes in and throws his hat irritably on the table.* ROGERS *looks at him with an amused smile*) What're you chirping about? Are you soused, too? Where have you

hidden the joy-water? Everyone in this bush-league
army seems all corned up tonight except me. Say,
I just got another flash at that dame I was telling
you about. She looked right through me at something behind my back. Some nerve to that greaser
chicken giving a real white man the foot! (*Scornfully*) I got a good slant at her this time. She isn't
much to look at after all. Back in God's Country
we'd use her photo for a before-taking ad.

ROGERS (*Indignantly*) Al, you always were a simp!
(*Grumblingly*) Better get a pair of cheaters for
those bum lamps of yours. (*Cheerfully*) Cheer up,
Al, you're all wrong, my son, you're all wrong!

(DEVLIN *gapes at him in open-mouthed amazement.*
ROGERS *commences to sing again: "Mexico, my bright-
eyed Mexico." The sentry grunts contemptuously*)

Curtain

THE SNIPER

A Play in One Act

❀

CHARACTERS

Rougon, a Belgian peasant

The Village Priest

A German Captain of Infantry

Four Privates of the Regiment

Jean, a peasant boy

Scene—*The main room of a ruined cottage on the outskirts of a small Belgian village. The rear wall has two
enormous breaches made by the shells of the artillery.
The right wall is partly hidden by a mass of wreckage
from the roof, which has caved in leaving a jagged hole
through which the sky can be seen. The ceiling slants
drunkenly downward toward the right, ending abruptly
in a ragged edge of splintered boards and beams which
forms a fantastic fretwork against the sky. The floor is
littered with all kinds of debris.*

*In the rear wall near the right corner, a window, its
panes of glass all broken, with a torn white curtain. No
trace of the doorway to the road remains. The larger
breach in the rear wall is used as exit and entrance.*

*The left wall, with a door in the middle, is uninjured.
Over the door a large black crucifix hangs from a nail.*

*In the center of the room, an overturned table. A
solitary chair, the only thing left standing, is beside it.
On the right of the table, a smashed armchair.*

*The time is about sundown on a September day.
Through the breaches in the wall a dark green vista of
rolling fields can be seen. Where they meet the horizon
they are already shimmering in the golden dust of the
sunset. Muffled and far-off, the booming of distant cannon reverberates slowly over the fields.*

The sound of shuffling footsteps is heard from the road before the cottage and a great hulking old man of sixty-five or so appears at the larger breach in the rear wall. He is dressed in the usual peasant fashion and wears wooden sabots on his feet. He is bent under some burden, which, as he enters the room, is seen to be the body of a young man dressed in the uniform of a Belgian infantryman. He lays the body down carefully in a cleared space between the table and the left wall, pillowing the soldier's head upon his knapsack. The body lies with its feet toward the rear wall.

He stands looking down at the still form, his attitude one of abject despair. A heavy sob shakes his round shoulders. He murmurs brokenly: "Charles! My little one!"; then turns abruptly and stumbles to the middle of the room, where he mechanically rights the overturned table. He sits down on the chair and stares at the ruins about him with an expression of dazed bewilderment on his broad face, his round, childlike eyes wandering dully from one object to another. His gaze finally rests on the smashed armchair on the other side of the table, and suddenly overcome by a flood of anguished horror, he hides his face in his hands, rocking from side to side on his chair, moaning to himself like a wounded animal.

The slight black-robed figure of a priest appears on the road outside. He casts a quick glance into the room and, seeing the bowed figure on the chair, quickly picks his way to the peasant's side. The priest is old, white-haired, with a kindly, spiritual face.

PRIEST Rougon!
ROUGON (*Not hearing him*) God, oh God!

PRIEST (*Laying a thin white hand compassionately on* ROUGON's *broad back*) There, there, my son! It is the will of God.

ROUGON (*Startled by the sound of a voice, he jumps up from his chair*) Eh?

(*He stares at the priest with dazed eyes*)

PRIEST (*With a sad smile*) Oh, come now, it isn't possible that you've forgotten me.

ROUGON (*Snatching off his cap respectfully*) Pardon, Father. I was—I didn't know—you see—all this—

PRIEST (*Gently*) I have heard of your loss. I understand.

ROUGON But take the chair, Father. (*Bitterly*) I am lucky to have it left to offer you.

PRIEST (*Sitting down*) You must not brood over your misfortunes. Many, a great many, have suffered even more than you. You must learn to bear these burdens as they come, at such a dreadful time as this, and pray to God for strength. We must all bow ourselves before His will.

ROUGON His will? Ha! No, the good God would not punish me so—I, who have harmed no one. (*Furiously*) It is all these cursed Pruss—

PRIEST Ssshh! (*After a pause*) Such thoughts may rest in the heart, but to let them rise to the lips is hardly wise—now.

ROUGON What matter if they should hear? I am finished, me! They can do no more but kill me.

(*He sits on the edge of the table. A heavy sob shakes his bowed shoulders*)

PRIEST (*After a pause during which he gazes sadly at the face of the dead young soldier*) You must not mourn his loss so bitterly. He has given his life for his country. He is at rest with God. You should feel proud of him.

ROUGON (*Dully*) Yes, he is—at rest—in heaven. And look you, Father, you remember, this was the day —today he was to have been married.

PRIEST (*In accents of deep grief*) True, true, I had forgotten. Poor boy, poor boy—and poor Louise!

ROUGON And my poor old woman. Ah, good God, what have we done? All this—in one day!

PRIEST Your wife—she doesn't know?

ROUGON No. This morning, look you, I sent her away. It was Charles who came to me this morning— in his new uniform—he who lies there so still now —he whom they have murdered, those cursed Prussians!

PRIEST Ssshh! Would you bring more misfortune upon yourself?

ROUGON (*Springing to his feet in a frenzy*) Ah, how I would love to slaughter them, to grind my heel in their fat faces, to—to—

PRIEST Calm yourself, for the love of heaven, my good Rougon! Will it improve matters, think you, to have you, too, shot? Do not forget your poor old wife. You must be careful for her sake, if for nothing else.

ROUGON (*Sullenly slouching back to his seat on the table*) It is hard, name of a dog, it is hard. I feel like a coward, me, to stand by and do nothing.

PRIEST (*In low tones*) Be comforted. The hour of retribution will yet strike. The end is not yet. Your son Charles will be avenged.

ROUGON (*Shaking his head doubtfully*) There are so many.

PRIEST But you were telling me about your wife. You
    sent her away this morning?

ROUGON If the good God so pleases, she is in Brussels
    by now. For, look you, Charles came to me this
    morning. "My father," he said, "I am afraid there
    will be fighting here today. I have warned the
    family of Louise and she is to flee with them to
    Brussels. I have arranged that Mother should go
    with them; and you, too, my father." "But no,"
    I said. "It is right for your mother. She shall go.
    As you say, it will be no place for women if there
    be fighting. But me, no, I shall stay." "Mind you,
    then, Father, no shooting!" Charles said as he
    kissed me good-bye and ran to join the regiment on
    the village place. "Or they will shoot you like a
    dog."

PRIEST You see! Your son gave you the best advice.
    Remember you are not a soldier.

ROUGON (*Proudly*) If I were not too old I should have
    been in a uniform this long time gone. Too old!
    The fools! As if I could not shoot straighter than
    all these boys!

PRIEST There are other things to consider, my poor
    Rougon. Someone must gather in the harvest if
    we are not all to starve.

ROUGON (*Fiercely*) The harvest? What is there left?
    First it is the French who take away my two fine
    horses that I have saved up every centime two
    years to buy—and leave me a scrap of paper;
    then—

PRIEST The French are our friends; in due time you
    shall be paid.

ROUGON Bah, promises!

PRIEST (*Earnestly*)   At a time like this all must bear their share of sacrifice.

ROUGON   All who wanted war, yes; but we who desired nothing more than to be left in peace to till our fields? Look you, my Father, why should we be robbed and plundered and our homes blown apart by their accursed cannon?

PRIEST (*Shaking his head sadly*)   God knows. Our poor country is a lamb among wolves.

ROUGON (*Raising his voice excitedly*)   The first shell that burst in our village—do you know where it struck?

PRIEST   No.

ROUGON   Out there—on my barn—setting it in flames —killing my two cows, one of which I was to have given Charles, with half of my farm, as a wedding present—burning up all my hay I had gathered for the winter. (*Stamping his foot in his rage*) Ah, those dirty beasts!

PRIEST   Ssshh! They are all around.

ROUGON   And then, look you, the cavalry ride over my fields trampling my grain beneath their horses, the artillery wheels tear up the earth, the cannon blow my home to pieces—as you see. (*Bitterly*) Harvest? There is nothing left to harvest but dirt and stones!

PRIEST (*To change the subject which is rapidly infuriating the old man*)   You may well give thanks to the good God that your wife is safe in Brussels.

ROUGON   They started early this morning, as I have said, and the family of Louise has relatives in Brussels. She is safe, God be thanked. (*With a grief-stricken glance at the body of his son*) But when she knows—and Louise, who also loved him so— Oh, my God!

(*He chokes back a sob*)

PRIEST   God give them strength to bear it.

ROUGON   (*Indicating his son*)   He wanted me to go with them. He was afraid I would do something rash if I stayed. But I have been calm. But, name of a dog, it has been hard—when I saw them trampling my wheat—those pigs—when I saw the ashes which had been my barn—and this house, as you see, where I had lived so many years—this finger itched to press the trigger and send at least one to hell for payment.

PRIEST   My son, my son!

ROUGON   Your pardon, my Father. Had it not been for the promise I had given Charles, I would have taken the old rifle from where I have it hidden in there (*He indicates with a nod of his head the room on the left*) and—

PRIEST   (*Casting an apprehensive glance toward the street*)   Ssshh! Be careful what you say in so loud a tone. Their soldiers are everywhere. But where were you when all this fighting was taking place?

ROUGON   I was hiding in the well. I had placed a board across, on which I could stand and see what took place through the chinks in the stones. I wanted to see—him.

PRIEST   See—Charles? How could—

ROUGON   His part of the regiment was behind the wall in the orchard not one hundred meters away. I could watch him clearly.

PRIEST   (*To himself, half-aloud*)   Poor man!

ROUGON At first it was all right. Their infantry came up so close to each other that not even a child could have missed them. Bang! and they were toppled over before they had even reached the foot of the hill. I laughed. I thought it was all finished. I could see Charles laughing and talking with his comrades—and then—

(*He stops, shaking his head despondently*)

PRIEST And then?

ROUGON One of their devilish flying machines which look like the great birds flew overhead, far up. All shot at it but it was too far away. It flew back to them, and a minute later, look you, I saw white puffs of smoke on all the hills over to the west; then bang! crash! I could not hear; my ears were cracked with the din. There was dust, and falling walls, and my barn blazing. Ah, those accursed cannon! I climbed out of the well and ran to the barn.

PRIEST In the midst of all those bursting shells?

ROUGON I trembled with rage. I had no fear of their cannon. I remembered only the cow, the pretty little cow I was to give to Charles. But I could do nothing. Not all the fire engines in Belgium could have saved it. I ran back to the well. Ssszzz! went the bullets all round. As I was climbing over I was stunned by a terrible crash. The roof of this house tumbled in—as you see.

PRIEST And you remained in the well all during the battle?

ROUGON Yes—until I saw Charles fall. He was just aiming his rifle over the wall when I saw him throw up his hands, spin around like a top, and fall on his face. I ran down and carried him back on my shoulders to the well—but it was too late. He was dead. (*He stops abruptly, choking back a sob*)

PRIEST (*After a pause*)   Requiescat in pace. His life was ever a happy one. He never knew the cares and worries that come with the years and the ceaseless struggle for bread. He loved and was loved. He died the death of the brave. (*Gently*) Is it not better after all—as it is? (ROUGON *does not answer*) Can you not console yourself with that thought?

ROUGON   Perhaps. Who knows? But, look you, it is hard for me—and for Louise—and most of all for his mother whose baby he was.

PRIEST   You all loved him, did everything in your power to make him happy. You have nothing with which to reproach yourselves.

ROUGON   But now—what shall I do? Look you, it was for him we worked and saved, his mother and I; that he might never have to know, as we had known, what it is to be poor and hungry. (*Despondently*) And now we are old—what use to work? There is nothing left but death.

PRIEST   You have each other.

ROUGON   Yes, we have each other. Were it not for the thought of my poor Margot, I had let these butchers kill me before this.

PRIEST (*Sternly*)   I do not like to hear you talk in that manner. You must realize well, that in its time of stress, your country has need of you; as much need of you as of her soldiers. You must not be rash. You must live and help and bear your part of her burden as best you can. It is your duty.

ROUGON   Yes, yes, I well know it; but—

PRIEST Above all, you have to exercise control over your hasty temper. You must realize that you will best serve your country and revenge your personal wrongs by living and helping, not by willfully seeking death. You must remember you are a civilian and, according to the rules of war, you have no right to fight. Your part lies elsewhere. Let others shoot the guns.

ROUGON (*Disgustedly*) Bah! The children they have as soldiers cannot shoot. With my little rifle in there I could pick off more Prussian swine than a whole regiment of youngsters like my poor Charles. (*Scornfully*) Yet they tell me I am too old to enlist! Dolts!

PRIEST (*Rising and laying his hand on* ROUGON's *back— with solemn earnestness*) My son, before I leave, I want you to swear to me before the God who watches over us, that you will remember what I have said and not allow your temper to force you to violence.

ROUGON (*Sullenly*) I promise. I swear it.

PRIEST (*Patting him on the back*) There, now you are sensible, more like yourself. (*He stands looking down at* CHARLES) I would advise you as to the burial of Charles. (ROUGON *groans*) Let it be done as secretly as possible. Let us avoid all provocation, and on their heads be it if misfortune happens. Perhaps tonight would be best.

ROUGON Ah, no, no, no! Please, my Father, not yet! Tonight let him remain here in his home, the house he was born in, with me.

PRIEST So be it. Tomorrow night then. You will let me know what time you wish it to be.

ROUGON   Very well, my Father.

PRIEST   And now I must go; but first let us kneel down
and humbly offer up a prayer for the repose of his
soul. (*They kneel down beside the dead body. The
PRIEST commences to intone a prayer in which the
words "Almighty God," "Merciful," "Infinite justice," "Infinite love," Infinite pity," "Thy son
Jesus," "We, Thy children," "Praise Thy infinite
goodness" stand out from the general mumble of
sing-song sentences. Perhaps a sense of the crushing irony of this futile prayer penetrates the sorrow-
numbed brain of ROUGON and proves the last straw
which breaks down his self-control; for he inter-
rupts the droning supplications of the PRIEST with
a groan of agony, throws himself beside the young
soldier's body and sobs brokenly: "Charles, Charles,
my little one! Oh, why did not God take me instead!" The PRIEST, after a pause, wipes the tears
from his eyes with his large handkerchief*) Come,
come, it is hard, I know, but you must bear it like a
man. God's will be done! He, too, had a Son who
died for others. Pray to Him and He will comfort
you in your affliction.

ROUGON   (*Placing his hand gently on his son's face*)
Cold! Cold! He who was so alive and smiling only
this morning.

(*A step is heard on the road outside. The two get
hastily to their feet as a young man in the gray uniform
of a German captain of infantry appears at one of the
gaps of the wall.*)

CAPTAIN   (*Entering and turning to the PRIEST*)   Are you
the— (*Seeing the body on the floor*) I beg your
pardon.

PRIEST (*Coldly*) What is your wish?

CAPTAIN (*Twirling his blond mustache fiercely to hide his embarrassment*) Again, I ask pardon. I meant no disrespect. (*Taking off his helmet impressively. He is a very young captain*) I honor the brave dead on whichever side they fall.

PRIEST (*Indicating* ROUGON, *who has slunk off to the other side of the table and is controlling his hatred and rage with very apparent effort*) It is his son.

CAPTAIN Ah! Too bad! The fortunes of war. Today, him; tomorrow, me, perhaps. Are you the *curé* of the village?

PRIEST I am.

CAPTAIN I have been seeking you ever since we occupied the place.

PRIEST I returned but a short time ago from Brussels, where I had been called to make my report to the Bishop. I knew nothing of the fighting here or I should have returned sooner. (*Sadly*) There were many, perhaps, who died needing me. But what is it you wish?

CAPTAIN I was sent by the Colonel to find you and deliver his orders. There seems to be no one of civil authority left in the village—else I should not intrude upon you.

PRIEST I am listening.

CAPTAIN (*Oratorically*) It is the Colonel's wish that you warn the inhabitants against committing any violence against our soldiers. Civilians caught with arms will be immediately shot. (*The* PRIEST *casts a significant glance at* ROUGON, *who scowls and mutters to himself*) Is that clear?

PRIEST Quite.

CAPTAIN On the other hand, all we demand of you will be paid for in cash. Let all your parishioners return to their work without fear of molestation. We make no war upon the helpless. (*With complacent pride*) I hope I make my meaning clear. I flatter myself my French is not so bad.

PRIEST (*With cold politeness*) You speak it very well, *monsieur.* You may tell your colonel that I will do all in my power to impress his words upon the minds of my people—not that I respect his orders or admit his right to give them to a man of peace, but because I have the welfare of my people at heart.

CAPTAIN Good. I will tell him. And now I will say *au revoir,* for I, too, have my duties to perform. We march from here immediately.

PRIEST (*Significantly*) Adieu.

(*The* CAPTAIN *goes out*)

ROUGON (*Raging*) Dog of a Prussian!

PRIEST Silence! Are you a fool?

(*While he is speaking, an awkward peasant boy of about fifteen with a broad face appears at the breach in the rear wall. His clothes are mud-stained and ragged and he is trembling with fear. He breathes in great shuddering gasps. There is a cut on his forehead beneath which the blood has dried in reddish-brown streaks*)

ROUGON (*Hears the noise*) What's that?

(*They both turn and see the boy*)

PRIEST Why, it's Jean! Whatever are you doing skulking around like that?

JEAN (*Stopping uneasily as if he intended to run away again*) Nothing, nothing.

PRIEST Come over here. (JEAN *does not move but*

stares at him with frightened eyes) Don't you hear me speaking to you? What is the matter with you?

JEAN (*Faintly*)   I am afraid.

PRIEST   Of me? Come, this is ridiculous.

JEAN (*His lips trembling*)   I am afraid—of them. Everything—blows up.

ROUGON   Come to the good Father when he speaks to you, stupid dolt! Or I shall find a good strong stick and—

PRIEST   Hush, you are only frightening him. Come to me, Jean, like a good boy. (JEAN *goes slowly to the* PRIEST, *who puts an arm about his shoulders*) Why, you're trembling like a leaf! Did the battle frighten you?

JEAN   No, no, no! I don't know.

ROUGON (*Contemptuously*)   The battle? He was never near the fighting. It was bad enough for we others without having this half-witted calf around. So we sent him away with the women this morning. (*To* JEAN) Answer me, you, how is it you are back here?

JEAN (*Trembling*)   I don't know.

ROUGON (*Roughly*)   Name of a dog, what do you know? Did we send you away with the women this morning or didn't we?

JEAN (*Uncertainly*)   Yes—I went away—this morning.

PRIEST   Hush, Rougon, you are only frightening the poor fellow. Jean, listen to me and stop trembling. I shall not let anyone hurt you. I have always been your good friend, have I not?

JEAN   Yes—you are my friend.

PRIEST   Of course I am; and while I am around, there is nothing you need fear. Come now, tell me like a good lad; you went away with the others this morning, didn't you?

JEAN   Yes, Father.

PRIEST   Then how do you happen to be here now? Why did you return to the village? Your clothes are in a shocking state. Where have you been hiding and how did you get that cut on your forehead?

JEAN   (*Feeling the cut on his forehead with a dazed air*) It hurts.

PRIEST   You will come home with me presently and we will wash that nasty cut and wrap it up in a nice clean bandage. Then you may be sure you will no longer feel any hurt at all. But first tell me—

JEAN   I don't know. I ran and ran—and I came here.

PRIEST   But something must have happened to make you run. Come, tell us, what was it?

JEAN   (*Vaguely*)   We left here and walked a long, long ways. Some rode in wagons but I was walking.

ROUGON   And did you see Mother Rougon there, and Louise?

JEAN   (*In a strange tone—with a shudder*)   Yes, I saw them, I saw them.

(ROUGON *gives a grunt of satisfaction*)

PRIEST   Go on, my son, tell us what happened next.

JEAN   We could hear shots. We hurried faster. The horses galloped. The women commenced to scream and cry. Always the firing was louder. We didn't see any soldiers for a long time. Then we came upon lots of bodies—men from our army and others dressed in gray.

ROUGON   (*In growing alarm*)   Name of a dog, why didn't you turn back, eh?

JEAN (*Vaguely*) I don't know. (*He drones on in his expressionless voice*) The women were praying. They were afraid. They wanted us to hurry up and get to Brussels. We beat the horses. The hills were covered with white spots like—like daisies; and they floated way up in the air.

(*He makes a queer awkward gesture upward*)

ROUGON Idiot! What is all this foolish talk?

PRIEST (*Gently*) It was the smoke from the guns you saw, my child.

JEAN (*Very slowly—trying his best to imitate the exact sound*) Boom! Boom! Boom! I couldn't hear what anyone was saying.

(*He pauses*)

ROUGON Why do you stop, stupid? Go on, go on, or—

(*He shakes his clenched fist at the boy*)

PRIEST Silence, Rougon! Give the poor lad a chance.

JEAN (*In flat, monotonous tones*) Something blew up in a field by the road and threw dirt and stones on us. The horses were afraid. They ran faster. Then we came to the top of a hill. Lots of the soldiers in our army were there hiding in a long ditch. They shouted for us to run away. Then—then—then—

PRIEST (*Anxiously*) Yes?

(ROUGON *stands tensely with averted face as if afraid to listen*)

JEAN (*Throwing both his arms into the air with a wild gesture*) Then everything around blew up. (*In flat tones*) Something hit me on the head. I laid down for a while. When I got up I couldn't see any of the rest. There were bodies all around. I saw Mother Rougon—

PRIEST (*Clinging to a last shred of hope*) Alive and
     unharmed?

(*But* ROUGON *has guessed the worst and stands as if
in a stupor, clenching and unclenching his big red
hands, his features working convulsively*)

JEAN She was lying on the ground. She had a big hole
     here (*Pointing to his chest*) and blood all over—
     bright and red like—like flowers.

ROUGON (*Dully*) Dead! She, too!

JEAN And Louise had a hole in her head, here (*Point-
     ing to his forehead*) and—

PRIEST (*Distracted with horror*) Enough! Stop! We
     have heard all we care to, do you hear?

JEAN So I ran, and ran, and ran, and ran, and ran.

(*His words die away into a murmur. He stares straight
before him like one in a trance*)

PRIEST Merciful God, have pity!

ROUGON (*Slowly—as if the meaning of* JEAN's *words
     were just commencing to dawn on him*) So—they
     are gone, too—the old woman—and Louise—
     (*Licks his lips with his dry tongue*) Everything is
     gone.

(*There is a long silence. The* PRIEST *dabs with his big
handkerchief at the tears which are welling into his eyes.*
JEAN *wanders over to the breach in the wall and stands
looking down the road. A loud bugle call is heard.* JEAN
darts back into the room)

JEAN (*Waving his arms, cries in terrified tones*) They
     are coming. They are coming this way!

(*He runs to the right corner of the room and crouches
there trembling, seeking to hide himself in the fallen
ruins*)

ROUGON   So—*they* are coming?

(*He strides resolutely across the room and enters the room on left*)

PRIEST (*Alarmed by the expression on* ROUGON's *face*) Rougon! Rougon! What are you going to do? (*He receives no answer. A moment later* ROUGON *re-enters the room carrying a long-barreled rifle. The* PRIEST *seizes him by the arm*) No, no, I beseech you!

ROUGON (*Roughly throwing the* PRIEST *aside*) Let me alone! (*He half-kneels beside one of the breaches in the wall—then speaks in a voice of deadly calmness*) They will not pass here. They are going to turn off at the fork in the road. It is near enough, however.

(*The rhythmic tramp of the marching troops can be faintly heard*)

PRIEST (*In agony*) In the name of God I implore you—

ROUGON   Bah, God! (*He takes careful aim and fires*) That for Margot! (*He loads and fires again*)That for Louise!

(*Cries of rage and running footsteps are heard.* ROUGON *is reloading his rifle when the* CAPTAIN *and four German privates rush in.* ROUGON *struggles but is disarmed and forced back to the wall. He stands proudly, calmly awaiting his fate. One of the soldiers seizes the* PRIEST)

SOLDIER (*To the* CAPTAIN) *Was mit dem Priester?*

ROUGON (*To the* CAPTAIN) The good Father did nothing. He but did his best to hold my arm and stop me. It is I alone who did the shooting, dog of a Prussian!

CAPTAIN   Is this true, priest?

PRIEST   It is as he tells you. I tried to restrain him—not
for your sakes, but for his own.

CAPTAIN   (*To the soldier*)   *Las den Priester gehen!*
(*The soldier releases the* PRIEST. *The* CAPTAIN *turns
to* ROUGON) If you have a prayer to say, be quick!

(*The four soldiers line up in front of* ROUGON *and face
him across the body of* CHARLES)

ROUGON   (*With angry scorn*)   I want no prayers!

PRIEST   Rougon!

ROUGON   (*Furiously*)   To hell with your prayers!

PRIEST   (*Supplicatingly*)   Make your peace with God,
my son!

ROUGON   (*Spitting on the floor, fiercely*)   That for your
God who allows such things to happen! (*To the*
CAPTAIN) I am ready, pig!

CAPTAIN   (*To the soldiers*)   *Gewehr! Heraus!*
(*The soldiers take aim*)

PRIEST   May God have mercy on—

CAPTAIN   *Feuer!* (*There is a crashing report.* ROUGON
*pitches forward on his face, quivers for a moment,
is still. The soldiers file out to the road. The* CAP-
TAIN *turns to the horrified* PRIEST)

CAPTAIN   (*Shrugging his shoulders*)   It is the law.
(*He follows the soldiers*)

PRIEST   (*Looking down with infinite compassion at the
still bodies of father and son*)   Alas, the laws of
men!

(*The sun has set. The twilight is fading grayly into
night. From the heap of wreckage in the right corner
comes the sound of stifled weeping*)

Curtain

A WIFE FOR A LIFE

A Play in One Act

❀

CHARACTERS

The Older Man

Jack, the Younger Man

Old Pete, a miner

SCENE—*The edge of the Arizona desert; a plain dotted in the foreground with clumps of sagebrush. On the horizon a lonely butte is outlined, black and sinister against the lighter darkness of a sky with stars. The time is in the early hours of the night. In the foreground stands a ragged tent, the flap of which is open. Leaning against it are some shovels and a pick or two. Two saddles are on the ground nearby. Before the tent is a smoldering campfire at which an elderly man of about fifty is seated. He is dressed in miner's costume: flannel shirt, khaki trousers, high boots, etc.—all patched and showing evidence of long wear and tear. His wide-brimmed Stetson hat lies on the ground beside him. His hair is turning gray and his face is the face of one who has wandered far, lived hard, seen life in the rough and is a little weary of it all. Withal, his air and speech are those of an educated man whose native refinement has clung to him in spite of many hard knocks.*

On one side of the tent stands a rough stool and a gold-miner's panning tub—a square box half filled with water.

OLDER MAN (*Stirring the fire in a futile attempt to start it into flame*) I wonder what can be keeping him so long? (*He hears a noise of someone approach-*

ing) Hello, Jack, I was just beginning to think you were lost.

(OLD PETE *enters. He is an old man dressed in rough miner's costume but he wears spurs and carries a quirt in his hand. He is covered with dust and has evidently been riding hard*)

OLD PETE   It ain't Jack. It's me.

OLDER MAN (*Disappointed*)   Hello, Pete. What brings you around at this time of the night?

OLD PETE (*Taking a telegram from his pocket*)   I was just leaving Lawson when the operator stopped me and give me this for Jack. I seen your campfire burning and reckoned I'd bring it right over.

OLDER MAN (*Taking the telegram*)   Many thanks, Pete. Won't you sit down and rest a bit?

OLD PETE   Much obliged but I reckon I'll travel along. I ain't slept none to speak of in the past few nights and I got to be up at sunrise. (*Grinning sheepishly*) That fool town of Lawson sure does keep you up nights. (*He starts to go, then stops*) Claim panning out as good as ever?

OLDER MAN   Better every day. This morning we took a sample from the upper end which we haven't touched so far. It looks good but we haven't panned it yet.

OLD PETE   You-alls ought to get rich. You know how to keep money. Now me and money never could get on noway. (*He pulls out pockets ruefully*) They cleaned me out in Lawson this time and I reckon they'll clean me again the next time. (*Shaking his head*) Cities is sure hell that-a-way. Adios. (*He exits*)

OLDER MAN   Good night. Poor Pete. Same old story.

Been bucking the faro bank again, I suppose. (*He looks at the telegram*) Hmm. Wonder what this is? Jack has had no correspondence in the five years I've been with him. May be something important in connection with the mine. I guess I'd better open it. He won't mind anyway. (*He opens the telegram and reads aloud*) "I am waiting. Come." No name signed. It comes from New York too. Well, it's too many for me. I give it up. (*He puts the telegram in his pocket*) Must be that fool operator got mixed up in his names. I wouldn't like to see Jack obey any summons like that. He's about all I've got now and I'd hate to see him leave just when we've struck it rich. (*Dismissing the subject*) I guess this wire is all a mistake anyway. (*He looks around yawning and his eye lights on the panning tub*) Now if only the upper part of the claim is as rich as that we've been working—(*The noise of someone approaching is heard*) Here he comes now. Welcome, wanderer! Where have you been all this time?

(JACK *enters. He is dressed about the same as the* OLDER MAN *but is much younger—in the early thirties*)

JACK   One of the horses slipped his hobbles and I had quite a hunt for him. I finally found him down by the spring wallowing around as if water was the commonest thing in this section of Arizona. Fool beast!

OLDER MAN   (*Forgetting all about the telegram*)   It's a strange thing we should run into water out here where the maps say there isn't any. It's the one blessing we've found in this land God forgot. We're fools for luck for once.

H

JACK (*Nodding*) Yes. (*Then, rather exultantly*) But we have small cause to kick about this lonely hole after all. Any place is God's country to a man if there's gold in it and he finds it. There's gold here and (*Taking a small bag from his pocket and shaking it*) we've found it. So long live the desert say I.

OLDER MAN Those are my sentiments. (*He rolls a cigarette paper and, setting it afire in the flame, lights his pipe*) It sure looks as if our ship has come in at last here on the rim of the world. The luck was due to change. We've had our share of the bad variety; just missing a strike in every jumping-off place from South Africa to Alaska. We've taken our hard knocks with the imitation of a laugh at any rate and (*Stretching out his hand to younger man, who grasps it heartily*) we've been good pals ever since that day in the Transvaal five years ago when you hauled me out of the river, saved my life, and our friendship began. (*As the younger man starts to speak*) No, you needn't try to stop me expressing my gratitude. I haven't forgotten that day and I never will.

JACK (*To change the subject*) I'm going to see what that prospect we took at the other end of the claim looks like. (*He goes into the tent and returns with a gold pan heaped with dirt under his arm, and sitting down in front of the panning tub, proceeds to test the prospect. He washes the heap of dirt down until there is but a handful of gravel left. The* OLDER MAN *comes over and stands behind him looking over his shoulder. Finally, after one quick flip of the pan,* JACK *points to the sediment left in the bottom in which a small heap of bright yellow particles can be seen*) What do you think of that?

OLDER MAN (*Reaching over and feeling them with his fingers*) O' course gold; just as I expected. The upper end of the claim is just as rich as it is down here.

JACK (*With growing excitement*) There's over a quarter of an ounce here at least. That's five dollars a pan—better than we've ever panned down here at any time since we made the strike four months ago. (*He lays the pan aside*) I tell you, this claim is too much for us to handle alone. One of us ought to go East and organize a company.

OLDER MAN Then it will have to be you. I'm too old. (JACK *smiles and makes a deprecating gesture*) Anyway I never could get along with civilization and (*Laughing*) civilization never cared overmuch for me. (*He goes over and sits down by the fire. After a pause*) You've seemed to be hankering after the East quite a lot in the last month or so. (*Smiling*) Getting tired of the company here, eh?

JACK (*Quickly*) No, you know that isn't so, after all the years we've been pals and all we've been through together.

OLDER MAN (*Jokingly*) Then what is the attraction the effete East has to offer? (*Mockingly*) It's a woman I suppose?

JACK (*With dignity*) An angel, rather.

OLDER MAN (*Cynically*) They're all angels—at first. The only trouble is their angelic attributes lack staying qualities. (*Then, half bitterly*) At any rate, you'd find them hard to prove by my experiences.

JACK (*Shrugging his shoulders a little impatiently*) You're a disgusting cynic and I refuse to argue.

You know we've never been able to agree on that subject. I'm going to hunt out that bottle we've carried about so long and we'll drink to the mine and future prosperity. (*He goes into the tent*) Here it is. (*He returns with a quart of whiskey, opens it with a knife and pours out two drinks in the tin cups. Laughing*) I think this is a proper occasion for celebration—the two prodigals welcome the fatted calf. Let's make it a christening also. Here's to the Yvette Mine!

OLDER MAN (*He has been laughing, but turns suddenly grim. His hand trembles as he clinks cups and he almost spills some of the whiskey. He speaks in harsh, jerky tones*) Why the Yvette?

JACK (*Not noticing his agitation*)   I know it sounds like rather a frivolous name for a mine but I have a hunch. There's a romance back of it—my romance. That was her name. One rarely speaks of such things. I've never told you but I will now if you care to hear it. It was over a year before I met you. I had just been out of mining school a short time and was prospecting around in the mountains of Peru hoping to hit a bonanza there. At the time I speak of I had returned to re-outfit at a small mining camp near the frontier of Ecuador. It was there I met her. She was the wife of a broken-down mining engineer from the States, over twenty years her senior. (*The* OLDER MAN, *who has been listening intently, is poking the fire nervously and his face becomes harsher and harsher*) According to all accounts he was a drunken brute who left her alone most of the time and only lived from one drunk to another. Personally I never saw him. It

was probably better that I did not. You see, I fell
in love with her on the spot and the thought of
how he treated her made my blood boil.

OLDER MAN (*In stifled tones*) What was the name of
the mining town you mention? I've been in that
country myself—many years ago.

JACK San Sebastien. Do you know it?

(*At the words "San Sebastien" the* OLDER MAN *seems
to crumple up. Nothing seems alive about him but his
eyes, staring horribly, and his right hand, which nervously fingers the gun in the belt around his waist*)

OLDER MAN (*In a hoarse whisper*) Yes. I know it. Go
on.

JACK (*Dreamily, absorbed in his own thoughts*) I
loved her. In the corrupt environment of a mining
camp she seemed like a lily growing in a field of
rank weeds. I longed to take her away from all that
atmosphere of sordid sin and suffering; away from
her beast of a husband who was steadily ruining that
beautiful young life and driving her to desperation.
I overstayed my time. I should have been back in
the mountains. I went to see her often. He was always away it seemed. Finally people began to talk.
Then I realized that the time had come and told her
that I loved her. I shall never forget her face. She
looked at me with great calm eyes but her lips trembled as she said: "I know you love me and I—I love
you; but you must go away and we must never see
each other again. I am his wife and I must keep my
pledge."

OLDER MAN (*Starting to his feet and half drawing the
pistol from the holster*) You lie!

JACK (*Rudely awakened from his dream, he springs to

his feet, his face angry and perplexed)   Why, what
do you mean? What is it?

OLDER MAN (Controlling his rage with a mighty effort
and sitting down again)   Nothing. Nerves, I
guess. It's my sore spot—the virtue of women. I've
seen but little of it in my mining-camp experience
and your heroine seems to me too impossible.

(Wonderingly JACK sits down beside him again)

JACK (Eagerly)   You wouldn't think so if you could
have seen her. (The OLDER MAN covers his face
with his hands and groans) Here's a picture of her
she sent me a year ago. (He takes a small photo
out of the pocket of his shirt) Look at it. (Handing
him the photo) Do you think a woman with a face
like that could be the regular mining-camp kind?

(He feels in his pocket again and goes into the tent
as if searching for something)

OLDER MAN (He looks at the photo with haggard eyes
for a moment, then whispers in a half sob)   My
wife! (Then, staring into vacancy, he speaks to himself, unconsciously aloud)   She has not changed.

JACK (Coming back from the tent with a soiled envelope in his hand in time to hear the last sentence.
Astonished)   Changed? Who? Do you know her?

OLDER MAN (Quickly mastering his emotion and lying
bravely)   No. Of course not. But she reminds me
of a girl I knew here in the States a long time ago.
But the girl I speak of must be an old woman by
this time. I forget my gray hairs.

JACK   Yvette is only twenty-five. Her parents were
poor French people. In a fit of mistaken zeal for
her welfare they forced her to marry this man
when she was too young to know her own mind.

They thought they were making an excellent match. Immediately after the marriage he dragged her off to San Sebastien, where he was half-owner of a· small mine. It seems the devil broke out in him before they were hardly settled there. (*After a pause*) I'd like to be fair to him. Maybe he realized that she could never love him and was trying to drown the memory of the mistake he had made. He certainly loved her—in his fashion.

OLDER MAN (*In a pathetic whisper*) Yes. He must have loved her—in his fashion.

JACK (*Looking at the letter in his hand, which he had forgotten*) Ah, I forgot. I have proof positive of her innocence and noble-mindedness. Here is a letter which she wrote and sent to me the morning I was leaving. It's only a few words. Read it, Mr. Doubting Thomas.

(*He hands the letter to the* OLDER MAN)

OLDER MAN (*His hands tremble. Aside*) Her writing. (*Reading aloud*) "I must keep my oath. He needs me and I must stay. To be true to myself I must be true to him." (*Aside: "My God, I was wrong after all"*) "Sometime I may send for you. Goodbye." Signed Yvette. (*He folds the letter up slowly, puts it back in the envelope and hands it to* JACK. *Suddenly he turns to him with quick suspicion*) What does she mean by that last sentence?

JACK When I left I gave her my address in the States and she promised to let me know if she changed her mind or if conditions changed.

OLDER MAN (*With grim irony*) You mean if the drunken husband died.

JACK (*His face growing hard*) Yes. That's what I
mean.

OLDER MAN Well, how do you know he hasn't? Have
you ever heard from her since?

JACK Only the one time when she sent the picture I
showed you. I received the letter from her in Cape
Town a year ago. It had been forwarded from the
States. She said her husband had disappeared soon
after I left. No one knew where he had gone but
the rumor was that he had set out on my trail for
vengeance, refusing to believe in her innocence.
(*Grimly patting his gun*) I'm sorry he didn't find
me.

OLDER MAN (*He has by this time regained control of
himself and speaks quite calmly*) Where is she
now?

JACK Living with her parents in New York. She wrote
to say that she would wait a year longer. If he did
not return to her by then she would become legally
free of him and would send for me. The year is up
today but (*Hopelessly*) I have received no word.

(*He walks back and looks into the darkness as if
hoping to see someone coming. The* OLDER MAN *suddenly remembers the telegram he has. He takes it from
his pocket as if to give it to* JACK; *then hesitates and
says in agony, "My God, I cannot!" as he realizes the
full significance of what the telegram says. Mastered by
a contrary impulse he goes to burn it in the campfire
but again hesitates. Finally, as* JACK *returns slowly to
the campfire, he turns quickly and hands the telegram
to him*)

OLDER MAN Cheer up! Here's a surprise for you. Read
this. Old Pete brought it from Lawson before you

returned and I forgot all about it. I opened it by
mistake thinking it might have something to do
with the mine.

(*He turns quickly away as if unable to bear the sight
of* JACK's *elation.* JACK *feverishly opens the yellow envelope. His face lights up and he gives an exclamation
of joy and rushes to the* OLDER MAN)

JACK It's too good to be true. Tell me I am not dreaming.

OLDER MAN (*He looks at* JACK *steadily for a moment,
then tries hard to smile and mutters*) Congratu-
lations.

(*He is suffering horribly*)

JACK (*Misunderstanding the cause of his emotion*)
Never mind, old pal, I won't be gone long and
when I come back I'll bring her with me.

OLDER MAN (*Hastily*) No, I'll manage all right. Better
stay East for a while. We'll need someone there
when the work really starts.

JACK When can I get a train?

OLDER MAN If you ride hard and start right away, you
can get to Lawson in time for the Limited at three
in the morning.

JACK (*Rushing off with his saddle under his arm*) My
horse is hobbled at the mouth of the canyon.

OLDER MAN (*He stands in front of the tent*) So I have
found him after all these years and I cannot even
hate him. What tricks Fate plays with us. When
he told me his name that first day I noticed that it
was the same as the man's I was looking for. But
he seemed such a boy to me and my heart went out
to him so strongly that I never for an instant har-
bored the idea that he could be the John Sloan I

was after. Of course, he never knew my right name. I wonder what he would say if he knew. I've half a mind to tell him. But no, what's the use? Why should I mar his happiness? In this affair I alone am to blame and I must pay. As I listened to his story this evening until no doubt remained that he was the John Sloan I had sworn to kill, my hand reached for my gun and all the old hate flared up in my heart. And then I remembered his face as he looked that day in the Transvaal when he bent over me after saving my life at the risk of his own. I could almost hear his words as he spoke that day when death was so near: "All right, old pal, you're all right." Then my hand left my gun and the old hatred died out forever. I could not do it. (*He pauses and a bitter smile comes over his face as at some new thought*) Oh, what a fool I have been. She was true to me in spite of what I was. God bless him for telling me so. God grant they may both be happy—the only two beings I have ever loved. And I—must keep wandering on. I cannot be the ghost at their feast.

JACK (*Entering hurriedly, putting on spurs, hat, etc.*) Good-bye, old pal. I'm sorry to leave you this way but I have waited so long for this. You understand, don't you?

OLDER MAN (*Slowly*) Yes. (*Grasping his hand and looking deep into his eyes*) Good-bye and God bless you both.

JACK (*Feelingly*) Good-bye.

(*He exits*)

OLDER MAN (*He sits down by the campfire and buries his face in his hands. Finally he rouses himself with an effort, stirs the campfire and, smiling with a whimsical sadness, softly quotes)* "Greater love hath no man than this, that he giveth his wife for his friend."

Curtain

SERVITUDE

A Play in Three Acts

✿

CHARACTERS

David Roylston, *playwright and novelist*

Alice Roylston, *his wife*

Davie ⎫
Ruth ⎬ *their children*

George Frazer, *a broker*

Ethel Frazer, *his wife*

Benton, *a manservant*

Weson, *a gardener*

Act One

SCENE—*The study in the house of* DAVID ROYLSTON *at Tarryville-on-Hudson, New York. In the middle of the far side of the room, a fireplace. To the right of it, a door. The remaining space of the back wall is covered by bookcases which frame the fireplace and door. In the left foreground another door. Next to it, a writing desk. Still farther back, a bookcase. On the right, a leather sofa and armchairs. On either side of the sofa, an open window looking out on the garden. In the center of the room, a table on which are a heap of books and an electric reading lamp with a green shade. A few framed prints of Old Masters are hung on the walls.*

It is about ten o'clock on a sultry night in early May.

DAVID ROYLSTON *is seated at the table, writing. He is a tall, slender, dark-haired man of thirty-five with large handsome features, a strong, ironical mouth half-hidden by a black mustache, and keenly intelligent dark eyes. He has taken off his coat, which hangs from the back of his chair. He wears a white shirt with soft collar and black bow tie, gray trousers and low tan shoes with rubber soles.*

BENTON *enters from the door at the rear and stands waiting for* ROYLSTON *to notice his presence. He is fifty-five, clean-shaven, discreetly soft-spoken. One of his eyes is badly crossed, giving him a look of sly villainy*

*quite out of keeping with his placid temperament. He
wears livery.*

ROYLSTON (*Looking up from his writing*) Well, Benton?

BENTON Shall I shut the windows, sir? It's started to
rain a little.

ROYLSTON No, I will close them myself when I go to
bed.

BENTON (*Reproachfully*) They were open when I
came down this morning, sir.

ROYLSTON Were they? I must have fogotten all about
them last night. Never mind; there's nothing much
worth the stealing in this house except ideas, and
the thieves of ideas are not usually housebreakers.
But if it will ease your anxiety, you may close
them. There's a draft in here.

BENTON Yes, sir.

(*He closes the windows*)

ROYLSTON Any telephone calls while I was out?

BENTON Mrs. Roylston called up, sir; wished me to
tell you that she and the children had arrived
safely in New York; had a very pleasant trip in the
motor; roads were fine all the way down. She said
the children were very excited to think they were
really going to the theatre.

ROYLSTON (*Abstractedly*) Ah, indeed. No one else
called up?

BENTON No, sir.

ROYLSTON Not even the young lady who has (*Ironically*) asked my advice so frequently of late?

BENTON No, sir.

ROYLSTON Well, whenever the young lady in question

calls up again, you are to tell her I am writing and cannot be disturbed.

BENTON   Yes, sir.

ROYLSTON (*Impatiently*)   She is becoming a bore; and I am in the midst of a play and have no time for such foolishness.

BENTON   Very good, sir. Anything else before I go to bed, sir?

ROYLSTON No, you may go. (BENTON *takes* ROYLSTON'*s light overcoat, hat and stick, wihch are lying on one the armchairs, and starts to go out*) Leave those here. I may take a walk later on to get a breath of the spring and blow the cobwebs out of my brain, and I don't care to be barking my shins in the dark hall. (BENTON *lays them down again. A doorbell is heard ringing somewhere in the house*) Who can that be at this time of the night? (*As* BENTON *hurries out through the door on the left*) Remember, Benton, I'm busy—too busy to be disturbed.

BENTON   Yes, sir.

(*He goes out.* ROYLSTON *bites his pen nervously, trying to concentrate on his thoughts. A minute or so later* BENTON *enters. He is visibly embarrassed and is turning over a card in his fingers*)

ROYLSTON Well?

BENTON   It's a lady, sir.

ROYLSTON Has she gone?

BENTON   No, sir, she—

ROYLSTON (*Frowning*)   Did you tell her I was busy?

BENTON   Yes, sir, but she said she must see you on a very important matter; said she wouldn't leave till she saw you. This is her card, sir.

ROYLSTON (*Looking at it*) Mrs. George Frazer—hm—
Mrs., eh? Never heard of her. An old crank of some
kind, I suppose?

BENTON Quite the other way, sir; young and pretty,
I should say, if I'm any judge.

ROYLSTON Anyone come with her?

BENTON I don't think so, sir.

ROYLSTON Alone, at this time of night, and (*Sarcastically*) a lady, you say?

BENTON (*Promptly*) No doubt of that, sir; but dressed
shabby almost, as if she'd seen better days—you
know what I mean, sir.

ROYLSTON (*Cynically*) Ah, then, I had better get my
checkbook ready.

BENTON Beg your pardon, sir, but she doesn't seem
that kind either; not like one that'd beg, I mean. I
couldn't make her out exactly.

ROYLSTON Perhaps she's another aspiring playwright
who wants me to write her last act for her. At any
rate you have aroused my curiosity; so show her in
here.

(*He takes his coat off the back of the chair and puts
it on*)

BENTON Very well, sir.

(*He goes out through the door on the left. A moment
later he shows in* MRS. FRAZER. *She is a tall, strikingly
beautiful woman about twenty-eight years old. Her complexion is pale; her eyes large, expressive, dark; her hair
black and wavy; her figure inclining a little toward vo-
luptuousness. There are shadows under her eyes and her
face is drawn. Her manner is troubled, nervous, uncertain. She has on a plain black dress such as is worn by
the poorer class of working women*)

ROYLSTON (*Getting up and staring at her with open admiration*) Ah! (*Turning to* BENTON) You may go, Benton. I shan't need you again. I will take Mrs.—er (*Looking at the card*) Mrs. Frazer to the door myself.

BENTON Yes, sir.

(*He goes out*)

MRS. FRAZER (*Uncertainly*) I hope you will pardon—

ROYLSTON (*Indicating the armchairs on the left*) Won't you sit down, Mrs. Frazer? (*She sits down in the one nearest to him*) And now, what can I do for you?

MRS. FRAZER I know this intrusion of mine is unpardonable. You must be terribly busy, and I have forced myself on you, interrupted your work—

ROYLSTON You must not feel conscience-stricken about that. I was only puzzling over a problem in construction. I am glad to have my mind taken off it for a time.

MRS. FRAZER But my coming here at this time of the night and alone? (*Forcing a smile*) What can you think of such a breach of all the conventions!

ROYLSTON (*Dryly*) You are the very first to accuse me of conventionality. I see nothing strange in your coming here when you wanted to, when you were able to. I have lived long enough in this suburb to know the difficulties of getting here at the time one wishes.

MRS. FRAZER (*Looking at him for a moment with a questioning smile*) Can't you remember ever having seen me before?

ROYLSTON No, I must confess—

MRS. FRAZER And yet you have met me. I can, at least,

plead that much justification for this encroachment
on your time.

ROYLSTON (*Trying to remember*)   It's no use. My brain
is too full of marionettes to recall flesh-and-blood
realities. I confess, to my shame, I will have to ask
you where it was.

MRS. FRAZER   Oh, I did not dream of your remember-
ing. We only spoke about two words to each other,
and it was at least a year ago. You remember the
ball Mr. Coleman, the artist, gave at his studio?

ROYLSTON   So it was there? It would be too trite for me
to say I knew I had seen you before; but I really did
have that feeling when you came in. One doesn't
forget a face like yours. So it was at Coleman's
studio? He and I have been friends for years.

MRS. FRAZER   He is a very dear friend of my—of mine,
also.

ROYLSTON   Do take off your hat now that we know
who's who. To see you sitting there with your hat
on gives me the uncomfortable impression that this
is a lawyer's office and you are consulting your at-
torney—and I warn you I am far from being a *legal*
adviser.

MRS. FRAZER (*She takes off her hat and puts it on the
sofa; leans back in her chair*)   I knew it. That is
why I came.

ROYLSTON   For advice?

MRS. FRAZER   Advice which I must have or—

ROYLSTON   Or?

MRS. FRAZER   The crowning disillusion.

ROYLSTON (*Smiling*)   I hope it is not about me, the illusion.

MRS. FRAZER (*Emphatically*)   It is about you but it is
   not an illusion.

ROYLSTON   Certainty goeth before disappointment.

MRS. FRAZER   In this case it must not. I have borne so
   much already—I could not bear it. I must have
   something firm to stand on.

ROYLSTON   Then it is not a play you come to consult
   me about? (*Seeing her mystified expression*) I beg
   your pardon, but you know there are so many play-
   wrights-in-embryo who come to me for suggestions
   about their work—as if I could help them; as if it
   were not absolutely necessary for them to work out
   their own salvation!—and I thought when you mentioned advice—

MRS. FRAZER (*Smiling*)   I see. No, I almost wish it
   were. I would like to be able to write a play even if
   it were only a very bad one. It would at least prove
   I was capable of creating something; I'm afraid
   even that is beyond my power.

ROYLSTON (*Perfunctorily*)   One never knows till one
   tries. The thing to do is to make a start; and then,
   if necessary, realize one's mistake smilingly.

MRS. FRAZER   I intend to try sometime. (*Apologeti-
   cally*)   I'm wasting your time and I will come to
   the point at once; or rather I will have to go back
   quite a ways to give you a clear idea of my present
   situation. (*Nervously*) Won't you smoke or appear
   occupied with something? I won't feel such an in-
   truder if you do.

ROYLSTON (*Laughing*)   I would have done so before if
   I had known you didn't object.

MRS. FRAZER   On the contrary, I like it. My hus— I

have always been accustomed to men who smoked.
My father was a great smoker.

ROYLSTON (*Who has taken a box of cigarettes from his
pocket and lighted one*)   There.

(*He leans back in his chair in an attitude of attention*)

MRS. FRAZER   To begin at the beginning. My father was
a prominent lawyer with a wide practice. He died
five years ago leaving a large estate to my mother,
who is still alive but in very feeble health. They had
only two children, my brother, five years older than
I am, and myself. I tell you all this because you lay
such stress in all your books and plays on the influence of environment, and I want you to understand thoroughly what mine was. Being the baby
and pet of the family you can readily guess how I
was brought up—governess, private tutors, and finally a finishing school. Of course, at the end of
their elaborate system of education I knew only
what a young lady of my position should know—
nothing of any value.

ROYLSTON   (*Smiling*)   Naturally; but you have pro-
gressed wonderfully since then.

MRS. FRAZER   If I have, I have paid for it; and whatever
progress I have made I owe to you.

ROYLSTON (*Wonderingly*)   To me?

MRS. FRAZER   We haven't come to that part of the story
yet. When I returned home from the finishing
school, my life became one long round of recep-
tions, parties, balls, and so forth, until, in spite of
the fact that at that time I was only interested in
the most superficial things, I became surfeited,

bored, and felt a longing to break away and experience something of more interest.

ROYLSTON   You wished to try your wings.

MRS. FRAZER   Yes, that was it. It was about this time I
met Mr. Frazer, the man who afterward became
my husband. He was then, and still is, a broker on
the New York Stock Exchange. He fascinated me.
I seemed to see personified in him all I had read
about the (*Sarcastically*) financial giants, the daring gamblers who fought their battles to the bitter
end of ruin. The house he was connected with is
one of the largest on the Exchange and some of the
so-called Napoleons of finance, whose names were
forever in newspaper headlines, did their business
through it. I thought of him doing his part in their
gigantic enterprises, laboring to effect ever larger
combinations in order that this glorious country
might thrive and become ever greater and more
productive (*With a short laugh*) You can see what
a child I was; but I'm afraid you're not listening.

ROYLSTON   (*Eagerly*)   I assure you, you are mistaken. I
am intensely interested. I was simply trying to recall something. Do you know when I watch you
and listen to you talk I am forcibly reminded of
some other woman. The likeness is so perfect it's
uncanny.

MRS. FRAZER   May I ask who it is?

ROYLSTON   That's exactly what I cannot recollect. I am
sure it's someone I know intimately and yet, for the
life of me, I cannot bring the exact person to my
mind.

MRS. FRAZER   How strange.

ROYLSTON   But I'm interrupting you. Please go on with your story.

MRS. FRAZER   Well, the inevitable happened. I fell in love with George—Mr. Frazer—and he with me, and after a short engagement we were married. My family approved of him in every way. I believe they cherished the same illusion about his business, in a modified form, perhaps, as I did.

ROYLSTON   Do you not think your husband also had the same illusions?

MRS. FRAZER   It would be hard to say. In justice to him I must acknowledge he always seemed to idealize it. He never could see his business in all its hideousness as I came to see it, and I don't think he wore a mask just for my benefit; but you never can tell.

ROYLSTON   Most of them can't see the unpleasant side. It becomes so much a part of themselves, you know. And after you were married?

MRS. FRAZER   Oh, the usual honeymoon trip to Europe with its inevitable visits to Westminster Abbey, the tomb of Napoleon, the Cologne Cathedral, and other points of interest.

ROYLSTON (*Ironically*)   How ideal!

MRS. FRAZER   And yet I was very happy, or thought I was happy, which is much the same thing. Of course, in the light of what I now know, of what you have taught me, I can see it was merely a stupid happiness, the content of the born blind who have never seen the light.

ROYLSTON   And I am to blame for your enlightenment?

MRS. FRAZER   To blame?

ROYLSTON   Since it has made you unhappy it must be blameworthy.

MRS. FRAZER (*With fine scorn*)   What is such sluggish content worth? When you had opened my eyes to the truth I repudiated it. I felt I must win to a higher plane—or remain unhappy.

ROYLSTON (*Bewildered—running his fingers through his hair. With laughing impatience*)   How you do remind me of someone! And yet I cannot remember— But tell me how this great change came about. After your return from your honeymoon I suppose your husband laid aside his role of lover and became the businessman once more, leaving you to ornament his home, and brood, and read my novels and plays.

MRS. FRAZER   That is what you would naturally think, isn't it? However, you are quite wrong. My husband was as much the lover on the day I left him as he had been when we were married seven years before.

ROYLSTON   Then you have left him?

MRS. FRAZER   Yes, eight months ago.

ROYLSTON   Have you no children?

MRS. FRAZER   No. I used to be very sorry we had not; but now I am glad. It would have made it so much harder for me when the time came to free myself.

ROYLSTON   You fell in love with someone else?

MRS. FRAZER (*Flushing*)   If I had ceased to love my husband it is no reason why—

ROYLSTON (*Smiling*)   You must not be offended. It usually happens that way you know.

MRS. FRAZER (*Earnestly*)   I was in love with an ideal—

the ideal of self-realization, of the duty of the individual to assert its supremacy and demand the freedom necessary for its development. You had taught me that ideal and it was that which came in conflict with my marriage. I saw I could never hope to grow in the stifling environment of married life—so I broke away.

ROYLSTON (*Gravely*) Please tell me in what manner I effected this change in you.

MRS. FRAZER I bought one of your novels one day about two years ago, more out of curiosity than anything else. It was the one about Wall Street.

ROYLSTON You mean *The Street*.

MRS. FRAZER Yes, that's the one.

ROYLSTON Then it was that book of mine which disillusioned you about your husband's business?

MRS. FRAZER Yes. When I first read it I couldn't believe it. I began to ask George questions about his deals, and so forth. He was surprised and happy to find me interested in his work and he finally used to explain all his transactions to me—and then I knew.

ROYLSTON Hm.

MRS. FRAZER I tried to persuade him to go into something else. He acknowledged there was a lot of truth in your book but said there were two ways of looking at everything. When I pleaded with him he laughed and called me his "dear little muckraker."

ROYLSTON (*Smiling*) So you became disillusioned about the broker—but how about the man?

MRS. FRAZER Your book made me long to read what you had to say about other things. I bought all your

published works, and went to see all your plays, not
once but many times. It dawned upon me gradually
that the life he and I were living together was the
merest sham; that we were contented because he
was too busy and I was too lazy to analyze our position, to stop and think. For a long time I was very
unhappy. I knew what I must do but I did not have
the courage to do it.

ROYLSTON (*Impatiently*) Why didn't you tell him
frankly how you felt?

MRS. FRAZER I couldn't. You see, he was so good and
kind to me and it seemed such heartless cruelty to
hurt him. All the time I felt myself being ground
smaller and smaller day by day. I discovered that
he and I had not a thought in common. Everything
he was interested in was so shallow. He never concerned himself with what lay beneath the surface
and I know my thoughts bored him although he
was far too kind to ever show it. He observed the
change in me and it worried him but the only rem-
edies he could suggest were (*With a short laugh*)
Southern California, a trip to Europe, or some
other change of air. When I refused to go away he
was at a loss what to do. I think toward the end he
suspected I was in love with someone else.

ROYLSTON (*With a cynical smile*)   I'll wager he did.

MRS. FRAZER I resolved not to think. I plunged into all
sorts of activities to try and forget myself. I learned
shorthand and typewriting—

ROYLSTON (*Interrupting her enthusiastically*) Good!
That is your salvation.

MRS. FRAZER (*Wearily*) My soul refused to be lulled
to sleep and there came a day when I left a note for

my husband and left the house. I had been to see your play *Sacrifice* the night before for the tenth time. It seemed to breathe a message to me over the footlights. You remember when Mrs. Harding in the play leaves her husband with the words "I have awakened!"?

ROYLSTON (*His eyes searching hers with keen questioning*) Yes, but Mrs. Harding has a lover to go to.

MRS. FRAZER (*Bearing his scrutiny unflinchingly*) And I have an ideal which I love. When I heard her say those words that night they impressed me as never before. I felt that I, too, had awakened; that the time had come to assert my—

ROYLSTON (*With a sudden exclamation—interrupting her*) The puzzle is solved. What a dolt I am! It is Mrs. Harding in my play you resemble so much.

MRS. FRAZER (*Surprised*) Oh, is it? I saw the play so many times, you see.

ROYLSTON And you left your husband the next day?

MRS. FRAZER Yes. I sold some things which I had a right to call my own and bought a plain black dress. I knew I would have to become a worker, a wage-earner, and I wished to take nothing with me to remind me of the old life.

ROYLSTON (*Sympathetically*) I can imagine the ordeals you have been through since then. When one is beautiful it is doubly hard.

MRS. FRAZER (*Blushing—hurriedly*) At first I missed all the little comforts and luxuries I had been used to. I never knew till I had to do without them how they had grown into my life. I got bravely over that. I found it very hard to get work and harder still to keep it. The men were all such beasts and

the women I had to come in contact with were so
unintelligent and ordinary.

ROYLSTON (*Dryly*)   You'll find most people are—rather
ordinary.

MRS. FRAZER   In my last position I really thought for a
time my employer was a gentleman. I discovered he
was only playing a part to throw me off my guard,
and he turned out the worst of all. And then the
unspeakably long nights in the dingy hall bedroom
of a boarding house with no one to speak to, no
money, no place to go; not able even to take a walk
alone on the streets for fear of the insults, the
smirking groups in the doorways and on the corners. Oh, yes, it has been hard! (*Her voice trembling*) It has been almost more than I could endure.

ROYLSTON (*Kindly*)   Come; it was your ordeal of fire
and you have borne up wonderfully. Have you
never received word from your husband?

MRS. FRAZER   That is the worst of all. He has haunted
me, waited for me at the doors of boarding houses,
at the entrance of office buildings where I worked,
pleading with me to come back, offering to do anything I wished, trying to force money on me, even
pushing it in under the door of my room. He cannot understand what has come over me. I think he
really believes I am the victim of a mad infatuation
for a married man; and yet he has had me followed
continually, to protect me, as he says, not to spy on
me, and he knows I have seen no one. (*Putting her
hands over her face with a sob*) And he looks so
unhappy, so miserable. I feel guilty whenever I see
him.

ROYLSTON (*Gently*) Are you sure you no longer love him?

MRS. FRAZER (*Hysterically*) Oh, love, love, what is love? How can I know? I am certain I could no longer live with him. How can you doubt it after all I have told you? I know that I like him very much and do not want to see him suffer on my account.

ROYLSTON (*After a pause—frowning*) Have you stopped to think that you might have been followed here?

MRS. FRAZER I am certain I was not. He has given up hope. I haven't seen him in over a month. Besides, I took special pains to throw anyone off the track. I went down to the office building where I used to work this morning and left by a side entrance. I used the freight elevator to come down in. No one could have seen me.

ROYLSTON Where have you been all day?

MRS. FRAZER Sitting on a bench in Central Park.

ROYLSTON But good heavens, Mrs. Frazer, why didn't you come during the day?

MRS. FRAZER I was afraid you might be out. You see, I had read in the paper that you always worked at night and I felt pretty sure of finding you. I could not afford more than one trip. To be quite frank with you, it was with the last dollar I had in the world that I came out here.

ROYLSTON But if I had not been at home?

MRS. FRAZER (*Firmly*) I should have waited until you came. No matter how, I should have waited.

ROYLSTON (*Plainly embarrassed—getting up and walking nervously about the room*) You have been frank with me, Mrs. Frazer. Will you permit me to be the same?

MRS. FRAZER   I wish you to be so.

ROYLSTON   You promise to take no offense at what I am going to ask you?

MRS. FRAZER   I am not afraid. I know you are trying to help me.

ROYLSTON   I am glad of that. What I want to ask is: Will you let me help you in—er—a pecuniary way?

MRS. FRAZER   (*Rather indignantly*) How could you think so?

ROYLSTON   I mean as a loan, you know. You really ought to—

MRS. FRAZER   You know I could not.

ROYLSTON   Then you have not freed yourself from all prejudices after all. You will certainly let me see to it that you get a position where you will be well paid and respected?

MRS. FRAZER   Gladly, and be more than grateful for your assistance.

ROYLSTON (*With a sigh of relief*)   Then that is settled. (MRS. FRAZER *suddenly breaks down and commences to sob.* ROYLSTON *goes to her and lays his hand on her shoulder*) There, there, Mrs. Frazer. I know it has been hard. It's bound to be, you know, for a woman in your position. The future will be much easier, you'll find. Please don't break down that way. (A *pause*) I feel as if I were responsible for all this and yet—

MRS. FRAZER (*Wiping her tears away and trying to control herself*)   You don't understand. You are only looking at the material side. I don't care about that. What I came here to demand—yes, demand, for I

have a right to do so—was certainty, the assurance
that I am on the right path. These past few weeks
with their sleepless nights have been terrible.

ROYLSTON How can I—

MRS. FRAZER Had I the right to do what I did? To
cause others so much suffering? Am I realizing the
best that is in me or the worst? My will to keep on
striving is being broken. I doubt the worth of my
action. When I see him so unhappy I say to myself: "Have you the right?" and I find no answer
to satisfy me. I can only argue and argue until my
brain aches. How can I bear hardship for a cause in
which my faith is wavering? That is why I come to
you.

ROYLSTON (*In a troubled voice*) I cannot tell you how
deeply grieved I am to have been even the indirect
means of causing you pain.

MRS. FRAZER (*Excitedly*) I have the right to come to
you, haven't I? Mentally I am your creation. That
you had no knowledge of my existence when you
wrote does not lessen your responsibility in my
eyes. I demand that you restore my peace of mind
by justifying me to myself.

ROYLSTON (*Deeply moved*) What I have written cannot apply to every case. (*With conviction*) But it
is my sincerest belief that you have found yourself,
that as things stand between you, it would be folly
for you to go back to your husband; that out of
your present distress will spring a higher satisfaction than you have ever before known or believed
possible. Therefore, I urge you not to give up the
battle, for in the end you will achieve a victory well
worth the winning.

MRS. FRAZER (*Extending both her hands to him—gratefully*)   You have given me new hope, new strength.

ROYLSTON (*Taking her hands and looking into her eyes*)   Promise me you will call on me whenever you need help in the future.

MRS. FRAZER (*Withdrawing her hands—simply*)   I promise to do so.

ROYLSTON (*Smiling*)   You must now, you know. You have charged me with the responsibility. You must let me pay off my debt.

MRS. FRAZER (*Forcing a smile*)   Whenever my supply of will power runs low I'll come a-borrowing, never fear.

ROYLSTON   By the way, I meant to ask you if your mother and brother know anything of all this?

MRS. FRAZER   No. My mother is in Switzerland. Her health is so feeble I have not dared to tell her about it; and I know she would never learn of it through Mr. Frazer. My brother is the manager of a railroad in Brazil and very seldom returns to this country or writes to me. So, of course, he knows nothing.

ROYLSTON   But your husband's family?

MRS. FRAZER   I believe he has told them something about my being in California for my health.

ROYLSTON   You have that in your favor. Family interference always complicates matters. As for the position I promised you, I will see what I can do when I go to the city in the morning. I have many influential friends and I have no doubt a real opportunity will be found for you some place. In the meantime I have lots of work which should be typewritten, and if you care to—

I

MRS. FRAZER   Oh, how good of you! Your encouragement has made me feel so hopeful, so full of energy, I am ready for anything. A new life of wonderful possibilities seems opening up before me.

ROYLSTON   It will be full of obstacles, too.

MRS. FRAZER (*Spiritedly*)   The harder the better. With your help I know I shall overcome them.

ROYLSTON   You are overrating me. Take warning!

MRS. FRAZER (*Picking up her hat from the sofa*)   And now I had better be going back to my little hall room.

ROYLSTON (*Looking at his watch—then turning to her with a quizzical smile*)   Yes, but how?

MRS. FRAZER   What do you mean?

ROYLSTON   I mean the little hall room will have to remain empty tonight. You have missed the last train.

MRS. FRAZER (*Apparently greatly astonished*)   Surely you don't mean it? And I never looked at the time-table! Why didn't you warn me?

ROYLSTON   I had no idea what time it was.

MRS. FRAZER   How stupid of me! That comes of living in the city, where you can always get the subway or something. I must get back some way.

ROYLSTON   It's impossible, I'm afraid.

MRS. FRAZER   Then what can I do?

ROYLSTON   You must stay here.

MRS. FRAZER   Here—in this house?

ROYLSTON   There is no alternative unless you wish to pass the night in the fields.

MRS. FRAZER   There must be a hotel.

ROYLSTON   There is only a roadhouse, a place of very

questionable character, frequented by joy-riders and their—companions. You could not go there; and I know of no other place. You see, there are nothing but summer residences around here and I am hardly acquainted with any of the neighbors. (*Gravely*) Think of the time of night, and the rain, of the conclusions which would be drawn. You are beautiful and people have evil minds. Don't you see the impossibility?

MRS. FRAZER Yes—but, oh—how can I stay here? What will your wife think?

ROYLSTON She will not think. She will never know.

MRS. FRAZER I—I don't understand.

ROYLSTON She is not here. Except for the servants I am all alone.

MRS. FRAZER (*Genuinely alarmed*) Then I must go, even if I do have to spend the night in the fields.

ROYLSTON Listen; there is rather a strange coincidence, or shall I say fatality in all this. My wife went with the children to see the fairy play in New York, and contrary to her usual custom—she doesn't care for motoring—she went down in the machine. Otherwise I could have had the chauffeur drive you home; but they won't return before tomorrow afternoon at the earliest.

MRS. FRAZER (*Frightened*) This is terrible. How can I—(*She hurries to the window and looks out*) It's pouring.

ROYLSTON Fatality.

MRS. FRAZER (*Imploringly*) Please, please suggest something! You know I can't stay.

(*She looks at him pleadingly—her lips tremble*)

ROYLSTON Why not? (*Slowly*) Don't you believe you would be as safe here in my house as in your dingy hall bedroom?

MRS. FRAZER (*Looking at him searchingly*) Yes—I know I would be—but—

ROYLSTON (*Impatiently*) But you are afraid of appearances, of what people might think if they knew. You never learned that fear from me. Is not the knowledge of your own innocence enough to raise you above such considerations? Or are you afraid I may be a Don Juan in disguise?

MRS. FRAZER No, I am not afraid of you.

ROYLSTON And even if you fear appearances? Who is to know?

MRS. FRAZER (*Wavering*) You forget your servant.

ROYLSTON He has been with me for years, was with my father before me, all his life has been in our service. I flatter myself he's a model of discretion.

MRS. FRAZER But what will he think of me? (*Seeing* ROYLSTON's *scornful smile*) But it doesn't matter. I will stay.

ROYLSTON Bravo! It would be foolish and cowardly of you to get soaked with the rain and be insulted, and perhaps worse, in the railroad station for the sake of a worn-out code of ethics.

MRS. FRAZER (*Smiling feebly*) Your wife might not think the ethics worn out

ROYLSTON (*Carelessly*) Oh, my wife; she would not think anything. If it would ease your conscience, I will tell her the whole thing. I'm sure she'd forget all about it ten minutes later (*Contemptuously*) when the butcher came for his order.

MRS. FRAZER (*Impulsively*) You do not love your wife, do you? (*As* ROYLSTON *looks at her in astonishment, she grows confused*) What an impertinent question! Forgive me!

ROYLSTON (*Lightly*) So impertinent I never dare ask it of myself. I have always rejected the temptation to analyze my home relations. They are pleasant enough and that is all I care to know.

MRS. FRAZER (*With a sad smile*) If I had looked at it that way—

ROYLSTON The family relationship was the most important thing in the world for you at that time. With me it is purely secondary. My work comes first. As long as my home life gives free scope for my creative faculty I will demand nothing further of it. Life is too meager, too stingy with its favors, for us to ask for perfection. So I accept my domestic bliss at its surface value and save my analytical eye for the creations of my brain. (*Smiling*) I see you are vainly trying to stifle a yawn, and I know you must be terribly tired and sleepy. Won't you let me direct you to your room?

(*He goes to the door on the left*)

MRS. FRAZER (*Forgetting her hat, which she leaves lying on the sofa, she smilingly walks over to him*) I am dismissed, then?

ROYLSTON Far from it. I merely wish to save you the embarrassment of falling asleep in the chair. (*Pointing*) You see the light at the top of the stairway? Well, turn to your left when you reach the top and boldly enter the first room on your left. You will find everything there you need, I imagine.

It is the official number-one guest chamber.

MRS. FRAZER   I suppose you won't retire for hours yet?

ROYLSTON   I have some work to finish up.

MRS. FRAZER   (*Catching herself in the act of yawning—with a laugh*) I can't deny I'm sleepy—for the first time in months. (*Giving him her hand*) If you only knew how grateful I am! How can I ever thank you?

ROYLSTON   (*With sudden passion*) By looking at me like that. How beautiful you are!

MRS. FRAZER   (*Withdrawing her hand—a note of warning in her voice*) Remember the princess in the fairy tales who was as good as—

ROYLSTON   She was beautiful. I understand. Pardon me. Good—but emancipated.

MRS. FRAZER   (*Smiling*) Free to be good.

(*She turns to go out the door*)

ROYLSTON   Good night.

(*He goes toward the table*)

MRS. FRAZER   (*Turning to him suddenly, a look of resolution on her face*) I must explain one thing before I go, before I accept your hospitality. I have told you a lie. (ROYLSTON *looks at her in surprise*) I never met you at the studio ball. I was there but I did not meet you. I knew I had missed the last train. That is the reason I came so late. I wanted to miss it. And I knew there was no hotel, for I made inquiries at the station. But I had no idea your wife would be away.

ROYLSTON   (*Staring at her in amazement*) But why, why?

MRS. FRAZER   I wanted to put you to the test, to see if you would help me and let me stay. I wanted to get a glimpse of your home life, to see if you were a real man with the courage of your convictions or just a theorist. (*Hesitatingly*) You see, in my agony of doubt it seemed necessary for me to get back of dry words to a flesh-and-blood reality. (*With a faint smile*) It all appears such a wild idea now; and the test turned out to be a test of myself after all, didn't it?

ROYLSTON (*Not able to recover from his astonishment*) You tell me this—now—that you purposely missed the last train?

MRS. FRAZER (*Flushing*) I am ashamed to say that is the exact truth. (*Avoiding his ardent gaze*) I wish there to be no deception on my part after all your kindness to me.

ROYLSTON (*Intensely*) Do you realize how beautiful you are? Are you not afraid to make such a confession to me—of the conclusions I might be vain enough to draw from it?

(*He moves a step toward her*)

MRS. FRAZER (*Looking straight into his eyes*) No— because I know now you *are* a real man.

ROYLSTON (*Moving still nearer to her*) Take care! The real men are usually the greatest sinners.

MRS. FRAZER But they protect the helpless. (*With a smile*) So you see how safe I am. Good night.

(*She goes out*)

ROYLSTON (*Going to the door*) Good night (*He watches her ascend the stairway*) Good night. (*He comes back and sits down at the table again; starts to look over his manuscript, glances upward in the direction of her room, throws his manuscript down with an exclamation of disgust, goes to the door on the left again and looks up at the top of the stairway, finally comes back to the table again and stands beside it for a moment, frowning thoughtfully and evidently weighing something in his mind)* Damnation! *(He takes his hat and light overcoat from the chair, puts them on, grabs his cane and hurries out through the door at the back)*

Curtain

Act Two

SCENE—*The same. It is about nine o'clock on the following morning. Bright sunlight streams in through the two open windows.* BENTON *is arranging the papers and books on the table. Having finished he turns and is going out the door in the rear when he catches sight of* MRS. FRAZER's *hat, which is lying on the sofa. He gives a low whistle of amazement. A shadow falls across the sunlight at one of the windows and a moment later* WESON, *the gardener, puts his head into the room and peers around near-sightedly. He is an old withered man with a drooping gray mustache stained yellow by tobacco juice.*

BENTON   Good morning, Weson.

WESON   Oh, it's you, is it?

BENTON   Who did you think it was?

WESON   I thought maybe Mr. Roylston—

BENTON   He isn't up yet. Want to see him about any-thing?

WESON   Nothin' special. When I first come out this mornin' I seen a feller hangin' round the house s'picious like. Soon's he seen me he turned round and walked off s'fast s'he could go. "D'you think this is a park?" I shouts after him, but he didn't pay no attention. Thinks I: I better tell Mr. Royl-

ston about you. With all them burglaries happenin'
nearabouts you can't be too careful.

BENTON   Hm—you're right about that. (*With an in-
voluntary glance at the hat*) Mr. Roylston ought
to be more careful.

WESON   Oughter hire a watchman, s'what I say. (*In
a whining voice*) T'ain't safe for me sleepin' all
alone in that house at the end of the drive. S'me
they'd tackle first. I was readin' in the papers
t'other day where robbers tortured an old gardener
same's me to make him tell them how to git into
the house; burned his bare feet with a red-hot
poker! (*With rising inflection*) Ain't that tur-
rible?

BENTON   Oh, I guess you're safe enough. (*Meaningly*)
It isn't burglars his nibs ought to be frightened of.

WESON (*Eagerly, scenting a scandal*)   What's he been
up to now?

BENTON (*Picking up* MRS. FRAZER'*s hat*)   Cast your eye
on this.

WESON   Wait till I git my specs. (*He reaches into his
pocket and pulls out a pair of steel-rimmed spec-
tacles*) I can't see nothin' without 'em no more.
(*He puts them on and looks at the hat. In disappointed tones*) What's that? One of the Missus'
hats?

BENTON   Guess again. She don't wear cheap truck like
that.

(*He throws the hat contemptuously on the sofa*)

WESON   You don't mean—? (*With an explosive
chuckle*)If he don't beat the devil! An' the Missus
in Noo York! Makes hay while the sun shines,
don't he? Don't the Missus never guess nothin'?

BENTON (*Scornfully*) She doesn't know enough; besides, usually he chucks 'em before the thing gets
serious. He likes to have them crazy about him
but when they get too mushy—he doesn't like
complications—they interfere with his work, he
says; and then when they call up I have to say he's
too busy to be disturbed.

WESON (*Admiringly*) Foxy, ain't he?

BENTON I don't know what's wrong with him this
time. I don't blame him, though; she's a beauty.
But he ought to be more careful. Once caught,
twice shy, they say; and he was caught once, good
and proper. (*With a short laugh*) It'll do the
Missus good to get a dose of her own medicine. It
broke the old man's heart when the young fellow
married her, and—(*Stopping abruptly as he sees
how avidly* WESON *is drinking his words in*) A fine
man to work for, the old gentleman; not that I'm
complaining of the son at all.

WESON What was you sayin' about the marriage?

BENTON Nothing that an old scandalmonger like you
ought to hear. There's lots of things I could tell if
I had a mind to; but I'll keep my mouth shut. It's
the best policy, Weson, especially when you're
around. You better get out of here. I think I hear
someone coming down the stairs.

(WESON *hurriedly withdraws.* BENTON *goes to the
table and pretends to be arranging the things on it.*
MRS. FRAZER *appears in the doorway on the left. She
stops uncertainly when she sees* BENTON)

BENTON (*Affably*) Good morning, ma'am.

MRS. FRAZER (*Embarrassed*) Good morning. I believe
I left my hat in here.

BENTON   Yes, ma'am. Here it is.

(*He picks up her hat from the sofa*)

MRS. FRAZER (*Walking over and taking it from him*) Thank you.

(*She goes to the window and stands drinking in the beauty of the spring morning*)

BENTON (*With an admiring glance at her figure framed in the sunlight*) Beautiful morning, ma'am.

MRS. FRAZER   Yes, isn't it? And what a lovely garden.

BENTON   Yes, ma'am, very fine. It has the gardener busy all the time keeping it in shape.

MRS. FRAZER   No doubt; they require a great deal of care. Has Mr. Roylston come down yet?

BENTON   Lord no, ma'am; won't be down for an hour yet, I should say. He's not what you'd call an early bird; stays up so late nights he couldn't be. (*Insinuatingly*) But he's been so queer and—hm— different from what he usually does, he might do anything this morning.

MRS. FRAZER (*Crushing him with a look of icy hauteur*) What do you mean?

BENTON (*Confused, fumbling with the books on the table*) Nothing at all, ma'am, only—

MRS. FRAZER (*Her curiosity getting the better of her— more kindly*) Only what?

BENTON (*Accepting her change of manner as a confession which equalizes their position*) Only, begging your pardon, he doesn't usually—he isn't in the habit of—he usually thinks that sort of thing too dangerous. Now, when the others—

MRS. FRAZER (*Horrified*) Others?

BENTON (*Grinning*) Loads of 'em. They're all crazy about him. He likes it, too—phone calls and letters

and flowers and all such stuff. He pretends not to
care, but it tickles him just the same to have them
adoring him, asking for his advice—

MRS. FRAZER   Stop! Is this the way you slander the man
who trusts you?

BENTON (*Offended*) It's no secret. He laughs and
talks about it himself. I've heard him read parts of
the letters to the Missus, Mrs. Roylston. I was only
saying it to you because it's never—he's never
taken any chances for the others. I thought you'd
like to know you were the only one—

MRS. FRAZER (*Her face crimson*)   How dare you?

BENTON (*Quickly*) Beg your pardon, ma'am, no offense intended. (*Slyly*) Of course I don't mean
anything wrong. (*The sound of a door closing is
heard from the hallway on the left, then children's
voices.* BENTON *turns excitedly to* MRS. FRAZER)
Good Gawd, it must be Mrs. Roylston and the
kids. Go in there where she won't see you.

(MRS. FRAZER, *too overcome with fear and shame to
stop and think, hurries through the door at the rear.*
BENTON *closes it after her and is busy with the papers on
the table when* MRS. ROYLSTON *enters with the children,
who are talking and laughing together.*

MRS. ROYLSTON *is a pretty woman of thirty or so, with
a mass of light curly brown hair, big thoughtful eyes,
rosy complexion, tiny hands and feet, and a slight girlish figure. She is dressed stylishly but with ostentation.*

DAVIE *and* RUTH, *aged nine and seven respectively, are
healthy, noisy, delightful children. Their clothes are
simple but of expensive material*)

MRS. ROYLSTON   Good morning, Benton. Mr. Roylston's not up yet of course?

BENTON   No, ma'am.

MRS. ROYLSTON   Telephone for Dr. Morse at once, will you, Benton? Tell him to come up at once.

BENTON   Yes, ma'am. Nothing serious, I hope, ma'am.

MRS. ROYLSTON   Oh no. Ruth was ill last night when we returned from the theatre. Mrs. Dexter sent for her doctor. He said it was nothing but (*Smiling and shaking an accusing finger at* RUTH) too much candy. However, I wanted to make sure. I have no confidence in strange doctors. So I took the first train out this morning and didn't wait for the machine.

RUTH   I didn't eat much, Mother.

DAVIE   I ate more'n she did, and I was'n sick.

MRS. ROYLSTON   But you're a man, dear.

RUTH   I feel puffictly well this morning, Mother.

MRS. ROYLSTON   (*Kissing her*)   Of course you do, dear. Mother wishes to make sure, that's all. So telephone right away, please, Benton.

BENTON   Yes, ma'am.

(*With an apprehensive glance at the door in back he hurries out to the left*)

DAVIE   Mother, can we go out and play in the sand-pile?

RUTH   I'm goin' to play I'm the princess in the play last night.

MRS. ROYLSTON   And are you going to be the prince, Davie?

DAVIE   Nope, I'm goin' to be the dragon.

MRS. ROYLSTON   But the dragon was very, very wicked.

DAVIE   Tha's why I wanta be him.

MRS. ROYLSTON   (*Laughing and kissing both of them*)   Run along then, and be sure and stay in the sun;

and come in when you see Dr. Morse drive up. Try
and be as quiet as you can. You know your father
isn't up yet.

(*The children answer:* "*Yes, Mother,*" *and skip out
through the door on the left*)

BENTON (*Appearing in the doorway on the left*) Dr.
Morse will be right up, ma'am.

MRS. ROYLSTON Very well. Thank you, Benton. (BEN-
TON, *unwilling to leave the room, and not knowing
any excuse for remaining, stands fidgeting nervously in the doorway*)Anything you wish to see me
about, Benton?

BENTON No, ma'am, nothing at all. So glad to hear it's
not serious—Miss Ruth, I mean.

MRS. ROYLSTON (*Smiling at him kindly*)Thank you,
Benton.

(*She sits down, picks up the manuscript from the
table and starts to read.* BENTON *turns reluctantly and
leaves.* MRS. ROYLSTON *glances over the pages of the
manuscript interestedly. The door in the rear is slowly
opened and* MRS. FRAZER *comes into the room. Her face
wears an expression of defiant shame. She coughs to
attract* MRS. ROYLSTON'*s attention. Startled by the sound,*
MRS. ROYLSTON *turns around and sees her. The two
women stare at each other in silence for a moment.*
MRS. ROYLSTON *grows very pale. Her lips tremble and it
seems as if she were shrinking up in her chair, becoming small and pitiful. A flush slowly spreads over* MRS.
FRAZER'*s face. She drops her eyes*)

MRS. FRAZER I beg your pardon.

MRS. ROYLSTON How did— Who is it you wish to see?

MRS. FRAZER I am waiting to speak to Mr. Roylston.

MRS. ROYLSTON How did you get in that room?

MRS. FRAZER (*Defiantly*) I hid there when I heard you coming.

MRS. ROYLSTON (*With a sigh that is like a moan*) I knew it! I knew it!

MRS. FRAZER (*Embarrassed*) I lost my head completely for a moment, and I ran away. I was so afraid of what you might think. In there I regained my senses. I had done no wrong. Why should I be afraid of you? So I came back.

MRS. ROYLSTON (*Slowly*) I am the one who should be afraid.

MRS. FRAZER I was sure you would misunderstand my presence here.

MRS. ROYLSTON (*Coldly*) I'm afraid I understand it only too well.

MRS. FRAZER Mr. Roylston was so positive you would ignore appearances. I knew better. I am a woman. I should never have allowed myself to be persuaded into remaining here against my better judgment.

MRS. ROYLSTON (*Trying not to understand*) Mr. Roylston? You have seen him? Is he up already?

MRS. FRAZER (*Unflinchingly*) No; I saw him last night.

MRS. ROYLSTON Last night? Then you— When did you come here—

MRS. FRAZER Last night about ten o'clock.

MRS. ROYLSTON (*Her worst fears realized*) Last night? Ten o'clock? Then you were here in this house— you and he—alone?

MRS. FRAZER Yes; but you must not draw any conclusions from that until I—

MRS. ROYLSTON (*Jumping to her feet, her eyes flashing*) Oh!

MRS. FRAZER You will be sorry if you form a hasty judgment.

MRS. ROYLSTON Hasty? As if I had not always a picture of this before my mind! I have known it was coming, dreaded it, for years. Hasty? Oh no! I have prayed this would never happen, but I have seen it drawing nearer every day in spite of my prayers; and I am prepared for it.

MRS. FRAZER If you will permit me to explain—

MRS. ROYLSTON (*With a mocking laugh*) Explain!

MRS. FRAZER (*Firmly*) I came here to ask your husband's advice.

MRS. ROYLSTON They all want advice—so they say.

MRS. FRAZER (*Flushing angrily but controlling herself*) I was in such desperate straits that only he could help me. I was wild with despair. I formed the mad idea of coming here. I never thought of your being away. And I missed the last train. (*She realizes how improbable this explanation must seem to* MRS. ROYLSTON *and continues uncertainly*) There was no hotel to go to; so your husband kindly—

MRS. ROYLSTON (*Her laughter breaking hysterically*) And you expect me to believe this! Do you think I have no intelligence at all? (*Furiously*) Lies! Lies! All lies!

(*Throwing herself in the chair by the table she sobs convulsively, her face hidden in her hands*)

MRS. FRAZER (*Calmly*) I will excuse your insults because I know how you must feel. (*Earnestly*) You will regret this when the truth comes out, when you know you have been insulting an innocent woman. You are judging by appearances and letting them deceive you.

MRS. ROYLSTON Lies, lies! Haven't I read your letters to him?

MRS. FRAZER (*Astonished*) I never wrote to your husband in my life.

MRS. ROYLSTON (*As if she hadn't heard*) "Will you give me permission to come out and see you sometime?" I suppose you never wrote that? Oh, how well I remember them—those letters!

MRS. FRAZER Mrs. Roylston, you are mistaken. I never—

MRS. ROYLSTON To take advantage of my being away with the children; oh, how could he!

MRS. FRAZER Mrs. Roylston, you must listen to me.

MRS. ROYLSTON I won't listen to you. What is there to say—now? You love him. I don't blame you for that; but what will become of me?

(*She breaks down and sobs unrestrainedly*)

MRS. FRAZER (*Waiting until* MRS. ROYLSTON *has regained control of herself*) Listen to me, Mrs. Roylston! I do not love your husband.

MRS. ROYLSTON The more shame, then, for he must love you.

MRS. FRAZER He never saw me before last night.

MRS. ROYLSTON (*Coldly*) I don't believe you.

MRS. FRAZER (*Angrily*) Ah, there is a limit to everything. Since you persist in insulting me, since you refuse to listen to anything, you may continue to believe whatever you please. I will leave Mr. Roylston to do the explaining.

(*She hurries toward the door on the left but* MRS. ROYLSTON *jumps up and reaches it before her, blocking her passage*)

MRS. ROYLSTON (*Fiercely*) You cannot go now.

MRS. FRAZER Cannot?

MRS. ROYLSTON I don't mean that. Please don't go yet, before he comes. There is so much which must be cleared up. I didn't mean to hurt you. If you knew how I am suffering, you wouldn't blame me. Please sit down, won't you, until he comes?

MRS. FRAZER (*On the verge of tears herself*) After the things you have said to me? No, I will not remain in this house a minute longer. Please let me pass.

MRS. ROYLSTON I am sorry. You are not to blame. No one is to blame. I implore you to stay until he comes. He ought to be down in a few minutes. It won't be long.

MRS. FRAZER (*After a moment's indecision*) Very well, I will stay; not because you ask me to but because I wish to hear my own justification.

(*She sits down in one of the armchairs near the sofa*)

MRS. ROYLSTON Thank you. It will help to clear up matters between the three of us once and for all.

(*She chokes back a sob and sits down in the chair by the table*)

MRS. FRAZER In the meantime, if you please, let us not talk about it. It will only make matters worse—if that were possible.

MRS. ROYLSTON (*Strangely*) How you said that! As if you were giving an order. And why shouldn't you? You have more right in this house than I have.

(*She sobs*)

MRS. FRAZER (*Moved in spite of herself—with great kindness*) Please, Mrs. Roylston, don't make yourself unhappy in this way. If you only knew how wrong you are.

MRS. ROYLSTON (*More calmly*) I won't break down

again. What must be, must be, I suppose. I have
known this was coming for a long time. The day
I was married I could foresee it. I should have had
the courage to refuse then; but I didn't. It all
seemed such a wonderful dream come true, I just
couldn't refuse even when I knew I was wronging
him. I was a coward then and I still am, I guess.
Eleven years of happiness and now I have to pay
and—I am afraid. (A *pause during which* MRS.
FRAZER *looks at her pityingly*) I've pretended not
to see a lot of things in those years. I wanted him to
be happy, and I knew he wouldn't be if he thought
he had a jealous wife prying into his affairs. All the
women who sent him flowers and wrote to him
and called him up on the phone—I knew they
loved him, and I hated them for it; but I never let
him think I suspected anything. Until lately I
never thought he considered them seriously.

MRS. FRAZER (*Interrupting her indignantly*)   And you
think I was one of those fools!

MRS. ROYLSTON   He used to read parts of their letters
to me. He never guessed how it hurt. For I could
see in spite of the way he joked they pleased him
just the same. Then all at once he stopped showing
them to me—and they kept coming, all in the
same handwriting. I had never read a letter of his
before but I brooded until I couldn't resist the
temptation any longer. Two of them were lying
open on this table one day and read them. Then I
could see the end coming. He had been writing to
her, meeting her in New York, and I knew from
the letters it was only a question of time.

MRS. FRAZER   And those are the letters you think I
wrote?

MRS. ROYLSTON (*Dully*)   Yes.

MRS. FRAZER   But when I swear to you I never wrote a
line to your husband in my life, never spoke a word
to him before last night!

MRS. ROYLSTON   I'd like to believe you. (*Intensely*)
Oh, I wish I could believe you! But how can I?

MRS. FRAZER (*Desperately*)   You will have to. He will
tell you the same thing.

MRS. ROYLSTON (*Her voice low and shaken with pain*)
What does it matter? You or someone else. She
said she had left her home to work out her own
salvation; and I thought you looked that way. I
thought she would be younger. Her letters sounded
girlish. What does it matter? *You* were here—last
night.

MRS. FRAZER (*Quietly*)   Mrs. Roylston, I really cannot
stay and listen to such implications.

MRS. ROYLSTON   I don't blame you or anyone. It's my
own sin coming back on me. Marriages like mine
are cursed.

MRS. FRAZER   Cursed? It seems to me yours has been a
very fortunate one.

MRS. ROYLSTON   Yes, cursed. Sooner or later the curse
falls. Retribution finds you out in the end. Forbidden love—you'll find out the curse of it like I have,
when you least expect it, when you think you're
happy and the future is all smiling.

MRS. FRAZER (*Interested*)   I fail to see how all this can
apply to your case.

MRS. ROYLSTON (*Continuing in a lifeless, monotonous*

voice as if all the spirit in her had been crushed and broken. Her face wears an expression of dazed, almost stupid, resignation) Give him up before it's too late, for your own sake. You'll have to pay. I'll be frank with you. You can't throw any stone. He married me because he had to, or thought he had to. I was his father's stenographer, we loved each other—too well. His father found out and discharged me. Then David asked me to marry him and I couldn't refuse. I loved him so.

MRS. FRAZER (*Bewildered*) Please, Mrs. Roylston, don't—

MRS. ROYLSTON I want you to understand—whatever happens to me afterwards—it isn't his fault.

MRS. FRAZER Do you know what you are telling me?

MRS. ROYLSTON (*Hotly*) I wouldn't be ashamed to tell it to the whole world. It shows how good he is. If he no longer loves me it's because I allowed him to make too great a sacrifice. His father cut him off and never spoke to him again. The old gentleman was kind enough generally but he had great plans for his only son, David, and I spoiled them all. He died soon afterward—of grief over our marriage, they say. I've always thought that perhaps in his heart David has never forgiven me for—killing his father.

MRS. FRAZER How can you imagine such a thing?

MRS. ROYLSTON When I married him I resolved that as soon as he was able to take care of himself—

MRS. FRAZER (*Astonished*) Take care of himself?

MRS. ROYLSTON He wasn't famous in those days. He hadn't even had a book published yet. He used to take positions in offices but he never held them

long and I could see how he hated them. He
wanted to write, write, write all the time. Every
once in a while he sold an article, but not often
enough to keep him alive. It must have been terribly hard for him—worrying and fretting how to
make two ends meet. He had been accustomed to
everything he wanted—and I had dragged him
down. He wouldn't have been human if he hadn't
had a sort of grudge against me for it.

MRS. FRAZER   He is hardly as mean as that.

MRS. ROYLSTON   I had to stay with him until he got on
his feet. I was considered a fine stenographer in
those days and my salary was enough to keep us
going. Then, too, he had to have someone to typewrite his manuscripts for him.

MRS. FRAZER   (*With wondering admiration*)   And you
did all that?

MRS. ROYLSTON   I had plenty of time at night to typewrite what he had written during the day. Those
were the happiest days of my life. How often since
then I've wished that he had never been successful,
that we could have gone on like that always. It was
selfish of me to feel that way but I couldn't help
it sometimes. (*Musingly*)   We had a small flat all
to ourselves.

MRS. FRAZER   And you did all the housekeeping, too?

MRS. ROYLSTON   (*Simply*)   Of course. I had made a re-
solve to leave him and let him get a divorce as
soon as he was successful and could get along without me. I saw clearly at that time, before the children came, what I see now—that he was never
meant for me. I knew he would come to regret his
sacrifice and I would become a dead weight hold-

ing him back. I knew nothing of what he knew.
Whatever I have learned since, he has taught me.
We had been married a little over a year when his
first play was produced and made a sensation—and
then—

MRS. FRAZER (*Eagerly*) Yes?

MRS. ROYLSTON (*Softly*) Little Davie came. I couldn't
think of going away then. It would have killed me.
I wasn't strong enough or brave enough for that.
I hoped he would love me more for Davie's sake,
and he did for a time. He was so kind to me; and
when our little girl was born he was so proud. As
he became famous he had less and less time to
spend at home, and he hated to be disturbed when
he was writing. He met so many people, women,
of his own kind outside, who could talk about the
things he was interested in, that I guess he commenced to despise me a little because I was so
stupid.

MRS. FRAZER (*With a strange smile, half to herself*)
No, no, he has never analyzed his home relations.

MRS. ROYLSTON (*As if she had not heard*) Lately he
has grown more and more indifferent to me and to
the children; so that now I'm afraid he only looks
on me as a sort of housekeeper. (*With a pitiful attempt at a smile*) He'll have to acknowledge I'm
a good one. I've protected him from all the small
worries he detests so much. I don't believe he realizes; he thinks things just run along by themselves.

MRS. FRAZER (*Eagerly*) Why have you never asserted
yourself, claimed your right as an individual? Why
have you never spoken to him, told him how you

felt? You have seen him slipping away and made
no attempt to hold him.

MRS. ROYLSTON (*Fiercely*) I have loved him, loved
him, loved him with all my heart and soul; loved
him more than you or any other woman will ever
love him. If that has no power to hold him—then
I have lost him.

MRS. FRAZER (*After a pause*) How unhappy you must
have been!

MRS. ROYLSTON (*Scornfully*) Unhappy? So that's what
you think! How little you know! I have been happy
in serving him, happy in the knowledge that I have
had my little part in helping him to success, happy
to be able to shield and protect him. In spite of all
you other women with your letters and flowers, I
have been happy. (*With a sad smile*) However, it's
all ended now. As long as I could pretend I didn't
know about you others, as long as I was sure he
didn't suspect I knew about you, I could remain
and love him and still preserve my self-respect. It's
different now. I can't pretend to be blind any
longer. I know, and you know I know, and he
knows I know. Besides, I see that his future happiness does not depend on me and (*Intensely*) above
all else in the world I want him to be happy.

MRS. FRAZER But he *is* happy—now—with you!

MRS. ROYLSTON (*Shaking her head sadly*) My useful-
ness is past. I can only thank God for granting the
beauty and joy of the past eleven years to a woman
who sinned and was too cowardly to pay. The payment was never canceled, only postponed, I see
that now—postponed until I had the courage to

pay. I have that courage now. I will pay. I will leave him to his happiness. (*Her voice thrilling with pride*) How many of you others love him as much as that? Not many, or one, I think. How many of you would make the sacrifice I will make? How many of you would be willing to give him up to another woman because your love was so great? Not one of you! (*Bitterly*) You the least of all—for him or anyone else! I can see it in your face.

MRS. FRAZER (*Slowly*)   It is true. Compared to you I am a weakling.

MRS. ROYLSTON   I do not boast of my strength, only of the strength of my love. I thank you just the same. You are the only person who has ever given me credit for being what I must be. Not even he ever saw it in all these eleven years.

MRS. FRAZER   But did you ever lay bare your soul to anyone, even to him, as you have to me?

MRS. ROYLSTON   Yes, to him, every day, every hour; but he never saw it.

MRS. FRAZER (*After a pause—thoughtfully*)   How much you have taught me! Happiness, then, means servitude?

MRS. ROYLSTON   Love means servitude; and *my* love is *my* happiness.

MRS. FRAZER   I should have come to you for advice, not to him.

MRS. ROYLSTON (*With a scornful smile*)   Advice? That word has been my torturer. You women of the flowers and letters have stolen him from me in the name of advice.

MRS. FRAZER (*Hurt*) Even now you have no faith in me.

MRS. ROYLSTON It isn't possible. How can I? How can I?

MRS. FRAZER I can't blame you; things are so mixed up. It must appear incredible. But can't you see that I, too, have suffered? Even if what you think were true, could you not pity me?

MRS. ROYLSTON (*Excitedly*) No, no, no, I can only hate you. How can the vanquished pity the victor? You ask too much.

MRS. FRAZER (*Rising from her chair*) I cannot wait any longer. I must go out into the fresh air and be alone for a while—to think.

MRS. ROYLSTON You are afraid to wait until he comes.

MRS. FRAZER I will wait outside. In this room the weight of your suspicion is crushing me. I begin to feel guilty.

MRS. ROYLSTON (*Savagely*) Ah!

MRS. FRAZER (*Weakly*) I will wait outside in the garden if I may.

(*She starts to go. The sound of a door slamming is heard.* MRS. ROYLSTON *goes to the door on the left and looks out. She gives an exclamation of surprise*)

MRS. ROYLSTON (*Slowly*) He has just come in. He must have been out for his morning walk. What could have got him up so early? (*Turning impetuously to* MRS. FRAZER) You must have known of this; and you wanted to sneak away before he came. Lies! Lies! Lies everywhere!

MRS. FRAZER (*Distractedly*) No, no, I swear to you—

MRS. ROYLSTON Ssshh! Here he comes.

(ROYLSTON *enters from the door on the left. He is dressed exactly the same as the night before*)

ROYLSTON (*Concealing his annoyance*)   Hello, Alice, what brings you back at this unearthly hour? Good morning, Mrs. Frazer.

MRS. ROYLSTON (*Falteringly*)   Ruth was sick last night and I didn't wait for the machine this morning but hurried out on the first train. She seems to be all right this morning but I've sent for Dr. Morse to make sure.

ROYLSTON (*Indifferently, shrugging his shoulders*) Stuffed full of candy, probably. I see you and Mrs. Frazer have already made each other's acquaintance.

MRS. ROYLSTON (*With a short laugh at what she thinks is his attempt to deceive her in the name*)   Oh, yes.

(MRS. FRAZER *does not reply but stares at him as if she were seeing him for the first time*)

ROYLSTON (*Searching through the things on the table*) God be thanked I haven't a jealous wife; for I must acknowledge that even to the most unprejudiced observer the events of last night would appear dubious. (*Irritably*)   Where did Benton put—? Oh, here it is. (*He finds the fountain pen he has been looking for and puts it in his pocket*) You see, Mrs. Frazer missed the last train, and when I explained that you were away it was all I could do to persuade her to occupy guest chamber number one instead of melting to death in the rain. Nice situation, wasn't it? Nothing if not compromising. Married man, married lady—not to each other—lonely country house—stormy night—wife returns home unexpectedly the next morning and—does not believe the worst. (*With a laugh which has a trace of mockery in it*) My dear Alice, you are really the perfect wife. (*He goes over to her and puts his arm around her carelessly and continues in the same bantering tone*) I told you, Mrs. Frazer, that Caesar's wife was above harboring suspicion. I welcome you to the model household, where truth reigns, where conventions are as naught, where we believe in each other implicitly because we have found each other so worthy of belief. And I salute you, my angel of trustfulness.

(*He bends to kiss his wife. She gently pushes him away*)

MRS. ROYLSTON Don't, David, please!

ROYLSTON (*Glancing from one to the other.* MRS. FRAZER *is looking at him with frank disgust*) Hm—I was too hasty in my reliance on mutual confidence, it seems. You two have had a run-in already, I see. (*To his wife, impatiently*) I am sorry you should have jumped at conclusions before you heard my explanation. Mrs. Frazer is going to do some work for me and—

MRS. ROYLSTON (*Her eyes filling*) Ah.

ROYLSTON Which will necessitate her being here for some time, and we must clear away all unpleasantness—

MRS. FRAZER (*Interrupting him coldly*) You are mistaken. I have decided I cannot accept the work you offer me.

ROYLSTON (*Perplexed*) Hm—it's as bad as that, eh?

MRS. ROYLSTON (*Turning to* MRS. FRAZER) But you must!

MRS. FRAZER (*Indignantly*) Must?

MRS. ROYLSTON What good can your refusal do now?

MRS. FRAZER (*To* ROYLSTON) Your wife has plainly told me that she is firmly convinced I am your mistress. She has read letters to you from someone and thinks I am the author. You see how plainly impossible it would be for me to work for you or accept your assistance in any way. Besides, there are other reasons. I have made a mistake, a great mistake, and it only remains for me to go. Before I leave I should like to have you try to convince Mrs. Roylston that her suspicions are groundless—as far as I am concerned.

ROYLSTON (*Turning to his wife*) So you read my letters?

MRS. ROYLSTON Yes; you left them on your table and I—couldn't resist the temptation. (ROYLSTON *turns away from her contemptuously*) I saw I was losing you, that you were becoming indifferent to me and the children—

ROYLSTON And you thought opening my letters would cure that?

MRS. ROYLSTON They were already open.

ROYLSTON Reading them, then.

MRS. ROYLSTON I did not stop to think. I love you.

ROYLSTON (*Coldly*) Indeed? You have strange ways of showing it.

MRS. ROYLSTON I wanted to fight for you. I had to know who my enemy was.

ROYLSTON Well, who was this so-called enemy of yours?

MRS. ROYLSTON   The letters were signed Julia Wainright.

MRS. FRAZER (*Eagerly*)   You see!

ROYLSTON   What has she to do with Mrs. Frazer? Why, in heaven's name, should you connect the two? Your insults to Mrs. Frazer are unpardonable and nonsensical. You are letting a narrow-minded suspicion blot out all that is best in you. Appearances have been against me before and yet you never took this attitude.

MRS. ROYLSTON   There is such a thing as the last straw.

ROYLSTON (*Sternly*)   Alice, what has come over you? You are not yourself. When I tell you we are both blameless, do you still persist—

MRS. ROYLSTON (*Frenziedly*)   I don't believe you or her or anyone. I can't, I can't! You call her Mrs. Frazer and expect me to believe her innocent—and she wears no wedding ring. (MRS. FRAZER *instinctively hides her hand behind her back*) Why are you up and out so early? You never get up before ten —Because she is up!

MRS. FRAZER (*Growing crimson*)   Oh!

(*The doorbell is heard ringing*)

ROYLSTON (*Bitingly*)   You need not tell your woes to the servants, Alice. Please try to control yourself. Here comes Benton.

(*A moment later* BENTON *appears in the doorway*)

BENTON   Dr. Morse is here, ma'am.

MRS. ROYLSTON (*Faintly*)   Very well, Benton. Tell him I'll be right out; and call the children in.

ROYLSTON (*Turning to his wife—cuttingly*)   Your conduct has been rather a revelation to me.

MRS. ROYLSTON (*Wincing*)   Don't, David!

ROYLSTON   You have called me a liar and you have insulted Mrs. Frazer, who is my friend. (MRS. FRAZER
makes an angry gesture repudiating this statement)
You will have no cause for any suspicions in the
future, for I shall not trouble you with my presence
in this house any longer. I will have Benton pack
up my things at once. I do not care to live with a
wife who is also an evil-minded spy. I could vindi-
cate myself beyond all possibility of doubt, in ten
words; but I prefer to have you think whatever your
jealous whim dictates. I will explain to Mrs. Frazer
and she may tell you if she considers your charges
against her worth the trouble of refuting.

MRS. ROYLSTON   (*Shrinking from him as if he had struck
her*)   Don't, don't, David! Please don't speak like
that—to me. You are killing me. I love you, you
must not go away. This is your home. It is I who
have no reason here. I will give you (*Sobbing and
walking toward the door on the left*) your freedom.
I want you to be happy, and—I know I'm only in
your way—now. Please forgive me if I can't believe. (*Stretching out her arms to him supplicatingly*) Please forgive me!

(*He turns away from her coldly*)

MRS. FRAZER   (*Indignantly*)   For shame, Mr. Roylston!

MRS. ROYLSTON   (*Turning to her furiously*)   How dare
you intercede for me! Don't you know how I hate
you?

(*She rushes out the door to the left*)

Curtain

Act Three

SCENE—*The same,* ROYLSTON *and* MRS. FRAZER *are still staring at the door through which* MRS. ROYLSTON *has just gone.*

ROYLSTON (*Shrugging his shoulders he turns to* MRS. FRAZER *with a short laugh*) I have lived with that woman for eleven years, and have never known her until ten minutes ago.

(*Benton appears in the doorway to the left. He stands there irresolutely for a second and is turning to go out again when* ROYLSTON *sees him*)

ROYLSTON (*Sharply*) Well, Benton? What is it?

BENTON (*Confused*) Nothing of any importance, sir —just something the gardener, Weson, asked me to tell you.

(*He hesitates, plainly indicating he does not wish to speak before* MRS. FRAZER)

ROYLSTON (*To* MRS. FRAZER) Excuse me. (*He goes over to* BENTON *in the doorway*) Well?

BENTON Weson says he saw a suspicious character hanging around and looking at the house early this morning. Weson shouted at him to find out what he wanted and he ran away.

ROYLSTON (*With a groan*) Damn Weson! Are you never going to get over your idiotic burglar scares, Benton?

K

BENTON (*Darkly*)   I wasn't thinking of burglars—this time. (*With a meaningful glance in* MRS. FRAZER's *direction*) Look out for the badger game, sir.

ROYLSTON (*Irritably*)   Go to the devil! (BENTON *smiles craftily and goes out.* ROYLSTON *comes back to the table*) When I outgrew a governess they gave me Benton. I thought it was a change for the better but it wasn't. I have never been able to outgrow him. He won't let me. (MRS. FRAZER *remains silent.* ROYLSTON *strides up and down nervously, clasping and unclasping his hands and scowling at his disagreeable thoughts. Suddenly he strikes his fist into the palm of his hand with an impatient exclamation*) What a blind fool I am! If there was anything in the world I would have trusted Alice not to do, it was to read my letters. What a contemptible thing to do—to read my letters! And what a trustful simpleton I was to leave them around! (*With an ironical smile*) Do you remember what I said last night about not caring to analyze my home relations provided the surface remained smooth? Well, your visit has stirred up the depths with a vengeance—the muddy depths.

MRS. FRAZER (*Sarcastically*)   What a crushing blow for you!

ROYLSTON   In all seriousness, it really is appalling. I feel as if the world were turned topsy-turvy. When you have taken a thing for granted for years, when a faith in it has been one of the main props of your life, although you might not have realized its importance at the time—and suddenly you make the discovery that you have trusted in a sham, that your prop is worm-eaten! It is rather a rough tumble, isn't it?

MRS. FRAZER (*In the same sarcastic tone*) I have found it so myself.

ROYLSTON That's so; I was forgetting. We're in the same boat, aren't we? (*With a sigh*) Well, I shall get bravely over it, as you have escaped from yours. A few bruises, I suppose, must be expected after such a hard fall.

MRS. FRAZER Yes, bruises on the soul.

ROYLSTON I will have to hunt a new illusion. You remember you said last night that when you came here you feared the crowning disillusionment?

MRS. FRAZER My fears were well grounded.

ROYLSTON Hm—you mean you have seen my illusion go up in smoke, too? It is discouraging—as if everything in life were founded upon false appearances. (*He quotes ironically*) "Yea, faileth now dream the dreamer and the lute the lutanist."

MRS. FRAZER You are deceiving yourself as to the nature of my awakening. I have come to regard the prop, as you call it, which I cast aside with scorn as the sound one. The new one, I find, is worm-eaten.

ROYLSTON The new one? Meaning that I am?

MRS. FRAZER Exactly! I asked you to guide my future because I though you were far-sighted. I have discovered you are only in-sighted—as pitifully in-sighted as I was.

ROYLSTON (*Surprised*) In-sighted?

MRS. FRAZER Yes, you see nothing beyond yourself. You are so preoccupied with the workings of your own brain that your vision of outside things is clouded. You are only a cruel egoist.

ROYLSTON Know thyself, sayeth the law.

MRS. FRAZER You make no allowance for the individual.

ROYLSTON Oh, come now, Mrs. Frazer; you have read what I have written. You know if there is one thing I harp on ad nauseam—

MRS. FRAZER It is the duty of the individual to triumph over environment; but in your life you regard yourself as the only individual in the world. You cannot see beyond that. You have reconstructed the world for yourself—well and good. Why try to force your conception on others? Why judge their thoughts by what you would think in their place? When you do so you deprive them of personality. You make them manikins and yourself the master of the show; and you care not a whit how you hurt their feelings when they fail to answer your pull of the string.

ROYLSTON (*With a bitter smile*) You too? It seems this is my day to be properly humbled in spirit.

MRS. FRAZER I know you will never pardon my effrontery in wounding your vanity so. Such colossal conceit!

ROYLSTON (*Flushing*) Mrs. Frazer!

MRS. FRAZER (*Calmly*) Your cruel vanity has torn off the mask. How could *you* help me? You can only help yourself. Perhaps if I were in love with you— but then you know, Mr. Naricissus, I would only be your reflection. However, I do not love you. Last night I thought—you were on such a high pedestal —I thought of the superman, of the creator, the maker of new values. This morning I saw merely an egotist whose hands are bloody with the human sacrifices he has made—to himself!

ROYLSTON (*Jumping from his chair—excitedly*) You are unjust, Mrs. Frazer.

MRS. FRAZER Now you are beginning to be angry.

ROYLSTON (*Indignantly*) Angry? Why should I be? You have a perfect right to your opinion, preposterous as it may be. Go on, let me hear the tale of my iniquities. It is very interesting.

MRS. FRAZER (*Teasingly*) You are losing your temper, you spoiled child.

ROYLSTON I am not losing my temper. (*Pettishly*) I am growing inured to insults this morning.

MRS. FRAZER Why, so am I! I must beg your forgiveness for one thing I said. It was too cruel of me.
   (*She pauses, smiling mischievously at him*)

ROYLSTON (*Sulkily*) To what are you alluding?

MRS. FRAZER (*Mockingly*) I was truthful enough to tell you I did not love you. That was horrible of me. How could you endure hearing a woman say she did not love you? And how bored you must be when you hear them say they do love you! Eternal repetition, you know. The petted favorite of fortune stands between the devil and the deep blue sea.

ROYLSTON (*Angrily*) Mrs. Frazer, these personalities are— (*Looking at her and catching the twinkle in her eyes—with an embarrassed laugh*) I'm beaten; I acknowledge defeat. I surrender to the superwoman—only don't hit me when I'm down.

MRS. FRAZER (*Contritely*) I shouldn't have said all this to you, but I had to cure myself of my attack

of hero-worship in some way. Besides, the wounds
I received in this morning's interview with your
wife cried aloud for vengeance. I had to vent my
spleen on someone.

ROYLSTON (*Bitterly*) I shall never forgive myself for
subjecting you to such a breach of hospitality. It
was shameful of her.

MRS. FRAZER (*Sternly*) No, it is shameful of you to
speak of her in that way. She is not to blame for
her suspicions. She loves you; how could she help
thinking what she did? She is the most wonderful
woman I have ever known—worlds above poor
blind creatures like you and me.

ROYLSTON I am afraid I cannot see it in that light.

MRS. FRAZER No, because in this case truth offends
your pride and you will not see. You never mis-
understood her as grossly as you do at the present
moment.

ROYLSTON And *I* think I have only just begun to understand her.

MRS. FRAZER Take care! You are doing exactly what
you rail against in others—judging by appearances.
Is the keen analytical eye obstinately closed by
wounded vanity?

ROYLSTON (*Impatiently*) No, no—but my letters?

MRS. FRAZER With such a wife you had no right to receive such letters.

ROYLSTON (*Scornfully*) Right?

MRS. FRAZER You'll admit that needless cruelty is
wrong, I hope?

ROYLSTON Yes, but I don't see what—

MRS. FRAZER Do you love this woman of the letters?

ROYLSTON No, of course not!

MRS. FRAZER Yet you persuaded her to leave her home—

ROYLSTON Persuaded? No, certainly not! She came to me for advice. She had been impressed by what I had written about the narrowing influence of the conventional home. She had practically the same environment you described to me as yours before your marriage. She was engaged to be married to some cut-and-dried young simpleton. Her life was unsatisfying, gave her no scope for realizing the best that was in her. I saw she had brains, ability. I advised her to learn some occupation which would make her self-sustaining, and then go out into life and see things for herself.

MRS. FRAZER She is young?

ROYLSTON Twenty-one.

MRS. FRAZER And pretty?

ROYLSTON Yes.

MRS. FRAZER You are sure you are not in love with her?

ROYLSTON (*Irritably*) I am sure, yes! (*With a bored smile*) I have been too busy to love anyone.

MRS. FRAZER But yourself. Then you have not even that justification.

ROYLSTON (*Coldly*) I see no necessity for justifying my actions.

MRS. FRAZER You cannot deny this girl loves you?

ROYLSTON (*Cynically*) She may think she does.

MRS. FRAZER And you think she does! It tickles your vanity to think so.

ROYLSTON You are breaking me on the wheel.
(*He laughs helplessly*)

MRS. FRAZER You are a poor blind bat, not a butterfly; you can stand it. It may open your eyes. Can't you see that you have forever ruined all chance of her being happy with her cut-and-dried simpleton or any of his kind? And where is she to find the super-man? Even if she gained your love, what a disappointment! What an awakening when she really came to know you!

ROYLSTON (*Forcing a laugh and looking down at his feet*) Poor clay feet!

MRS. FRAZER There is only one salvation for her. You must write to her at once and say—

(*She hesitates*)

ROYLSTON Say what?

MRS. FRAZER Reveal your true self.

ROYLSTON (*Smiling confidently*) You guarantee that will cure the infatuation?

MRS. FRAZER Absolutely!

ROYLSTON Are you sure she won't read her ideal into my words?

MRS. FRAZER (*Biting her lip*) Perhaps you are right. That won't do. I must go to her and tell her—

ROYLSTON She would think you were jealous. She would not believe you.

MRS. FRAZER Tell her flatly you don't love her.

ROYLSTON How about needless cruelty?

MRS. FRAZER (*Alarmed*) But you see yourself you must end it someway.

ROYLSTON I have a way (*Smiling at her*) tried and proved by experience.

MRS. FRAZER (*Scornfully*) I have no doubt.

ROYLSTON (*In a bantering tone*) Shall I tell you what it is? Don't try to look so indifferent. You know you're dying with curiosity. (MRS. FRAZER *shakes her head indignantly*) Well, I write a letter to this effect: "I love you but we must see each other no more."

MRS. FRAZER (*Contemptuously*) Oh!

ROYLSTON (*Continuing with a great show of affected pathos*) "I cannot make you unhappy. Our love is forbidden by cruel, man-made laws and it is on your frail shoulders their punishment would fall, etc., ad nauseam. So you must forget me—or rather, do not forget. Remember in my heart of hearts, my soul of souls, etc., ad lib, your image will remain, the inspiration of my work; that in spirit all my work will be dedicated to you—" And so on ad infinitum.

MRS. FRAZER That is disgusting drivel.

ROYLSTON Of course it is! But don't you know, haven't you ever been in love?

MRS. FRAZER Why?

ROYLSTON Love is the world upside down. Sense is drivel and drivel is sense.

MRS. FRAZER You mean to tell me she will be ridiculous enough to believe that?

ROYLSTON She will revel in it. She will telephone—I cannot be found. She will write—no answer. She may even try to see me—I am invisible. Then she will say: That wonderful man has the strength to sacrifice himself for my sake. *Voilà!* She goes home, marries the cut-and-dried simpleton, adopts a superior air which holds him in awed servitude, pities him—pity is love without jealousy—and whenever his uncouth matter-of-factness grates on her sensitive nerves she reverently takes my image from the inner shrine and indulges in the sweet happiness of melancholy retrospection. The memory of another's sacrifice for love of oneself— That is the most soothing narcotic a woman can possess. I recommend it to you.

MRS. FRAZER (*Dryly*) Thank you.

ROYLSTON (*Enthusiastically*) Just think of the ecstatic joy of a woman grown old and fat when she remembers that in her younger days a discarded lover committed suicide because she refused him. What a recompense for a double chin the memory of such a corpse must be!

MRS. FRAZER (*Controlling an impulse to laugh—coldly*) I was attempting to consider this matter seriously.

ROYLSTON What! Consider love seriously? Set your mind at rest. I have written the letter and I have ordered Benton to stifle the appeals of the telephone. You see, you need not have warned me.

MRS. FRAZER She had become serious, then?

ROYLSTON Why do you say that?

MRS. FRAZER When they become serious you grow afraid of complications. A little bird told me.

ROYLSTON A little bird?

MRS. FRAZER A man is never a hero to his—

ROYLSTON (*Groaning*) Valet! That scoundrel Benton! The model of discretion. Another illusion gone! My house of cards is tumbling about my ears.

MRS. FRAZER No more than you deserve.

ROYLSTON I admit it, Mrs. Frazer. (*Eagerly*) I may mock but I see it just the same. In the future I will send my tickled vanity a-packing and have done with such foolishness. After all, it was only an amusing flirtation—nothing more.

MRS. FRAZER Go and tell Mrs. Roylston that.

ROYLSTON (*His expression grows hard and cold*) Thank
you for reminding me.

(*He goes to the electric bell-button in the wall near
the door on left*)

MRS. FRAZER (*Anxiously*) What are you going to do?

ROYLSTON Ring for Benton to pack my things.

MRS. FRAZER Please don't!

ROYLSTON Why not?

MRS. FRAZER (*Pleadingly*) Not yet at any rate. Please
sit down again. I have something to say to you.

ROYLSTON (*Sitting down*) Whatever you may say,
Mrs. Frazer, will not alter my opinion in the least.
I have my own ideas of the way Alice has acted and
what I must do. With your permission I will go
back to New York on the train with you.

MRS. FRAZER No, no, no! Think of how that would
hurt her? Have you no pity? I will not allow it. Fur-
thermore, you will never see me again when I leave
this house. I have been the cause of too much unhappiness already.

ROYLSTON Don't accuse yourself. I have only gratitude
to you for opening my eyes, and I want to help you
in every way, as I promised I would.

MRS. FRAZER (*Vehemently*) No!

ROYLSTON Surely you don't mean you refuse—

MRS. FRAZER Yes, I refuse your assistance in any way,
shape or manner. I am not going to take any position and I will not need your help; so let us drop
that part of the matter. And as for opening your
eyes, you have never been as sightless as you are
now, poor blind mole!

ROYLSTON (*With smiling protest*) Odious compari-
sons! First I am a bat, then a mole!

MRS. FRAZER   Would you like to see clearly?

ROYLSTON   Granted that I am blind—will sight make me any the less miserable?

MRS. FRAZER   (*Enthusiastically*) It will make you happy, truly happy. (ROYLSTON *smiles skeptically*) Have I your permission to teach you the lesson I was given this morning.

ROYLSTON (*Frowning*)   Lesson?

MRS. FRAZER   Yes, a lesson in life your wife gave me this morning.

ROYLSTON (*Icily*)   My wife also gave me a lesson in life, if you will remember. (*Dryly*) Her first lesson was not so pleasing that I crave for a second.

MRS. FRAZER   For her sake, for my sake, for your own sake you must.

ROYLSTON (*Indifferently*)   Very well. (*He gets up from his chair*) In the meantime Benton can be packing up my things.

MRS. FRAZER   No, please, not yet. Hear me out first— then pack away if you still care to. (*He hesitates uncertainly*) Come, I ask it as a favor.

(*He sits down in his chair again*)

ROYLSTON   I warn you, Mrs. Frazer, I am not to be cajoled into altering my plans. You are wasting your time and eloquence.

MRS. FRAZER   We shall see. Remember you are to hear me from beginning to end—of the lesson. All ready? When I came down this morning I found the irreproachable Benton in this room.

ROYLSTON   And he showed you the crack in my armor.

MRS. FRAZER   He convinced me, without meaning to do so, that the idol's feet were—well—at least only plated.

ROYLSTON (*Sarcastically*) Of course, he meant well.

MRS. FRAZER He meant to flatter me. He had his own
convictions as to my status in this household, and
when I saw him growing confidential I did not attempt to show him his mistake.

ROYLSTON (*Accusingly*) You wanted to listen to his
gossip?

MRS. FRAZER (*With a frank laugh*) I wanted to play
detective and find out if my you was the real you.
Benton, having approved of your choice of a mistress, flattered me by revealing the fact that you
had never cared enough for any of the others to
dare to install them in your household.

ROYLSTON (*Raging*) The evil-minded wretch! Others,
indeed! I tell you that there never have been any
others in the sense he meant. And you allowed him
to talk to you like that?

MRS. FRAZER I was making an ineffectual attempt to
put him in his place when we heard Mrs. Roylston
coming in with the children. And what do you
think I did—I, the bold emancipated woman? I
ran and hid in that room like the guiltiest of cra-
vens. When I regained control of myself I was
furious, and to prove I was not a coward I came in
to face your wife. I went to the other extreme in
my display of daring. She was not certain I had
been here all night but I immediately told her the
truth of the whole affair.

ROYLSTON What else could you have done?

MRS. FRAZER Oh, I could have lied a little for the good
of her soul. Just consider how damning the facts
are! She returns unexpectedly to find me sneaking
out of a darkened room, the picture of guilt. I

brazenly acknowledge I have been here all night and tell her an absurd story of missing a train, and so forth. She has read letters and—

ROYLSTON (*Impatiently*) I know how sadly the circumstantial evidence is against the truth. I was relying on the implicit trust she has always seemed to have for me.

MRS. FRAZER Trust? After she had read those letters— letters which seemed all the more guilty because you had never mentioned them to her? Trust! You want an angel for a wife, not a human being.

ROYLSTON She had no business to read those letters. The whole thing rests upon that.

MRS. FRAZER You had no business to receive the letters. The whole thing rests upon that. But to go on with my lesson: I asserted my innocence. Your wife refused to believe me—naturally enough. She spoke despondently of having expected something of the sort for a long time because you had been growing indifferent to her and the children.

ROYLSTON (*Indignantly*) That is not so. It's true I haven't had much time. I have been very busy, but—

MRS. FRAZER (*Looking at him searchingly*) Are you sure what you are saying now is the truth. Come, be frank! Remember your statement to me last night when I asked you if you loved her.

ROYLSTON (*After a pause—grudgingly*) Well, I confess I may have seemed indifferent; but, good heavens—

MRS. FRAZER She said she blamed no one but herself for what had happened. How could it be expected that a brilliant genius like you could continue to love a poor ignorant creature like herself?

ROYLSTON (*A bit shamefaced*) She said that?

MRS. FRAZER Those are almost her exact words. She blamed herself for marrying you in the first place. Marriages like yours were cursed, she thought.

ROYLSTON Marriages like ours?

MRS. FRAZER (*Meaningly—looking steadily into his eyes*) She told me of the events which preceded your marriage—of the discovery of your love affair.

ROYLSTON (*Gripping the arms of his chair tensely, and speaking hoarsely*) Good God, she told you that! Poor Alice! (*Half to himself*) What could have made her do that?

MRS. FRAZER She said she thought that perhaps you blamed her for your father's death.

ROYLSTON What an absurd idea!

MRS. FRAZER She described your early life together—the days of struggle with poverty before your first play was produced; the days when you remained home in the little flat to write while she worked in an office as stenographer. She used to typewrite what you had written during the day when she came home at night—after she had cooked dinner and washed the dishes.

ROYLSTON (*His face slowly flushing crimson*) You are right! I see what you are driving at. Whatever I am she has made me. I have been forgetting those early days for the past few years. They do not chime well with the tickled vanity. (*With sudden ingenuousness*) But I did use to dry the dishes, you know.

MRS. FRAZER (*Laughing*) Bravo! Richard is himself

again. You only sold a few articles that first year,
she said.

ROYLSTON   She flattered me. I never sold one. Every
cent came through her.

MRS. FRAZER   She said those days were the happiest of
her life. She had often been selfish enough to wish,
since you became indifferent, that you had never
succeeded and it could always have been as it was
in the little flat.

ROYLSTON   Good heavens, she was nothing but a slave
in those days.

MRS. FRAZER   She knew how hard it must have been
for you, who had been used to having everything,
to have her drag you down into privation and—

ROYLSTON (*Deeply moved*)   What a horribly mistaken
thought! I joyed in losing everything for her. It was
like paying off part of my debt.

MRS. FRAZER (*Continuing as if he had not interrupted*)
So she resolved that as soon as your first book or
play was published or produced, and you did not
need her any longer, she would leave you, permit
you to regain your freedom.

ROYLSTON (*Stupefied—his voice trembling*)   Why,
that's what she proposed to do—for me—when she
was here a little while ago!

MRS. FRAZER   Oh yes, she only desires your happiness
and, as she thinks you love me, she is perfectly willing to give you up to me—because she loves you so
much.

ROYLSTON   How is it possible to lose oneself like that—
I cannot grasp it—there is too much clay in my
make-up— For me, too! Good heavens! She in-

tended to leave me when my first play was produced, you say? But she didn't.

MRS. FRAZER For a very good reason. It was about that time your son was born, wasn't it?

ROYLSTON (*Getting up from his chair and walking nervously about the room—in great agitation*) I see, I see! Poor Alice! What a woman she is! And I— good heavens! You threatened to open my eyes— I've lived with her all these years and forgotten how much I owed to her. She has protected and shielded me from everything—made my opportunity for me, you might say—and I took it all for granted—the finest thing in my life! Took it all for granted without a thought of gratitude, as my due. Lord, what a cad I've been! What a rotten cad!

(*He throws himself into the chair and stares moodily before him*)

MRS. FRAZER (*With a faint smile*) I'd like to deny your statement but I'm afraid it's only too true.

ROYLSTON What I cannot get through my head is why she should tell you all this. Alice is proud. To reveal all this to you, a stranger—it must have humbled her spirit to the breaking point.

MRS. FRAZER I cannot quite understand, myself. She wished to justify you, of course, to prove you were in no way to blame.

ROYLSTON (*Groaning*) Oh!

MRS. FRAZER You see she persisted in regarding this misfortune as the retribution for her sin in the beginning.

ROYLSTON (*Jumping up—excitedly*) Ah, by heavens, that is going too far! Retribution for *her* sin! What

a preposterous idea! As if the blame, the sin if it
was one, were not all mine! (*Looking at his hands*)
Bloody with sacrifices at my own altar—yes, you
were right—and she is the woman whom I tortured
with my blind egotism not half an hour ago—the
woman who pleaded for forgiveness—and I refused
and was going to desert her. I am beginning to hate
myself for a monster! Those letters! If any woman
ever dares to write to me again I'll have her letters
burned by the—no, we haven't one—I'll hand
them over to the police. (MRS. FRAZER *bursts out
laughing*) And my children— Good God, do you
know the horrible thought came to me just now
that I do not even know my own children?

MRS. FRAZER (*Protestingly*)   Now you are carrying your
self-accusation too far.

ROYLSTON (*Vehemently*)   I tell you it's the truth. I
speak to them, I kiss them sometimes; but I do the
same for other people's. For all the loving interest I
have taken in them they might just as well be the
gardener's—or Benton's.

MRS. FRAZER   You have the whole future before you for
retribution.

ROYLSTON (*Catching at the word eagerly*)   Yes, retribution, joyful retribution every day, every hour! Pay
off a part of this enormous debt of love which has
accumulated against me! Why, life is going to
mean more, be finer and happier than I ever
dreamed!

MRS. FRAZER   Happiness is servitude.

ROYLSTON (*Enthusiastically*)   Of course it is! Servitude
in love, love in servitude! Logos in Pan, Pan in
Logos! That is the great secret—and I never knew!

Thank you, thank you! But how did you guess it?

MRS. FRAZER Mrs. Roylston told me this morning—her lesson in life.

ROYLSTON That, too! Her love is great enough to solve all enigmas.

MRS. FRAZER (*Laughing*) But your work? The sovereign individual? The superman? The great lonely one?

ROYLSTON My love will be a superlove worthy of the superman, and— (*Hesitating*) Besides, this is the exceptional case which proves the contrary rule— what are you laughing at?

MRS. FRAZER At your determination to be exceptional though the heavens fall.

ROYLSTON (*Laughing himself*) I have to be exceptional to be worthy of such an exceptional wife.

MRS. FRAZER (*Rising from her chair*) And now I must go. My mission is accomplished.

ROYLSTON Your mission?

(*The doorbell is heard ringing*)

MRS. FRAZER Remember what you said about fatality? I am convinced I had to accomplish something here. It was not what I thought it was, but no matter. I, too, have learned the secret. It was my mission to open your eyes—and my own.

ROYLSTON You are going back to your husband?

MRS. FRAZER Yes, back to the chains which have suddenly become dear to me. Like you I had grown so accustomed to the best things in life that I scorned it. I, too, have my joyful retribution to make, my debt of love to pay.

ROYLSTON (*Going to her and taking her hand*) And how can I ever thank you for my awakening?

MRS. FRAZER   The fact that you have wakened is thanks enough.

ROYLSTON   And will you not become—my wife's friend?

MRS. FRAZER   With all my heart—if she will allow it.

(BENTON *appears in the doorway on the left. He is greatly excited*)

BENTON   Excuse me, sir, but there's a man who insisted on seeing you and—

(GEORGE FRAZER *pushes* BENTON *roughly aside and steps into the room. He is a man of about thirty-five, thick-set, of medium height, black hair gray at the temples, square jaw, irregular features, broad clean-shaven face and shrewd blue eyes. His face is haggard and shows plainly the traces of deep-rooted grief and anxiety with their consequent sleepless nights. He is dressed in a business suit of dark material*)

FRAZER   (*He gives a groan of suppressed rage as he sees the two standing together*)   Ethel!

MRS. FRAZER   George!

(*She makes a movement toward him. He throws himself at* ROYLSTON, *pulling a revolver from his coat pocket.* MRS. FRAZER *springs between them*)

MRS. FRAZER   For my sake! George!

(FRAZER *hurls the revolver on the floor and sinks into the chair by the table, hiding his face in his hands and sobbing heavily.* MRS. FRAZER *goes to him and puts her arm around his shoulder. He makes a feeble effort to shake her off.* BENTON *creeps stealthily over and picks up the revolver*)

ROYLSTON   (*Severely*)   You may go, Benton.

(BENTON *looks at him irresolutely, then goes out.* FRAZER *finally regains his composure somewhat and turns his grief-stricken face to his wife*)

SERVITUDE [297]

FRAZER   Ethel—why? My God!

MRS. FRAZER   (*Distractedly*)   Will this misunderstanding never be cleared up!

ROYLSTON   Yes, I will clear it up.

FRAZER (*Furiously*)   Shut up, you— You lie! I know what I know. You have done me harm enough without trying to treat me like a fool. I'd have shot you for the skulking liar you are—but—it wasn't for your sake I didn't—

ROYLSTON (*With calm dignity*)   I choose to ignore your insults for the present, Mr. Frazer. When you are calmer you will hear what I have to say and this ludicrous melodrama will end.

(*He turns to go out the door in back*)

MRS. FRAZER   No, please stay; you must. (ROYLSTON *remains standing by the door*)

MRS. FRAZER (*Her voice trembling*)   George, how did you find out?

FRAZER   I always knew you'd wind up here sooner or later. Before you left, when I was certain you didn't care for me any more, I suspected you were in love with this (*With bitter scorn*) gentleman. His books, his plays all over the place, his photograph on the middle of your dresser. (MRS. FRAZER *flushes.* ROYLSTON *looks at her in astonishment*) That was why I had you followed.

MRS. FRAZER (*With a frown*)   I thought you had given up spying on me.

FRAZER (*Pleadingly*)   It wasn't spying. You mustn't think that, Ethel. It was for your own sake I did it.

MRS. FRAZER (*With a hard laugh*)   For my sake!

FRAZER   I wanted to protect you. You don't know the world. I knew you'd do something foolish sooner

or later with your head full of his crazy ideas. You
don't know the game these gentlemen play.

ROYLSTON (*Angrily*) Oh!

(*He turns and goes out the door in back*)

MRS. FRAZER So I was followed to this house?

FRAZER Yes.

MRS. FRAZER When I came—last night?

FRAZER (*With a groan*) Yes.

MRS. FRAZER How is it you gave up waiting for me?
Why haven't you tried to see me yourself—it's
nearly two months.

FRAZER I could see you didn't want me bothering you
—and I've been sick.

MRS. FRAZER (*Alarmed*) Sick?

FRAZER (*Lightly*) Nothing serious—overwork—nervous breakdown, the doctor said. Had to go to bed
—he prescribed perfect rest. (*Ironically*) Perfect
rest!

MRS. FRAZER (*With tender anxiety*) But you're all
right now, de— (*She bites back the term of en-
dearment at his wondering look*) George?

FRAZER (*Sarcastically*) Fine—as you can see.

MRS. FRAZER Why couldn't you have sent me word? It
would have changed things so.

FRAZER You mean you wouldn't be here? Well, I
couldn't. I didn't want you to come back because
you pitied me. (*Bitterly*) I didn't think you'd care.

MRS. FRAZER (*Wincing*) Oh. (*After a pause*) Why
did you come here this morning?

FRAZER The detective telephoned me—when he was
sure. I wanted to kill this man and you too, at first.
I didn't know what I was doing.

MRS. FRAZER (*Sadly*) And now I suppose it's all over

—forever—between us. You can't want me any
longer—believing what you do.

FRAZER (*Turning away from her to hide his emotion*)
Don't say that, Ethel. I can't give you up—this
way. Life is too hard to bear—without you. I can't
help loving you—in spite of everything. I shouldn't
—I suppose—now. (MRS. FRAZER *is looking at him
with eyes full of tenderness*) If you'd only—love
me a little—I could forget this foolishness—not
your fault—if we'd had children—you were always
alone—my fault.

(*A sob shakes his shoulders*)

MRS. FRAZER (*Softly*) So you still want me—to come
back?

FRAZER Yes, that's why I came—to ask you—if you
would.

MRS. FRAZER (*Kneeling down beside him—eagerly*)
Then look into my eyes quick—now! (*He looks
down at her*) I swear to you I am innocent—that I
love you more now than I ever did, even on our
honeymoon; and I am as innocent of wrong now as
I was then. Can you believe me?

FRAZER (*Wonderingly*) Then you don't love him?

MRS. FRAZER No, no, a thousand times no! I love you,
and he loves his wife. My presence here is folly,
nothing more. Let me explain the whole thing to
you.

FRAZER (*Joyfully*) No, no, I believe you without that.
(*He takes her into his arms and kisses her.* MRS.
ROYLSTON *enters from the door on the left. She has a
small traveling bag in her hand. Her eyes are red from
weeping. She stops in astonishment and her bag drops
from her hand when she sees the* FRAZERS)

MRS. ROYLSTON (*Timidly*)   I beg your pardon.

(*Startled, they both jump to their feet and face* MRS. ROYLSTON *in confusion*)

MRS. FRAZER (*Joyfully*)   I want you to meet my husband, Mrs. Roylston. George, this is Mrs. Roylston.

MRS. ROYLSTON (*Astonished*)   I'm very happy—

FRAZER   A great pleasure—

MRS. FRAZER   Mrs. Roylston is the most wonderful woman in the world. (MRS. ROYLSTON *smiles feebly*) If you don't believe me, ask her husband. (*As* FRAZER *stammers and* MRS. ROYLSTON *is equally nonplussed*) And now you and I will be going— home! (*She walks over toward the door on the left*) Good-bye, Mrs. Roylston. I hope when you understand everything you will become my friend. (*She holds out her hand, which* MRS. ROYLSTON *takes uncertainly as if in a daze*) Come, George, out into the open air. I have so much to say to you.

(*She goes out.* FRAZER *follows her but stops at the door and turns to* MRS. ROYLSTON)

FRAZER   Mrs. Roylston, will you tell your husband I wish to take back all I said to him a while ago. He'll understand.

MRS. ROYLSTON (*Dully*)   I'll tell him.

FRAZER   Thank you; good-bye.

(*He goes out. A moment later the front door is heard closing*)

MRS. ROYLSTON (*Mechanically*)   Good-bye.

(*She takes her bag and sets it down beside the table; then sinks wearily into the chair and leans both elbows on the table, holding her face in her hands in an attitude of deep dejection.* ROYLSTON *enters from the door in the rear. He gives a joyful exclamation on seeing his wife)*

ROYLSTON (*Coming over quickly, he stands beside her*) Alice.

MRS. ROYLSTON (*Startled, she turns and looks up at him —dully*) Yes.

ROYLSTON They have gone—Mr. and Mrs. Frazer—together?

MRS. ROYLSTON Yes.

ROYLSTON (*Jubilantly*) Good! And without hearing my explanation! That is a proof of love and trust on his part which I would hardly have expected of him. You see, Alice, the most ludicrous part of this whole misunderstanding is the fact that I did not spend last night in this house.

MRS. ROYLSTON (*Slowly—as if she could not believe her ears*) You—were not here?

ROYLSTON No. After I directed Mrs. Frazer to her room I ran away—spent the night at the roadhouse. I was afraid to stay, I must confess—afraid of myself—afraid of how the situation might be misconstrued. I didn't want to be the cause of any more trouble to Mrs. Frazer, who had suffered enough already.

MRS. ROYLSTON (*Her eyes brimming with happy tears*) Oh, I'm so glad!

ROYLSTON I want you to prove my statement—to be completely satisfied that I am speaking the truth. My name is on the register at the roadhouse and they all know me and can testify to my story. I wanted to explain before but your doubts hurt my obstinate pride—I had boasted to Mrs. Frazer that you would not judge by appearances, you know. As for Frazer's detective, he must have taken everything for granted—as you and all the rest did. I'll have to write to Frazer and tell him. In spite of his fine confidence there might be some secret suspicions in the back of his mind.

MRS. ROYLSTON   David—forgive me.

ROYLSTON   (*Impetuously*)   Forgive you? What nonsense! (*He bends down to kneel beside her and knocks his knee against her bag. He holds it up wonderingly*) What's this? Your bag all packed! Then you were really going to leave me?

MRS. ROYLSTON   (*Tremblingly*)   I thought you loved her. I wanted you to be happy.

ROYLSTON   And the children?

MRS. ROYLSTON   I had no right— It was best for them to stay.

ROYLSTON   You were going to leave them, too—and all for my sake! Good heavens! And you ask for forgiveness! (*Kneeling down beside her and putting his arms around her*) Ah, my dear, my dear, how deeply you make me feel my unworthiness! I am the one who must plead for pardon, pardon for a lifetime of selfish neglect, of vain posing, of stupid conceit—

MRS. ROYLSTON   (*Kissing him*)   Ssshhh!

ROYLSTON   (*His voice vibrating with tenderness*)   Dear, the future will be all that the past has not been, I swear it. We start on our honeymoon today—a lifelong honeymoon. (*Jumping to his feet, with mock severity*) But haven't you read your husband's books, you wonderful, foolish woman? Don't you know it was your duty to claim your right as an in-

dividual, to shake off the shackles my insufferable
egotism had forced upon you? Don't you understand that you have stifled your own longings,
given up your own happiness that I might feel self-
satisfied.

MRS. ROYLSTON (*Interrupting him—softly and tenderly*)
That was my happiness.
(*He bends down and kisses her reverently*)

Curtain